Universes

Universes

John Leslie

ROUTLEDGE
London and New York

First published 1989 by Routledge
11 New Fetter Lane, London EC4P 4EE
29 West 35th Street, New York, NY 10001

Set in 10 on 11 point Times by Columns of Reading

Printed in Great Britain by
Richard Clay Ltd, Bungay, Suffolk

British Library Cataloguing in Publication Data
Leslie, John
   Universes.
   1. Nature – Philosophical perspectives
   I. Title
   113

Library of Congress Cataloging in Publication Data
Leslie, John
   Universes/John Leslie.
   p.cm.
   Bibliography: p.
   Includes index.
   1. Cosmology.   2. God — Proof, Teleological.   3. Teleology.
   I. Title.
   BD511.L48   1989
   113 — dc 19   89–5941
ISBN 0-415-04144-9

Contents

Acknowledgements

Thanks are due to the editors of the *American Philosophical Quarterly*, *Mind*, *Philosophy*, *Religious Studies*, the *International Journal for Philosophy of Religion*, and other journals for making space available for testing the book's ideas; to the editors of nine books for inviting papers on cosmology; and to Paul Edwards and the Macmillan Publishing Co. for asking me to edit and introduce *Physical Cosmology and Philosophy* (1989), a book of readings which could form a useful background to this one. Also to the Social Sciences and Humanities Research Council of Canada for a Leave Fellowship; to the University of Guelph, for a Forster Fellowship; to the Department of Religious Studies, University of Calgary, and the Research School of Social Sciences, The Australian National University, for periods of visiting fellowship; to the Vatican Secretariat of State for airfares to and from Australia, allowing me to join a workshop at Castel Gandolfo; to universities which invited lectures and short visits; to the Vatican Observatory for hospitality in Poland; and to my wife. Many others helped the book on its way – sometimes by attacks on points developed in my papers, which often led to fairly major revisions. The book is particularly indebted to J. Baker, J. D. Barrow, B. J. Carr, L. J. Cohen, W. L. Craig, P. C. W. Davies, R. H. Dicke, J. Earman, G. F. R. Ellis, P. Forrest, G. Gale, D. Goldstick, I. Hacking, C. J. Isham, F. Jackson, M. J. M. Leask, D. Lewis, J. J. MacIntosh, H. Meynell, D. Page, D. Parfit, A. R. Peacocke, J. C. Polkinghorne, K. W. Rankin, M. J. Rees, I. L. Rozental (and P. Zavrel, who translated his Russian for me), D. W. Sciama, J. Simpson, J. J. C. Smart, E. J. Squires, R. Swinburne, R. Sylvan, and F. J. Tipler. Above all, I thank everyone at Routledge, and in particular R. Stoneman, A. Price, and M. Litvinoff for their enthusiasm, professionalism, and speediness.

Chapter One

World Ensemble, or Design

(i) Did God create a universe specially suited to life's evolution? (ii) Alternatively, Do there exist vastly many universes with very varied properties, ours being one of a rare kind in which life occurs? (iii) Or again, May there be nothing too surprising in our universe's life-containing character? (Perhaps more or less any universe would be life-containing, or perhaps there is some other ground for us to feel no surprise. Might we reason that if the cosmos weren't life-containing then nobody would be around to ask whether to be astonished, and that this shows there is nothing to be astonished at?) The chapter introduces some main arguments in reaction to these, the book's three main questions. 'God or Multiverse' is a phrase taken from Henry Adams.[1]

God or Multiverse

1.1 The Argument from Design is an argument for God's reality based on the fact that our universe looks much as if designed.

The Argument for Multiple Worlds starts from the same fact. But it concludes instead that there exist many small-u universes – Soviet cosmologists sometimes call them 'metagalaxies' – inside the capital-U Universe which is The Whole of Reality.

These 'universes', 'mini-universes', 'Worlds' with a capital W to distinguish them from mere planets, can be of immense size. There may be immensely many of them. And their properties are thought of as very varied. Sooner or later, somewhere, one or more of them will have life-permitting properties. Our universe can indeed look as if designed. In reality, though, it may be merely the sort of thing to be expected sooner or later. Given sufficiently many years with a typewriter even a monkey would produce a sonnet.[2]

Suppose there existed ninety-seven trillion universes, all but three of them life-excluding. Obviously, only the three life-permitting universes could ever be observed by living beings. This suggests that an interesting kind of observational selection effect could underlie our seeing of a world whose conditions permit life to evolve. (Recognizing this is not the same as proposing paradoxically that the world is a causal consequence of human existence.)

1.2 While the Multiple Worlds (or World Ensemble) hypothesis is impressively strong, the God hypothesis is a viable alternative.

1

Rightly or wrongly, however, this book shows no interest in the kind of God who designs the structures of individual organisms, plague germs perhaps, or who interferes with Nature's day-to-day operations. If God exists then of the various ways in which he may act on the universe there are only two which will be considered in these pages.

First, he makes the universe obey a particular set of laws (I prefer to think of them all as laws *of physics*), also 'sustaining' it in existence if this is necessary: recreating it, so to speak, from moment to moment, to prevent it from vanishing.

Second, he creates its initial state in such-and-such a fashion. He starts it off with this or that many particles in this or that arrangement; or at least he does this just so long as it has not been done already through his specifying what Nature's laws are to be. It might be that the laws themselves dictated the number and arrangement of the particles.

If the universe has existed for ever, replace 'creating its initial state' by something like 'deciding the number of its particles, and their arrangement at at least one time'.

1.3 Referring to God as 'he' or 'him' is just following convention. If God is real then his reality seems to me most likely to be as described by the Neoplatonist theological tradition. He is then not an almighty person but an abstract Creative Force which is 'personal' through being concerned with creating persons and acting as a benevolent person would.

To be more specific, Neoplatonism's God is *the world's creative ethical requiredness*. Or, which comes to the same thing, he is *the creatively effective ethical requirement that there be a good universe or universes*. Or again, he is the Principle that the ethical need for a universe or universes *is itself responsible for the actual existence of that universe or those universes*.[3]

However, it might instead be that God was a divine person creating everything else. Such a person might owe his existence and creative power to the fact that this was ethically required, a position suggested by the philosopher A. C. Ewing.

It is no insult to a divine person to suggest that he exists for that kind of reason. If anything, what would be uncomplimentary would be to call his existence utterly reasonless.

The Fine Tuning

1.4 This chapter introduces some of the book's chief arguments. One is that it looks as if our universe is spectacularly 'fine tuned for Life'.

By this I mean *only* that it looks as if small changes in this universe's basic features would have made life's evolution impossible. Thus talk of 'fine tuning' does not presuppose that a divine Fine Tuner, or Neoplatonism's more abstract God, must be responsible.

In the modern cosmological literature you find many claims like the following. (More details of them and full references to the literature will be given in Chapter 2.)

- Large regions coming out of a Big Bang could be expected to be uncoordinated since not even influences travelling at the speed of light would have had time to link them. When they made contact tremendous turbulence would occur, yielding a cosmos of black holes or of temperatures which stopped galaxies forming for billions of years, after which everything would be much too spread out for them to form. Placing a pin to choose our orderly world from among the physically possible ones, God could seem to have been called on to aim with immense accuracy. Cosmologists refer to this as *the Smoothness Problem*.

- The cosmos threatened to recollapse within a fraction of a second or else to expand so fast that galaxy formation would be impossible. To avoid these disasters its rate of expansion at early instants needed to be fine tuned to perhaps one part in 10^{55} (which is 10 followed by 54 zeros). That would make Space remarkably 'flat', so this is often called *the Flatness Problem*.

- Smoothness and Flatness Problems might be avoided through what is known as 'Inflation': after initial deceleration, a short burst of *accelerating* expansion at very early times could have increased the universe's size by a factor of as much as $10^{1,100,000}$. This could mean that everything now visible to us had grown from a region whose parts were originally well co-ordinated, which would give the observed smoothness. Also, a greatly expanded space might be very flat like the surface of a much inflated balloon.

  However, *Inflation could itself seem to have required fine tuning* for it to occur at all and for it to yield irregularities neither too small nor too great for galaxies to form. Thus, besides having to select a Grand Unified Theory (GUT) or Theory of Everything (TOE) very carefully, a deity wishing to bring about life-permitting conditions would seemingly need to have made two components of an expansion-driving 'cosmological constant' cancel each other with an accuracy better than of one part in 10^{50}. ('Bare lambda', the cosmological constant as originally proposed by Einstein, has to be in almost but not quite perfect balance with 'quantum lambda'. With a balance that was perfect, Inflation would probably not occur.) A change by one part in 10^{100} in the present strengths either of the nuclear weak force or of gravity might end this cancellation, disastrously.

- Had *the nuclear weak force* been appreciably stronger then the Big Bang would have burned all hydrogen to helium. There could then be neither water nor long-lived stable stars. Making it appreciably weaker would again have destroyed the hydrogen: the neutrons formed at early times would not have decayed into protons.

    Again, this force had to be chosen appropriately if neutrinos were to interact with stellar matter both weakly enough to escape from a supernova's collapsing core and strongly enough to blast its outer layers into space so as to provide material for making planets.

- For carbon to be created in quantity inside stars *the nuclear strong force* must be to within perhaps as little as 1 per cent neither stronger nor weaker than it is. Increasing its strength by maybe 2 per cent would block the formation of protons – so that there could be no atoms – or else bind them into diprotons so that stars would burn some billion billion times faster than our sun. On the other hand *de*creasing it by roughly 5 per cent would unbind the deuteron, making stellar burning impossible. (Increasing Planck's constant by over 15 per cent would be another way of preventing the deuteron's existence. So would making the proton very slightly lighter or the neutron very slightly heavier, as it would then not be energetically advantageous for pairs of protons to become deuterons.)

- With *electromagnetism* very slightly stronger, stellar luminescence would fall sharply. Main sequence stars would then all of them be red stars: stars probably too cold to encourage Life's evolution and at any rate unable to explode as the supernovae one needs for creating elements heavier than iron. Were it very slightly *weaker* then all main sequence stars would be very hot and short-lived blue stars.

    Again, a slight strengthening could transform all quarks (essential for constructing protons, and hence for all atoms) into leptons or else make protons repel one another strongly enough to prevent the existence of atoms even as light as those of helium.

    Again, strengthening by 1 per cent could have doubled the years needed for intelligent life to evolve, by making chemical changes more difficult. A doubled strength could have meant that 10^{62} years were needed – and in a much shorter time almost all protons would have decayed.

Again, there is this. The electromagnetic fine structure constant gives the strength of the coupling between charged particles and electromagnetic fields. Increasing it to above 1/85 (from its present 1/137) could result in too many proton decays for there to be long-lived stars, let alone living beings who were not killed by their own radioactivity.

- The need for electromagnetism to be fine tuned if stars are not to be all of them red, or all of them blue, can be rephrased as a need for fine tuning of *gravity* because it is the ratio between the two forces which is crucial. Gravity also needs fine tuning for stars and planets to form, and for stars to burn stably over billions of years. It is roughly 10^{39} times weaker than electromagnetism. Had it been only 10^{33} times weaker, stars would be a billion times less massive and would burn a million times faster.

- Various *particle masses* had to take appropriate values for life of any plausible kind to stand a chance of evolving. (i) If the neutron–proton mass difference – about one part in a thousand – had not been almost exactly twice the electron's mass then all neutrons would have decayed into protons or else all protons would have changed irreversibly into neutrons. Either way, there would not be the couple of hundred stable types of atom on which chemistry and biology are based. (ii) Super-heavy particles were active early in the Bang. Fairly modest changes in their masses could have led to disastrous alterations in the ratio of matter particles to photons, giving a universe of black holes or else of matter too dilute to form galaxies. Further, the superheavies had to be very massive to prevent rapid decay of the proton. (iii) The intricacy of chemistry and the existence of solids depend on the electron's being much less massive than the proton. (iv) The masses of a host of scalar particles could affect whether the cosmological constant would ever be the right size for Inflation to occur appropriately, and whether it would later be small enough to allow space to be very flat – failing which it would be expanding or contracting very violently. Today the constant is zero to one part in 10^{120}. (v) Forces can vary with range in seemingly very odd ways: the nuclear strong force, for instance, is repulsive at extremely short ranges while at slightly greater ones it is first attractive and then disappears entirely. The explanation for this lies in force 'screening' and 'antiscreening' and in how force-conveying 'messenger particles' can vanish before having had time to deliver their messages. These effects are crucially dependent on particle masses. The actual masses make forces enter into intricate checks and balances which underlie the comparatively stable behaviour of galaxies, stars, planets, and living organisms.

1.5 No doubt some of these claimed facts are mistakes – although many seem as well established as facts about the reality of quarks or black holes or neutron stars, or of the Big Bang itself. Others, again, may be dictated by physical principles so fundamental that they are not fine tunable. But clues heaped upon clues can constitute weighty evidence despite any doubts attaching to each element in the pile. Important, too, is that force strengths and particle masses are distributed across enormous ranges. The nuclear strong force is (roughly) a hundred times stronger than electromagnetism, which is in turn ten thousand times stronger than the nuclear weak force, which is itself some ten thousand billion billion billion times stronger than gravity. So we can well be impressed by any apparent need for a force to be 'just right' even to within a factor of ten, let alone to within one part in a hundred or in 10^{100} – especially when nobody is sure why the strongest force tugs any more powerfully than the weakest.

Ways of Getting a World Ensemble

1.6 As indicated earlier, one way of accounting for fine tuning of the world's properties to suit Life's needs would be suppose that there exists an ensemble of vastly many 'Worlds' or 'universes' with very varied properties. Ours would be one of the rare ones in which living beings could evolve. There is no need to say 'infinitely many universes' or 'all possible universes' instead of 'vastly many', although people often write as if this were essential. For a car number plate such as 'LOOK 1234 WOW' to be explained, *rendered unmysterious*, it can be enough that very numerous permutations of letters and numbers appear on cars. Again, a sufficiently mighty army of monkeys at typewriters could type a page of poetry unmysteriously without having to type infinitely many pages or all possible pages.

People have proposed a wide variety of mechanisms for generating multiple universes. Many such mechanisms will be discussed in detail in Chapter 4. They include these:

(a) The cosmos oscillates: Big Bang, Big Squeeze, Big Bang, and so on. As was suggested by J. A. Wheeler, each oscillation could count as a new World or (small-u) universe because of having new properties, or because the oscillations are separated by knotholes of intense compression in which information about previous cycles is lost – or in which Time breaks down entirely so that we cannot talk of other cycles as being 'previous'.

(b) Many-Worlds quantum theory, originated by H. Everett III, is usually understood as giving us a capital-U Universe which branches into more and more Worlds that interact hardly at all. Each World represents one choice among the sets of events which quantum mechanics views as having been truly possible.

Some people treat such branching as an offence against Simplicity. They prefer to regard Worlds other than our own as useful fictions at best. But various experiments – for instance, the double slit experiment in which we see what looks like interference between two separate sets of waves – seem to show that these supposed fictions are *complexly active*. The paths which particles *might have taken* appear able to affect in complex ways the paths which they actually take, setting up what looks like a 'jostling' of all the possibilities. It is then doubtful whether Simplicity is served by denying that the Worlds are all of them fully real.

(c) Worlds, small-u universes, could occur as quantum fluctuations, as was suggested by E. P. Tryon in 1973. Maybe such fluctuations would occur from time to time in a Superspace, although some have denied the need for any such already existing background.

That an entire universe could occur as a fluctuation can seem absurd. In fact, however, it forms the basis of what is fast becoming the accepted account of how our universe began. Quantum fluctuations, in which particles spring into existence at unpredictable places and times, are happening constantly even in empty space. A fluctuation can be long-lasting if its energy is very small. And it is very ordinary physics to treat binding energies – for instance, the energy which binds an electron to a nucleus – as *negative energies*. Now, gravitational energy is binding energy, and our universe is richly supplied with it. It may be a universe having a total energy of zero or nearly zero when this is taken into account. Moreover even a small fluctuation could give birth to hugely much, because at very early times more and more new matter could spring into existence without 'costing' anything: its mass-energy could be exactly balanced by its gravitational energy.

(d) If Space is 'open' instead of being 'closed' like the surface of a sphere then on the most straightforward models it is infinitely large and contains infinitely much material. Gigantic regions situated far beyond our 'particle horizon' (the horizon set by how far light can have travelled to us since the Bang) could well be counted as 'other universes', particularly if their properties were very different.

(e) Even a 'closed' cosmos could be of any size, and the nowadays very popular Inflationary Cosmos is in fact gigantic. It is quite probably split into hugely many domains, markedly different in their properties. A. H. Guth and P. J. Steinhardt suggest that our own domain stretches 10^{25} times further than we can see,[4] so of course we can see none of the others.

1.7 Even granted ideal conditions, life might evolve only with great difficulty: its first beginnings could depend, for instance, on tremendously lucky molecular combinations in some primeval soup. If so, then multiple universes could help produce it by sheer force of numbers: toss fifty coins sufficiently often and some day the lot will land heads together. However, a multiplicity of universes could be all the more helpful if the universes varied widely, so making it more likely that conditions would somewhere be ideal. Now, modern Unified Theories do suggest that very wide variations could be expected.

Why? Well, at early times there may have been only a single force and a single general type of particle. As the Big Bang cooled this unity would have been destroyed by a process known as 'symmetry breaking'. It would have become energetically advantageous for a scalar field (or more probably *fields*) to take a non-zero value (or values). The choice of any such value in any particular region may have been a random affair. Alternatively, field values may have varied from region to region not randomly but deterministically. Now, interacting with a field can make particles take on mass – and particle masses, besides being of great direct importance to the possibility of Life, also underlie the differences between the strengths of Nature's four main forces. Hence *any theory giving us multiple universes might also fairly readily provide multiply different combinations of force strengths and masses*.

When many scalar fields were involved and when each affected different particles in different ways, the range of variations would be enormous.

This way of looking on things is favoured by, for example, A. D. Linde, who speaks of the multiple domains of an Inflationary Cosmos as forming 'a lunch at which all possible dishes are available'.[5] It could then be unsurprising that at least a few of the dishes were food for intelligent living beings.

Observing only a single domain inside that cosmos, a single small-u universe, any such being could be greatly puzzled by how that domain's properties were accurately tuned to Life's requirements. Unless suspecting the existence of the greatly many other domains whose properties were life-discouraging, the being could feel forced to believe in a divine Fine Tuner.

A Few Stories

1.8 Let us ask, however, whether a life-containing universe really does stand in special need of explanation, and if so, whether a multiplicity of Worlds or universes with varied properties could provide the best explanation.

An initial point to notice is that neither a Multiple Worlds explanation nor an explanation by reference to a Fine Tuner would supply a substitute for a long, scientifically very ordinary causal account of Life's evolution. What these explanations could instead provide would be insight into how it came to be inevitable, likely, or very possible that there would be, *somewhere*, a situation whose characteristics – force strengths, particle masses, etc. – made Life's evolution inevitable or likely or very possible.

Next, I find it helpful to tell a succession of stories.

1.9 First comes the Fishing Story. You know that a lake's impenetrably cloudy waters contained a fish 23.2576 inches long, for you have just caught the fish in question. Does this fact about the lake stand in specially strong need of explanation? Of course not, you tend to think. Every fish must have some length! Yet you next discover that your fishing apparatus could accept only fish of this length, plus or minus one part in a million. Competing theories spring to mind: the first, that there are millions of differently lengthed fish in the lake, your apparatus having in the end found one fitting its requirements; and the second, that there is just the one fish, created by someone wishing to give you a fish supper. Either explanation will serve; and so for that matter will the explanation that the well-wisher created so many fish of different lengths that there would be sure to be one which you could catch. (God and Multiple Worlds are far from being flatly incompatible.) In contrast, *that the one and only fish in the lake just happened to be of exactly the right length* is a suggestion to be rejected at once. Similarly with the suggestion *that the lake contains many fish, all of a length which just happens to be the right one*.

1.10 The tale has countless variants: for example, the Poker Game Story. (This is a nice response to those who say that the 'improbability' of our universe is no more impressive than that of just any hand of cards, every possible hand being equally improbable.) You seem to see mere rubbish in your opponent's poker hand of an eight, six, five, four, and three. It is natural to assume that Chance gave it to him. But you then recall that poker has many versions; that you had agreed on one in which his Little Tiger ('eight high, three low, no pair') defeats your seemingly much stronger hand; that a million dollars are at stake; and that card players occasionally cheat. At once your suspicions are aroused.

Again, an old arch collapses exactly when you pass through. You congratulate yourself on a narrow escape from purely accidental death – until you notice your rival in love tiptoeing from the scene.

Again, consider a tale told by Ernest Bramah about an ingenious merchant. 'Mok Cho had been seen to keep his thumb over a small hole in a robe of embroidered silk'; now, 'although the tolerant-minded pointed out that in exhibiting a piece of cloth even a magician's thumbs must be somewhere . . .'.

1.11 The main moral must by now be plain. Our universe's elements do not carry labels announcing whether they are in special need of explanation. A chief (or the only?) reason for thinking that something stands in such need, i.e. for justifiable reluctance to dismiss it as how things just happen to be, is that one in fact glimpses some tidy way in which it might be explained.

In the case of catching the 23.2576 inch fish, a fish of the only length which can be caught and observed, the first of the tidy explanations which suggested themselves could be called a Fish Ensemble explanation. It runs parallel to the World Ensemble (or multiple universes) explanation of how it came to be at all likely that anyone would ever observe a cosmos.

1.12 There are subsidiary morals too. Thus, notice how you cannot account for catching your fish by considering many *merely possible* fish, remarking that only fish of just about exactly 23.2576 inches could be caught, and then declaring that this would sufficiently explain the affair even if yours had been the only fish in the lake. What you instead need is either a benevolent fish-creating person or else a lake with many *actual* fish of varied lengths. The fish, really existing fish, of lengths which cannot be caught, help to render unmysterious the catching of the fish which can be.

Is this wildly paradoxical? Surely not. Firing an arrow at random into a forest, you hit Mr Brown: persuasive evidence, surely, that the forest is full of people, despite how the other people gave Mr Brown no greater chance of being hit. You may need a well-populated forest to have much likelihood of there being somebody precisely where your arrow lands. You may need fish of many different lengths to have much likelihood that at least one of them will be of precisely the right length for your fishing apparatus.

When the fish is captured then the details of how it came to be captured and of how it came to be of the right length will form a long causal story perhaps entirely unaffected by the other fish in the lake. The complex details of how Mr Brown came to stand precisely where he stood may be uninfluenced by the others in the forest. But I have already (in section 1.8) drawn attention to this kind of point. I said, remember, that a Multiple Worlds explanation *would not be a substitute for* a long, scientifically very ordinary causal account of Life's evolution. Instead it would offer insight into why it was inevitable, likely, or very possible that Life would evolve *somewhere*.

1.13 But aren't there *infinitely many* infinitesimally different fish lengths which the fishing apparatus could accept? *Just as many*, in fact, as the lengths which it would reject?

Well, there being infinitely many points inside a bull's-eye is no ground for optimism that a dart will hit this tiny target.

One sometimes meets with the flat announcement that there could be nothing impressive in the supposed evidence of fine tuning unless among all possible sets of force strengths and particle masses *only one* could lead to Life's evolution. I see no excuse for such an announcement. Surely the fine tuning could be impressive if the Life-permitting possibilities constituted, say, only a thousandth of the range of possibilities under consideration. To deny this is almost as bad as announcing that the evidence could be impressive only if every single aspect of our universe were fine tuned, or only if the fine tuning made Life's evolution 100 per cent certain.

1.14 Would you protest that if fish appeared one after another with randomized lengths then there would be nothing particularly unlikely in the right length's being had by the very first fish of all?

You would be trading on an ambiguity. Yes, the very first fish would be no more unlikely to be 'just right' than the second or the millionth. *In that sense* its just-rightness 'wouldn't be particularly unlikely'. But it could still be particularly unlikely where this meant that it was very, very unlikely. Assuming that no benevolent fish-creator is at work, no just-right fish is likely to exist unless there are many fish.

1.15 Yet, you exclaim, aren't we in fact virtually compelled to accept the God hypothesis? The alternative is to assume, so to speak, that the lake contains many fish and that we had been waiting until a catchable fish – a universe we could observe – came along. Yet surely we weren't *disembodied spirits lying in wait* until there came to be a universe containing bodies for us!

Isn't *our being specifically us* tied to our being in this specific universe, a universe in which our minds are just parts or aspects of the bodies which we say they inhabit? So aren't we forced to believe in a divine hand which made our universe one in which life was likely to evolve?

Not so, I think. Let us agree that in God's absence our births could only be a matter of tremendous luck. Let it be supposed that if the breaking apart of Nature's four main forces had occurred slightly differently in our universe then living beings could never have evolved in it, and that exactly how it occurred was a random affair. So what? The hypothesis of many universes shows how it could be likely that *some* set of living beings should have the luck of being born. While they could be extremely lucky, their luck would not be unbelievably amazing.

Remember Mr Brown's sad case when the arrow hits him. Extremely unlucky? Yes. But his bad luck is unmysterious if there were many people in the forest. It is unmysterious despite how the others in the forest could in no way have increased the chance that he, Mr Brown in particular, would be hit.

Here we could tell a story of a lottery. When the hundred thousand lottery tickets were being printed one of them was given a number which made it worth a million dollars. Most of the tickets were actually sold. Anyone winning the million dollars – Mr Green, perhaps – should presumably feel no compulsion to seek some very special explanation for having won: some explanation of a kind inapplicable to just any other winner. Yes, the absence of such an explanation would mean that he personally had enjoyed immense good luck, but it was very likely that somebody would enjoy it. The greater the number of tickets sold after Mr Green purchased his, the less amazing his win, although the improbability of his winning would have been precisely as great no matter how many were sold.

True enough, Mr Green's immense good luck is firmly tied to the specific fact that he is Mr Green. If someone else had won the million dollars then Mr Green would be groaning. But the amazingness or otherwise of his win is not firmly tied to the luck involved. For if enough tickets were sold then it would be utterly unamazing that somebody or other – somebody who would be forced to be a specific somebody because nobody can avoid being somebody specific – should be the lucky winner.

1.16 This particular lottery story, however, fails to reflect an important extra element in the cosmological case: namely, that it is a case in which (so to speak) the winning of a lottery *is a prerequisite of observing anything*. Given this extra element, we cannot argue in the following style:

While it would not be unbelievably amazing that somebody had won a million dollars by mere chance, it could still be very amazing *to me* that the somebody should be *specifically me*. Not, perhaps, unbelievably amazing – because one presumably ought to be reluctant to say that *no matter who* wins a lottery by mere chance, that person ought to be flatly unwilling to believe that it was Chance that settled the affair – but still amazing enough to make me doubt whether Chance, rather than, say, my girlfriend who works at lottery company head-quarters, really did give me my victory. For *what I should expect to be observing* is a situation in which I hold a non-winning ticket.

One cannot argue in this style because in the cosmological case a queer kind of observational selection effect guarantees that a 'non-winning ticket' – a lifeless universe – will never be seen by anyone.

To highlight this extra element we might tell a new version of the Fishing Story. A mad scientist allocates numbers to millions of human ova, fertilized and then frozen. She fishes for ten seconds with an apparatus able to catch only a 23.2576 inch fish. If unsuccessful she destroys ovum number one. She then fishes for another ten seconds on behalf of ovum number two; and so on. Any test-tube boy baby born because 'his' fishing period led to success can (after mastering mathematics) be extremely thank-ful to have survived this savage weeding. He has been extremely lucky. But not unbelievably lucky. He presumably need not feel compelled to reject the mad scientist's report on how he came to be born. For with respect to *believability* this report is much on a par with a report that the scientist fished repeatedly on behalf of the same ovum for successive ten-second periods until triumph crowned her efforts. It is just that the two cases differ markedly with respect to how *fortunate* he is to have been born. In the case of the many ova it would have been only through immense good fortune that *his* ovum gave rise to a conscious being.

If, in contrast, the mad scientist reported to him that she had set aside only a single ovum for the fishing experiment and fished for just one ten-second period, then he should refuse to believe this. It would not be enough for him to comment, 'If that ovum hadn't had such tremendous luck then I shouldn't be here to ask whether to be surprised, so there's nothing for me to be surprised at.'

1.17 The Firing Squad Story can help us to see the correctness of that last point. When the fifty sharpshooters all miss me, 'If they hadn't all missed then I shouldn't be considering the affair' is not an adequate response. What the situation demands is, 'I'm popular with the sharpshooters – unless, perhaps, immensely many firing squads are at work and I'm among the very rare survivors.'

1.18 The proposed observational selection effect which inspires these stories – namely, that the universe which we observe must be in the class of life-permitting universes since how otherwise could we living beings be observing it? – cannot operate unless there is *more than one actual universe*. (No Observational Selection Effect without Actual Things from Which to Select! Section 1.12 in effect made this the second moral to be drawn from the Fishing Story. The tale of the Firing Squad is just another way of making the point.) But equally, a multiplicity of actual universes cannot help us much *unless the observational selection effect is joined to it*. Given vastly many universes very varied in their properties, we could be less puzzled that some universe or other was life-containing; but mightn't we be tempted to feel almost as astonished as ever that *our* universe was a life-containing one? Well, the temptation could disappear when we reflected that any universe which wasn't life-containing could not be 'our universe' to anybody. As 1.16 pointed out, we must not say things parallel to, 'What I personally should expect to be observing is a non-winning ticket.'

1.19 Perhaps a Typing Monkey Story will make things clearer. Contemplating the World Ensemble hypothesis we are not like Mr Henry who is called into a room, shown a monkey and a typewritten sonnet, told that the monkey has typed the sonnet just by chance, and then invited to feel less astonished – or else much less deeply suspicious that he has been told a lie – when he is further informed that vastly many men have been called into similar rooms at the same moment: sufficiently many men to have made it likely that at least one of them would be looking at a monkey-written sonnet.

Nor again are we like Mr Richard who is instead told that this was the one and only time that a monkey had been given a typewriter to play with, but that if no sonnet had been typed – faultlessly and without any prior errors – then he would have been unable to observe or think anything. 'You would have been shot as soon as the monkey made its first error, and therefore the sonnet is nothing for you to be astonished at.'

Rather, we are like Mr Thomas who is told both that there were vastly many monkeys typing away in different rooms and that each monkey was paired with a different Mr So-and-So, the arrangement being that no Mr So-and-So would remain unshot unless 'his' monkey generated a sonnet.

'There exist many universes, very varied in their properties', is of little use if in splendid isolation. The same applies to, 'Without life-permitting conditions we shouldn't be here to discuss a universe.' The two must work in harness.

How could the existence of other universes have affected the situation *here*? The answer is that it couldn't have affected it. The existence of countless other universes couldn't have made it any more likely that *this* universe, which in point of fact became 'ours' to living beings through (let us say) a breaking apart of Nature's four main forces which just chanced to take a fortunate turn, would have its forces break apart in that fashion so that life could evolve in it. But on the other hand the existence of countless universes may well have made it virtually sure that at least one universe would become 'ours' to living beings, thanks to the forms which its forces chanced to take when they broke apart. Those living beings, while having cause to thank their luck, could seem to have little ground for astonishment. Beings like them may have been practically bound to evolve somewhere – and wherever they evolved would be their 'our universe', '*this* universe', 'here'. An observational selection effect would guarantee that the particular universe which they observed was life-containing; and the existence of the many universes could have meant that there had been more than just a faint possibility that such a selection effect would operate. If the universes really were sufficiently many then there would have been a virtual certainty that it would operate.

(Even if there were only a single universe, mightn't that universe be 'subject to an observational selection effect' in the following strained sense, that it was only through its being life-containing that it could be observed? Perhaps so. But as the Firing Squad Story shows, this strained sense could not enter into any satisfying explanation.)

1.20 Yet – you protest – we have no firm reason to think that universes really could have any of a wide range of features much as fishes can have many lengths. Mightn't only the one kind of universe be possible? Or mightn't only universes like ours be at all likely?

Let us not linger over the idea that only the one kind of universe is logically possible. Today, 'the logically possible' means what could be described without self-contradiction; and *that only the actual universe could be described non-self-contradictorily* looks a very odd claim. Its charms are so few that its refutation can safely wait until Chapter 4.

How, though, should we react to the idea that there is something about Nature's actual force strengths, particle masses, and so forth which makes them alone '*really* possible or likely'?

While it looked to us as if God had very skilfully hit a bull's-eye, a tiny 'window' of life-encouraging force strengths, particle masses, etc., mightn't hitting this window have been hard or impossible to avoid? When we represented the situation on graph paper, couldn't we be using the wrong kinds of scale? Mightn't a truly appropriate graph show the so-called window as filling most or all of the field of real possibilities?

1.21 My answer is that all this might conceivably be so but that it ought not to trouble us much.

A fanciful example could illustrate the point. Suppose that the words MADE BY GOD are found all over the world's granite. Their letters recur at regular intervals in this rock's crystal patterns. Two explanations suggest themselves. Perhaps God put the words there or perhaps very powerful visitors from Alpha Centauri are playing a practical joke. Both explanations might account for the facts fairly well, yet along comes a philosopher with the hypothesis that the only 'really possible' natural laws are ones which make granite carry such words. And in that case, says he, there is no need for anything to be 'fine tuned' in order for there to be such words. Nothing else is genuinely possible! Explanation fully provided! So-called bull's-eye, tiny window, in fact fills the entire field! Yes, there are countless logically possible natural laws, but the only *really possible* ones are the laws which yield electrons, pebbles, stars, and MADE BY GOD.

Surely this would be ingeniously idiotic. We must not turn our backs on tidy explanations, replacing them by a hand waved towards the obscure notion of 'limits to what is really possible'. Prior to our discovering that there are messages in granite or that any of a hundred small changes in force strengths, particle masses, and so forth would seemingly have prevented Life's evolution —*prior to* our discovering this, I agree, it might be attractive to theorize that only the one kind of granitic crystal pattern or the one set of strengths and masses 'is really possible'. But afterwards? Surely the attractiveness has vanished. Blind Necessity must be presumed not to run around scattering messages or making a hundred different factors each look exactly as if chosen in order to produce living beings.

1.22 It might still be that all force strengths, particle masses, etc. were dictated by the laws which applied to our cosmos, laws cohering elegantly in some Totally Unified Theory or Theory of Everything. For these laws could be due *not* to Blind Necessity but to divine selection of a Totally Unified Theory which provided automatically the results which lead people to talk of fine tuning. (Rather similarly, a very carefully chosen Theory might perhaps yield granitic messages automatically. We might then say that 'the real fine tuning' was a matter of God's very careful choice.) Or again, it might just conceivably be that immensely many such Totally Unified Theories happened to be correct, each in a different universe. There would then be no Blind Necessity stating that all universes must be life-permitting – although it would of course be necessary that any universe in which living beings found themselves was in fact life-permitting.

1.23 Concluding that it was no Blind Necessities that gave life-permitting forms to a hundred factors, we should be showing cheerful disregard of the possibility that it was 'a priori tremendously likely' that such Necessities had dictated those factors. (Or else that they had made them highly probable – so that, in the cases of absolutely all the factors, the seeming needs for fine tuning were mere artefacts of graphs wrongly scaled. Or else, perhaps, that they had set up a situation in which those factors, while apparently so multitudinously distinct, in truth formed a web such that every attempt to ruin Life's prospects by changing one factor would only produce compensatory changes in others.) Yet such a cheerful disregard can be reasonable even if we grant that some clear sense can here be attached to the words 'a priori tremendously likely'. The Story of the Granite is an attempt to show how very reasonable this sort of disregard could sometimes be.

Again, consider the following case. Feeling two balls in an urn but knowing nothing about their colours, you draw a ball, replace it, draw again, replace, and so on for a hundred draws. Every single time a red ball is drawn. A tidy explanation suggests itself: that both the balls are red. Would you resist this on the grounds that 'maybe it was tremendously likely' that one of them was blue?

1.24 But, you object, wouldn't it be silly to suppose that we can, albeit only in thought or on computer screens, inspect absolutely all possible universes so as to be able to find that only a very tiny proportion would be life-permitting?

It would indeed be silly. However, the Story of the Fly on the Wall shows that we need inspect only the universes of 'the local area': the possible universes which are much like ours in their basic laws yet differ in their force strengths, particle masses, expansion speeds, degrees of turbulence, and so on. A wall bears a fly (or a tiny group of flies) surrounded by a largish empty area.

The fly (or one of the group) is hit by a bullet. With appropriate background assumptions – e.g. our not knowing that short-sighted frugal Uncle Harry was the one and only firer – we might fairly confidently say, 'Many bullets are hitting the wall and/or a marksman fired this particular bullet', without bothering about whether distant areas of the wall are thick with flies. All that is relevant is that there are no further flies locally.

The point of this story *is not* that the Many Bullets or Else Marksman theory is undeniably superior to the Uncle Harry theory. Instead it is that the latter theory would get no support from any mere fact that the wall was crawling with flies, if there were only the one fly locally.

When telling the story I have sometimes suggested that the alternative to the marksman would be that many bullets *were hitting the wall near the fly*. This was a blunder. For suppose the wall carried many solitary flies each surrounded by a largish empty area. There could now be a good chance of a bullet's hitting some solitary fly provided only that many bullets *were hitting the wall*. So from the fact that there is only one fly locally (only one life-permitting kind of possible universe inside 'the local group' of possible universes, those much like ours in their basic laws) we have no firm right to conclude that in the absence of a marksman (God) there are probably many bullets locally (many actually existing universes much like ours in their basic laws). It need only be supposed that there are many bullets hitting the wall at varying places: many actually existing universes with differing characters. Although the basic laws of these other universes could plausibly be thought to be much like those of our universe, they might conceivably be very different.

1.25 It is often objected that only one universe is open to our inspection and that judgments of probability cannot be made on the basis of a single trial. The Telepathized Painting Story is a suitable reply. After doing his best to paint a countryside, Jones tries to transmit the horrid results to Smith by mere power of thought. Behold, Smith reproduces every messy tree and flower and cloud. Whereupon a philosopher reacts as follows: 'Can't conclude anything from *that*! Must have more than one trial!'

Faced by such a reaction we ought to protest that Smith's painting is complex. Although only a single painting it is many thousand blobs of paint. Much could be learned from it. And experiencing many thousand billion parts of our universe, mightn't we rather similarly gain some right to draw conclusions about the whole? After learning about ordinary messages we could be justifiably reluctant to dismiss as mere chance, or even as 'neither probable nor improbable because we haven't experienced other universes', any MADE BY GOD messages which we found in the rocks. *After a little acquaintance with physics and biology* we could fairly confidently perform thought-experiments showing how dim Life's prospects would have been, had various force strengths and particle masses been slightly different; now, couldn't this well encourage us to believe in God or in an ensemble of universes? (Yet philosophers have argued solemnly that a Creator would find it impossible to leave any signs of his creative action because, poor fellow, he would be limited to showing us just a single universe. Hence, one presumes, even writing MADE BY GOD all over it would have no tendency to prove anything. And if that were so then of course the mere fact of its containing living beings could give us no reason to believe in God – or in Multiple Worlds, for that matter.)

Hostile Stories: Little Puddle etc.

1.26 Let us now turn to a story apparently damaging to my case: the oft-told tale of the Great Rivers Flowing through the Principal Cities of Europe. What superb evidence of the Creator's action!

A variant points to the Mississippi. See how wonderfully it threads its way under every bridge!

Another concerns pond life. The rotifers of Little Puddle marvel at the deity who has provided filthy water and mud. Had their ancestors evolved in arsenic-filled waters then they would be marvelling at the Creator's benevolence in supplying arsenic. An atrocious case of thinking backwards! How blind to Darwin's point that just as cities and bridges conform to the positions of rivers, so organisms adapt themselves to their environments! What parochial concern with the prerequisites of rotiferhood!

My reply is that even those defending the unfortunately named Anthropic Principle (see Chapter 6) often take pains to deny that their concern is only with *anthropos, homo sapiens*, mankind. As was made plain enough by B. Carter, who baptized the Principle and so has a right to be heard on the subject, what is involved is a possible observational selection effect stemming from the nature not of manhood but of *observerhood*. The Anthropic Principle reminds us that if there were many actually existing universes most of which had properties utterly hostile to the evolution of intelligent life then, obviously, we intelligent products of evolution could be observing only one of the rare universes in which intelligent life could indeed evolve. The fact that such a selection effect could be helpful in explaining any observations of fine tuning – could help them to become unmysterious since (section 1.8) such observations would have been likely to occur somewhere, and (1.16) no situations tuned in life-excluding ways could ever be observed – provides by far the strongest reason for believing in multiple universes. The mere truth that a slightly different universe could not be seen *by mankind* is much less interesting. It could be ludicrous to view that truth as any reason at all for accepting more than one universe. And similarly, those who believe in God rather than in multiple universes could be being absurd if their grounds for belief were that various natural conditions seemed crucial to human existence in particular. The key point is instead that *intelligent life of any plausible kind* seems crucially dependent on those natural conditions. People who tell sarcastic tales about rotifers could seem to have missed the point.

1.27 Alternatively, perhaps these people do not miss it but instead have minds dominated by the curious idea that intelligent life could evolve just about anywhere: for instance, in frozen hydrogen or near neutron star surfaces or in the interiors of ordinary stars like the sun or deep inside planet Earth, or in interstellar gas clouds.[6] But they then invite responses such as the following.

First, there are quite powerful reasons for thinking that frozen hydrogen, neutron stars, etc. would be inhospitable environments. There are for instance grounds for thinking that chemistry – impossible in neutron stars or inside the sun – is very special in the intricate structures which it makes possible. And our sort of life, at any rate, is chemical life. Are we to suppose that this, the only kind of life we know, is highly unusual, *other kinds* being nowhere near as suggestive of fine tuning? That could look too reminiscent of an argument which Bertrand Russell thought he heard voiced by various eighteenth-century optimists: that since, so to speak, the oranges at the top of the barrel looked rotten, those underneath were probably delicious.

Second, if intelligent life were as easily achieved as such people fancy then Fermi's celebrated 'Where are they?' conundrum, the puzzle of why we have no evidence of extraterrestrial intelligent beings, could become very hard to solve. Maybe the solution would now be that it is a huge step from mere *life processes*, perhaps something pretty simple going on in frozen hydrogen, to *intelligent life*. But in this case a multiplicity of universes or a divine Fine Tuner could be needed to make intelligent life at all likely to evolve.

Third, there could never have been any frozen hydrogen, neutron stars, ordinary stars, interstellar gas clouds, or even individual atoms, if the Big Bang had been followed by recollapse within ten seconds or if any of a large number of other unfortunate happenings had happened – happenings seemingly avoidable only by tuning that is extremely accurate. (See parts of section 1.4 and much of Chapter 2.) So even if living beings of many very different kinds filled our universe, a universe very slightly differently tuned would still be utterly lifeless.

1.28 'If rotifers could talk . . .' is sometimes replaced by 'If carbon could talk . . . .' The sceptic may say that the prerequisites of intelligent life are just whatever are the prerequisites of carbon, of water, of long-lived stable stars, and maybe of a handful of further things. Now, how would matters look to a Philosophical Club consisting of carbon atoms, water molecules, long-lived stable stars, and so forth? Instead of an Anthropic Principle, wouldn't there be a Carbonic Principle? Instead of worshipping a Creator benevolent towards humans, wouldn't club members pray to one who loved stellar stability?

In reply it can be helpful to insist that intelligent life seems to depend on a very lengthy list of things. When the Philosophical Club came to its grand conclusion that carbon, water, long-lived stars, and so forth are what are truly important here, or are at any rate just as important as the intelligent life which so obsesses humans, then surely the length of the list, plus the fact that all the items listed *were listed because of being prerequisites of intelligent life*, would show the wrongness of this.

1.29 Still, suppose for argument's sake that nothing but carbon was required for producing living intelligence. The prerequisites of carbon and of living intelligence thus being identical, might it not be arbitrary to concentrate on the latter?[7] Why not forget about the Difficulty of Generating Intelligence? Why not talk instead of How Hard It Is to Produce Carbon? Now, the existence of carbon might indeed act as a 'selection function' picking out our kind of universe from the field of all possible universes. Many scientific theories might fail through being incompatible with the observed fact of there being carbon. Yet – says the sceptic – this is all very ordinary science. Compare how the theory that rock becomes fluid at a pressure of two tons per square inch is refuted by the existence of Mount Everest whose lower regions would in that case have flowed away. There is nothing in this to justify talk of God, of a multiplicity of universes, or of the 'Mount Everestic Principle'! This seems to me very wrong. It overlooks the point of the Fishing Story, the Poker Game Story, the Collapsing Arch Story, and the tale of the Silk Merchant's Thumb. It forgets that carbon particles do not talk, observe nothing, and could not plausibly be loved for their own sakes by a benevolent deity.

How are those tales relevant, and what is so special about observerhood or about being such as a benevolent deity could well love? It is all a question of tidiness of explanation. Every thumb must be somewhere, but the placement of the silk merchant's is 'special' because it suggests a plausible ground – a love of money – for its being where it is and not elsewhere. Likewise, the reason why a 23.2576 inch fish is special is that nothing else can be observed with the help of your fishing apparatus and that this, when combined with belief in many fish of varied lengths swimming by the apparatus, very neatly explains why the fish is being observed. In place of a mere 'selection function' we have a possible observational selection effect: one which operates if there are many actual fish from which the apparatus can select.

1.30 True, the catching of the fish *also* gives grounds for believing in a benevolent fish-creator. But such double suggestiveness need not dismay us. Bob's empty treasure chest, on an island whose only inhabitants are Bob, Mike, and Jim, can fairly powerfully suggest that Mike is a thief despite also suggesting just as powerfully that theft has been committed by Jim. (In fact, the two of them may have committed it in partnership.)

Some Conclusions

1.31 Contemporary religious thinkers often approach the Argument from Design with a grim determination that their churches shall not again be made to look foolish. Recalling what happened when churchmen opposed first Galileo and then Darwin, they insist that religion must be based not on science but on faith. Philosophy, they announce, has demonstrated that Design Arguments lack all force.

I hope to have shown that philosophy has demonstrated no such thing. Our universe, which these religious thinkers believe to be created by God, does look, greatly though this may dismay them, very much as if created by God. Many of its basic features seem fine tuned to Life's requirements. Various parables ('Stories') suggest that this is indeed a ground for belief in God so long as we use reasoning such as serves us well in ordinary affairs. Let us trust it even here. The question of whether our universe is God-created is no ordinary question, but that cannot itself provide any strong excuse for abandoning ordinary ways of thinking. Theology is not a call to reject common sense.

Still, we must bear in mind two main points.

First: World Ensemble plus Observational Selection could provide a powerful means of accounting for any fine tuning which we felt tempted to ascribe to Divine Selection. Now, this does not say that belief in God could gain no support from fine tuning. (Remember the empty treasure chest of section 1.30.) Still, fine tuning could not point towards God in an unambiguous way. Of my various Stories, not one gives any support to the God hypothesis which it does not also give to the World Ensemble hypothesis.

Second: A cosmos too very obviously God-made might tend to be a cosmos not of freedom but of puppetry. This is one of several grounds for thinking that God's creative role would not be made entirely plain.

It would be quite another matter, though, for God to avoid every possible indication of his existence even when this meant selecting physical laws and force strengths and particle masses which were prima facie far less satisfactory than others he would otherwise have chosen. A God of that degree of deviousness looks uncomfortably close to the kind of deity who creates the universe in 4004 BC complete with fossils in the rocks.

1.32 A frequently heard protest is that no amount of finite evidence could support a belief in God, who is infinite.

A balance pan contains butter to the weight of one kilogram. The pan rises. What can we conclude about the weight in the balance's other pan? Answer: It is above one kilogram. We certainly cannot conclude that there is an infinite weight there.

My reply is that in science and elsewhere we should seek simplicity, and *infinity* can at times be simpler than, say, *five million and seventy*. Consider the theory that only five million and seventy universes will ever appear as quantum fluctuations (section 1.6[c]). It could seem simpler to believe that infinitely many would appear in this way.

In the case of the divine infinity, what is crucial to a Neoplatonist like me is God's infinite power to create what is good. But why should I prefer to think that this power is only finite? Why suppose that a creatively effective ethical requirement (1.3) could be responsible for a world's existence but only if that world were a non-intricate world, or a world containing no more than sixty million and thirty-one cabbages? (Would intricacy tax the intelligence of Neoplatonism's God? No. Creatively effective ethical requirements *act as if* intelligent but are not themselves intelligent in any way that could encourage us to speak of an intelligence which could be taxed. Among Neoplatonists, Plotinus was specially clear on that sort of point.)

1.33 Later chapters will expand the arguments of this first one. Sometimes it will be at the cost of making things look more complicated than they actually are.

In reading them, please remember section 1.4's point about words like 'fine tuned for producing Life'. Such words must not be read as begging the question of whether there is anything like a divine Fine Tuner. Physicists often say such things as this: that a particular theory might account for various facts, but only if various numbers which the theory allows to have any of many values are 'fine tuned', i.e. *fall within certain narrow limits.*[8] Nothing about a Fine Tuner there! – and the business need have nothing to do with Life. True, the fine tuning talked of in this book will almost always have to do with it; yet context will sometimes show otherwise. Assuming, for example, that fish must have lengths falling within narrow limits if they are to be caught by your fishing apparatus, then any fish which it catches are 'fine-tuned fish' even if the reason why there are any such fish is just that the lake contains vastly many fish of randomized lengths. In this context, calling the fish 'fine tuned' clearly says only that ones slightly different in length would not have been caught. Again, the fact that many of my Stories have involved the suspicion that *conscious agents* have been fine tuning things – the position of a thumb, say, or the constitution of a hand of cards – is of no particular significance. Any explanations given for 'fine tuning' need not be *agent*-explanations. If all natural pearls have grit grains at their centres then the positions of those grains are fine tuned in ways suggesting the theory that pearls are secreted by oysters to envelop irritating grit. The positions count as 'fine tuned' for suggesting this theory just because very slightly different ones wouldn't suggest it – and not because oysters are conscious beings intent on minimizing their irritations. Oysters aren't.

1.34 Please bear in mind also that satisfying various of Life's prerequisites (its necessary conditions) may often be fairly far distant from guaranteeing Life's presence. While this should be plain enough, the line between the two affairs can be difficult to draw; it will usually be left to your good sense to draw it in a flexible way. In this region, making the philosopher's beloved distinction between necessary and sufficient conditions can often be both a hard and a pointless task. For on the one hand, virtually nothing is 100 per cent guaranteed in a world of quantum uncertainties let alone in the realm of great chemical complexities (where luck can be very important). And on the other hand, in a large enough Reality anything which is at all possible could be expected somewhere or other.

Chapter Two

The Evidence of Fine Tuning

The chapter develops points of the kind summarized in section 1.4 of Chapter 1. Our universe does seem remarkably tuned to Life's needs. Small changes in the strengths of its main forces, in the masses of its particles, in its degree of turbulence, in its early expansion speed, and so forth would seemingly have rendered it hostile to living beings of any plausible kind. It risked recollapse within a fraction of a second, or becoming a universe of black holes, or a universe of matter much too dilute to form stars and planets, or even one composed of light rays alone.

Newton made points on much the same general lines. I discuss how he could reformulate them today.

Like others, the chapter is designed to be readable in isolation. Remember, though, that Chapter 1 tried to defend in advance against objections which may spring to a reader's mind.

Newton's Design Argument

2.1 In Lecture 7 of *Modes of Thought* (1938), A. N. Whitehead attacks a 'Hume–Newton' picture of Nature as a 'self-sufficient, meaningless complex of facts'. What a misleading impression this can give of Newton's thinking! The General Scholium to his *Principia* said that the 'most beautiful system of the sun, planets and comets could only proceed from the counsel and dominion of an intelligent and powerful Being'; that God placed stars 'at immense distances from one another' so that the cosmos would not collapse; that 'blind metaphysical necessity' could not produce 'all that diversity of natural things which we find suited to different times and places'. Can Whitehead have been ignorant of all this?

Perhaps Whitehead's real target is those 'Newtonians' who think always of the following words of the General Scholium: 'I frame no hypotheses. . . . It is enough that gravity does really exist and act according to the laws which we have explained.' Such people avert their gaze from the passages surrounding these famous sentences, from Newton's letters to Bentley, and from the Queries he added to the *Opticks*, all of which abound in theistic hypotheses. (The hypothesis, for example, of a divine plan in 'that Order and Beauty which we see in the world' and above all in such organs as the eye.[1] The hypothesis that 'the mere Laws of Nature' could never induce the world to 'arise out of a Chaos'.[2] The hypothesis that the reason why 'matter should divide itself into two sorts' and why 'that part of it which is fit to compose a shining body should fall down into one mass and make a sun' could lie only in 'the counsel and contrivance of a voluntary Agent'.)[3] Newton's reputation supposedly demands that this orgy of hypothesizing be quietly forgotten. People recall the scorn Leibniz poured on the Newtonian idea that God would from time to time 'rewind', 'clean', 'repair' the cosmos, imparting impulses to the planets to correct their perturbations.[4] Did not Laplace show the solar system to be stable despite those perturbations? Has not Darwin removed all need for God's hand? Newton can appear to seek God in the gaps of our scientific understanding, gaps which have had an embarrassing habit of snapping shut.

2.2 My argument will be that Newton's blending of science with theism is something glorious. I shall not defend him against Leibniz and Darwin, though, since the notion that God constantly intervenes in the world's workings seems unfortunate. (As Leibniz said, God seems here portrayed as 'an unskilful workman, oft obliged to mend his work'. And the Problem of Evil – of reconciling worldly disasters with divine beneficence – looks overwhelming unless God has strong moral reasons for *not* perpetually correcting how the world operates.) Yet the forms taken by the laws of physics, and perhaps also the distribution of material early in the Big Bang, suggest God's creative activity. When we illustrate the point with facts unknown to Newton this is precisely as he would have wished. He lacked, he said, 'that sufficiency of experiment which is required' for the proper development of his system.

My appeal will be chiefly to recent evidence, often discussed in connection with what is known as the Anthropic Principle. Many people suggest that basic characteristics of the observable cosmos are strikingly 'fine tuned' for producing Life. (a) Very often they conclude that there exist countless 'universes' – largely or entirely separate systems, perhaps of immense size – and that force strengths, particle masses, expansion speeds, and so on vary from universe to universe. Sooner or later, somewhere, conditions permit living beings to evolve. The Anthropic Principle reminds us that, obviously, *only such a somewhere could be observed by living beings*. (b) Yet an alternative interpretation could be offered. This is that there exists just a single universe, or else that while there are many universes, they are all very much alike. Force strengths and particle masses are the same everywhere, as is suggested by the *Principia*'s second Rule of Reasoning which

Newton illustrated with the remark that 'the light of our culinary fire and of the sun' should be regarded as governed by the same laws. And those strengths and masses, and no doubt many other factors also, were selected with a view to making Life possible. They were selected by a Mind or by a more abstract Creative Principle[5] which can reasonably be called 'God'.

Would there then be 'a God of the Gaps'? That might depend on the sense you gave to those ambiguous words. Many scientists would say they were not in the business of explaining why there was any universe, why its initial state was such-and-such, and why it obeyed any physical laws at all, let alone ones specifying these or those force strengths. A deity deciding such affairs would fill no gaps in science as they understand it. The gap-filler they reject is the one whose fury is the thunder or who dropped the first living cell into the primeval seas.

Low Turbulence; Life-permitting Expansion Speed

2.3 'Blind Fate', said Newton, could never produce the 'wonderful Uniformity' of planetary movements. 'Gravity may put the planets in motion, but without the divine power it could never put them into such a circulating motion as they have.'[6] Well, while wrong about the planets he could be right about the order of the universe in general. Run a model cosmos backwards. Unless its parts are very carefully positioned, chaos ensues. Now, Newton reasoned[7] that if one would expect chaos through trying to run a cosmos backwards – for example, by giving to 'the matter of the earth and all the planets and stars' a motion causing it to 'fly up from them', so attempting to reverse any process whereby this matter had come together to form these heavenly bodies – then divine power would have been needed to prevent that same cosmos from developing chaotically while it ran forwards. And reasoning much like this finds favour today. It is commonly argued that a chaotic Big Bang, probably beginning in a singularity (a region beyond which the past histories of light rays cannot extend) which is 'ragged' rather than point-like, could be expected because chaos would result from running a randomly selected universe backwards; and further, that the chaos of such a Bang could evolve towards cosmic smoothness only at the price of producing vastly much disorder on a smaller scale – vastly much heat or vastly many black holes. (Black holes are very disorderly, 'very high entropy' systems.)

Here, special importance attaches to the fact that instantaneous action at a distance is impossible. Lack of instantaneous communication would mean that regions coming out of a Big Bang could not know of one another until light had been given time to pass between them. Thus they could not be like runners signalling to one another so as to maintain an evenly expanding ring. Their movements could be expected to be thoroughly uncoordinated. When they made contact, friction might bring about some large-scale uniformity; the faster runners, so to speak, would meet with the most resistance, making them slow down; but the friction could be expected to produce life-excluding temperatures or a universe of black holes. This is the Smoothness Problem.

P. C. W. Davies wrote that frictional smoothing away of even a tiny amount of early roughness 'would increase the primeval heat billions of times', disastrously. And 'if the primeval material was churned about at random it would have been overwhelmingly more probable for it to have produced black holes than stars': 'the odds against a starry cosmos' become 'one followed by a thousand billion billion zeros, at least'.[8] R. Penrose similarly calculated that in the absence of new physical principles which ensured a smooth beginning 'the accuracy of the Creator's aim' when he placed a pin to select our orderly world from the space of physically possible ones would need to have been 'at least of the order of one part in $10^{10^{123}}$', an unimaginably gigantic figure.[9] (It is 1 followed by 10^{123} zeros.)

The Smoothness Problem remains of great magnitude even if mechanisms active at early instants adjusted the ratio of photons (Newton's 'particles of light') to matter particles in ways reducing its magnitude. For such mechanisms would operate only at very early times, whereas regions which had never before interacted could keep coming over one another's horizons for billions of years.

2.4 Any solution to the Problem must allow for life-encouraging local departures from smoothness: the galaxies. Volumes of gas must condense into stars. Yet if the entire universe behaved similarly, collapsing upon itself, then this could yield swift disaster. What hinders the stars from falling upon one another? Newton answered, as we saw, that God placed them 'at immense distances', but a more complete answer would be that our cosmos was from very early instants expanding at a speed placing it very close to the line dividing continued explosion from gravitational implosion. Tiny early deviations from this line would grow immensely, as was stressed by R. H. Dicke in 1970. He calculated that a 0.1 per cent early speed increase would have yielded a present-day expansion thousands of times faster than what we find.[10] A similarly paltry decrease would have led to recollapse when the cosmos was a millionth its present size.

Such calculations have since been refined. In 1978 Dicke said that a speed decrease of one part in a million when the Big Bang was a second old would have produced recollapse before temperatures fell below 10,000 degrees;[11] with an equally small increase 'the kinetic energy of expansion would have so dominated gravity that minor density irregularities could not have collected into bound systems in which stars might form'. And S. W. Hawking estimated that a decrease by as little as one part in a million million when the temperature was 10^{10} degrees 'would have resulted in the Universe starting to recollapse when the temperature was still 10,000 degrees'.[12] The fine tuning seemingly needed (i.e. for the universe to come to expand at a life-permitting speed) must be more accurate, the more one pushes back the time at which it is carried out.

2.5 Another way of coming to appreciate the fine tuning is to consider early cosmic densities, which are closely related to expansion speeds. If we can trace things back to the Planck time, 10^{-43} seconds after the Bang started, then the density must seemingly have been within about one part in 10^{60} of the 'critical density' which would have made space precisely flat (precisely Euclidean), so placing it precisely on the line between collapse and continued expansion.[13] Temperatures (measured in terms of energies) would then have been around 10^{19} GeV. At a later, 10^{17} GeV stage about which we can be more confident, the fine tuning would still have been accurate[14] to about one part in 10^{55}. The Expansion Speed Problem can thus be restated as a Flatness Problem. Why is space not more curved?

Inflation, and the Need to Tune it

2.6 Many now claim that Smoothness and Flatness Problems can both be solved by an 'inflationary' scenario. A. H. Guth and others developed such a scenario to explain the absence of magnetic monopoles. At very high temperatures the four main forces of Nature – gravity, electromagnetism, and the nuclear strong and weak forces – are thought to have been only aspects of a single force. There may also have been just one basic type of particle. As temperatures dropped this simplicity was destroyed ('symmetry breaking'). The forces split apart in phase transitions (radical changes of state): compare how water on undergoing freezing loses its complete rotational symmetry – its property of looking the same in all directions to an observer immersed in it –

and takes on the more limited symmetry of ice crystals. Now, the phase transitions could proceed in different ways. It would be highly probable that in areas that were causally separated, light rays not having had time to link them, they would in fact proceed differently. (A million monkeys are unlikely to type always the same sequence of letters.) The outcome would be vastly many domains with different symmetries, and topological knots where these came into contact. Such knots would be magnetic monopoles. They would be so heavy and so numerous that the universe would recollapse very rapidly.[15] But this disaster could have been averted if any monopole-creating phase transition were associated with a sudden, fast-accelerating inflation of space. And such inflation – like the growth of a warren in which the rabbits of every new generation each give birth to a dozen others – might have occurred at early instants. It could have pushed monopoles and domain walls far beyond the reach of any telescope.

Inflation might give us extremely flat space: a greatly inflated balloon can have a very flat surface. And the Smoothness Problem might find much the same answer as the Expansion Speed or Flatness Problem. In the absence of Inflation the visible universe would have grown from perhaps 10^{83} initially separated regions, tremendous turbulence resulting when these made contact. Inflation, though, could mean that the horizon to all that we can now see is deep within a single such region, one whose parts form a co-ordinated whole because of having interacted at pre-inflationary moments.

2.7 However, the two Problems would seem to have been solved only by introducing others. Model-builders have difficulties in getting Inflation started, in persuading it to end without excess turbulence ('the Graceful Exit Problem'), and in having it produce irregularities neither too small nor too large to allow galaxies to grow. Even when a Grand Unified Theory is selected cunningly to achieve the desired results – which (cf. section 1.22) can look suspiciously like the 'fine tuning' which the inflationary hypothesis is so often praised for rendering unnecessary – you may still be forced to postulate a gigantic space containing rare regions in which Inflation of the right type occurs. These regions may have to be very unusually smooth, for instance. In that case we can scarcely claim that Inflation rids us of the Smoothness Problem.[16]

If smoothness is instead classified as 'natural' our difficulties are still not over. Inflation of a very special kind may then be needed to make the universe just sufficiently lumpy for galaxies to be able to grow. Indeed, without it there would risk being no significant thermodynamic 'arrow of time', and without *that* life of any kind would seem very obviously impossible. One approach is to suppose that early very tiny irregularities, mere quantum fluctuations, were inflated just enough to provide the required lumpiness.

2.8 In the most popular models the inflationary process is powered by repulsion of the sort Einstein introduced when he gave a non-zero value to *the cosmological constant*. Although appearing naturally in General Relativity's equations, this constant was long treated as being zero and thus disregarded. Einstein remarked that his use of it had been his greatest blunder: instead of employing it to keep everything static he should, he said, have predicted the cosmic expansion. Yet Einstein's puzzle of how the cosmos could be kept static has come to be replaced by that of how it could avoid immediate collapse, as today's physics fills space with fields of so great an energy density – in particular in the form of quantum vacuum fluctuations in which particles attain a fleeting existence – that gravity could very quickly be expected to roll everything up into a sphere measuring 10^{-33} cm. To deal with this new puzzle two components of the cosmological constant, 'bare lambda' and 'quantum lambda', are viewed as cancelling each other with an accuracy of better than one part in 10^{50}. How this beautiful result is achieved is totally unclear. While we could invent mechanisms to perform the trick it can appear best to treat such precise cancellation as a question of Chance – i.e. of what would be quite likely to happen somewhere or other inside any sufficiently gigantic Reality – or else of Divine Selection. For it could seem that the cancellation cannot be dictated by any fundamental law since the quantum activity of the vacuum involves many fields each contributing in a temperature-dependent way, the masses of a host of scalar particles appearing crucial to the outcome.[17] Nor could one explain it as a product of an inflationary process which occurred appropriately, as this would put cart before horse. Inflation could occur appropriately only if the cancellation were already enormously accurate,[18] although it would be still more accurate afterwards. (Today the cosmological constant is zero to one part in 10^{120}.)[19]

Might 'supersymmetric' theories remove the difficulty? If the fields contributing to quantum lambda could be treated as closely allied ('incorporated into a multiplet') then weighting them in fairly simple ways might conceivably yield the cancellation. But this is at present only a very pious hope. And there is the problem that a cancellation too exact could hinder more than it helped because, as said earlier, a non-zero cosmological constant is typically viewed as needed for driving the inflationary process.

A change in the presently measured strengths either of gravity or of the nuclear weak force by as little as one part in 10^{100} could entirely ruin the cancellation,[20] making space expand or contract furiously. And it seems that Inflation would result in galaxy-producing density fluctuations only if a Grand Unified Force had a coupling constant (a measure of how strongly this Force affected particles) of only 10^{-7}, which could be thought 'unnaturally small'.[21]

2.9 Assuming, though, that it managed to inflate appropriately, then the cosmos could be dilute enough to escape collapse for the billions of years which intelligent life probably needs for its evolution, and also smooth enough to permit life-encouragingly low temperatures. And these would be no mean achievements. As J. A. Wheeler has emphasized, 'no universe can provide several billion years of time, according to general relativity, unless it is several billion light-years in extent',[22] which can be so only if it has an average density no higher than about ten hydrogen atoms per cubic metre.

Besides, one needs a very dilute cosmos to solve Olbers's paradox: *Why is the sky dark at night instead of being hot enough to fry us*, when each line of sight could be expected to end in a star or in some dust particle heated by that star? Many books wrongly appeal to the fact – which, as E. R. Harrison has shown, makes little difference to the problem – that the universe is expanding. The correct answer is that matter is so dilute that even were it all converted to radiation the sky would not be hot. A more major threat is from cosmic rays, so destructive that we can only be very thankful that their sources are so far spread out.

Inside each galaxy far greater densities occur without disaster. Even so, stars must not be much more closely packed than in our galaxy if they are to avoid frequent near-collisions spelling ruin to planetary systems (one of the points made by G. M. Idlis in the earliest major statement of what we now know as the Anthropic Principle) and to the galaxy as a whole, whose collapse is speeded whenever a near-collision occurs.[23] Again, were galaxies clustered more densely then their collisions could make things very difficult for Life.

2.10 Difficulties, furthermore, in making the step from mere chemistry to something like DNA biochemistry may be so great that the 10^{22} stars of the visible universe are needed to provide a fair chance of Life's appearing so much as once. Now, an inflationary era could be characterized by matter-producing mechanisms giving rise to those 10^{22} stars. The mechanisms would exploit the fact that gravitational energy, like all physical binding energies, is *negative energy* (point [c] of section 1.6). This could balance the positive energy of vastly much newly created matter.[24]

Stars, Planets, and Force Strengths (A): the Nuclear Forces

2.11 'Motion', Newton noted, 'is always upon the Decay': 'there is a need of conserving it by active Principles', for instance those 'by which the sun continues violently hot'. But the details were 'not yet discovered'.[25]

Have we now discovered them? Well, we now know energy is never lost entirely. When, to borrow Newton's example, two masses of clay collide, they become hotter. And while heat itself is energy in a 'disorderly' – 'high entropy' – form, heat differences can produce the orderliness of living things. The world's rush towards disorder, proceeding at different speeds in different places, sets up eddies. Thus local order is often increased.

Still, what originated the differences which are in this way exploited, granted that the Big Bang had no cold region into which to expand since it filled all space? Gravitational entropy may have come to the rescue. On large scales at least, all may have started off with extreme gravitational orderliness – a fact in which a modern Newton might see God's hand. On a microscopic scale there could have been extreme disorder, this cancelling itself out on a slightly less microscopic scale; compare how a coloured gas in a high-entropy state can appear smooth to the eye; but in the absence of divine planning it could remain hard to understand how on still larger scales the Bang was a gravitationally smooth affair rather than a ragged chaos giving rise to a cosmos of black holes or to temperatures that remained searing for billions of years. If, however, by divinely accurate pin-placement (2.3) or otherwise, large-scale gravitational smoothness could be had, then this could give rise to stars which generated heat in a steady way. For whereas thermodynamic entropy increases through dissipation, as when a gas expands, gravitational entropy increases through *concentration* as when a large mass of gas falls together to form a star.[26]

2.12 Newton was wrong in supposing that matter would need to 'divide itself into two sorts', the one forming the planets and the other a sun or suns. (Our sun is mainly hydrogen, but so is Jupiter.) Yet he was right in seeing the sun's immense size as the key to its long-lasting activity.[27] He was right, too, in his weird speculation – his conviction that the Creator could establish absolutely any physical laws must have helped make it seem acceptable to him – about 'the changing of Bodies into Light',[28] which we now know to be the source of the sun's power.

Suns and planets can be thought to depend on impressively much fine tuning of kinds which Newton could not have guessed at. For a start, the Big Bang needed to deliver atoms usable in stellar fusion reactions, not ones which had already undergone fusion. Here two things were crucial: the high expansion speed when atoms first formed – they were rushed apart before they could fuse – and *the extreme weakness of the nuclear weak force.* The weak force controls proton–proton fusion, a reaction 10^{18} times slower than one based on the other nuclear force, the strong force. Were it not for this, 'essentially all the matter in the universe would have been burned to helium before the first galaxies started to condense',[29] so there would be neither water nor long-lived stable stars, which are hydrogen-burning. (Helium-burners remain stable for times much too short for the evolution of living beings as we know them.)

Again, the weak force's weakness makes our sun 'burn its hydrogen gently for billions of years instead of blowing up like a bomb'.[30]

Had the weak force been appreciably stronger then the Big Bang's nuclear burning would have proceeded past helium and all the way to iron. Fusion-powered stars would then be impossible.

2.13 Notice, though, that the weak force could not have been much *weaker* without again giving us an all-helium universe. (There are thus *two* threats to hydrogen, one setting an upper and the other a lower limit to the values of the weak force compatible with life as we know it.) For at early moments neutrons were about as common as protons, things being so hot that the greater masses of the neutrons, which made them harder to generate, had little importance. The weak force, however, can make neutrons decay into protons. And it was just sufficiently strong to ensure that when the first atoms formed there were enough excess protons to yield roughly 70 per cent hydrogen. Without a proton excess there would have been helium only.[31]

Again, weakening the weak force would ruin the proton–proton and carbon–nitrogen–oxygen cycles which make stars into sources of the heat, the light, and the heavy elements (all those heavier than helium) which Life appears to need.[32]

2.14 How do these heavy elements get to be outside stars, to form planets and living things? The weak force helps explain this.

When stars explode as Type II supernovae they lose their heavy-element-rich outer layers. (Also, elements heavier than iron, which play an important role in Earth's organisms, can be synthesized in supernova explosions only.) Now, these layers are blasted off by neutrinos which interact with them via the weak force alone. Its extreme weakness, which allows neutrinos to pass through our planet more easily than bullets through air, permits also their escape from a supernova's collapsing core. Still, the force is just strong enough to hurl into space the outer-layer atoms needed for constructing astronomers! Strong enough, also, to fuse electrons with protons during the core's collapse, thus enabling the collapse to continue. The result is an implosion whose violence – the core shrinks thousands of times in under a second – gives rise to a gigantic explosion.

It is often held that the formation of our solar system, and presumably also of many or all other such systems of star and planets, was triggered by a nearby supernova explosion. Meteorites contain oxygen of just a single isotope, seemingly creatable only by such an explosion.

While the calculations are hard, it seems a safe bet that weakening the weak force by a factor of ten would have led to a universe consisting mainly of helium and in which the life-producing explosions could not occur.[33]

2.15 The *nuclear strong force*, too, must be neither over-strong nor over-weak, for stars to operate life-encouragingly. 'As small an increase as 2 per cent' in its strength 'would block the formation of protons out of quarks', preventing the existence even of hydrogen atoms,[34] let alone others. If this argument fails then the same small increase could still spell disaster by binding protons into diprotons: all hydrogen would now become helium early in the Bang,[35] and stars would burn by the strong interaction[36] which, as noted above, proceeds 10^{18} times faster than the weak interaction which controls our sun. A yet tinier increase, perhaps of 1 per cent, would so change nuclear resonance levels that almost all carbon would be burned to oxygen.[37] A somewhat greater increase, of about 10 per cent, would again ruin stellar carbon synthesis, this time changing resonance levels so that there would be little burning beyond carbon's predecessor, helium.[38] One a trifle greater than this would lead to 'nuclei of almost unlimited size',[39] even small bodies becoming 'mini neutron stars'.[40] All which is true despite the very short range of the strong force. Were it long-range then the universe would be 'wound down into a single blob'.[41]

2.16 Slight *de*creases could be equally ruinous. The deuteron, a combination of a neutron and a proton which is essential to stellar nucleosynthesis, is only just bound: weakening the strong force by 'about five per cent' would unbind it,[42] leading to a universe of hydrogen only. And even a weakening of 1 per cent could destroy[43] 'a particular resonance in the carbon nucleus which allows carbon to form from ^{4}He plus ^{8}Be despite the instability of ^{8}Be' (which is however stable enough to have a lifetime 'anomalously long' in a way itself suggesting fine tuning).[44] 'A 50% decrease would adversely affect the stability of all the elements essential to living organisms':[45] any carbon, for example, which somehow managed to form would soon disintegrate.

I. L. Rozental estimates that the strong force had to be within 0.8 and 1.2 times its actual strength for there to be deuterons and all elements of atomic weight greater than four.[46]

Stars, Planets, and Force Strengths (B): Electromagnetism and Gravity

2.17 The nuclear forces were unknown to Newton. How about those with which he was more familiar: electromagnetism (which he of course did not think of as a single force) and gravity?

Electromagnetism, it turns out, also needs to fall inside narrow limits if the stars are to encourage anything like life as we know it. For one thing, it is the strong force's strength by comparison with electromagnetism (it is some hundreds of times stronger) which is the real topic of the above remarks about carbon synthesis and about the deuteron's being luckily just bound while the diproton is equally luckily just unbound. Again, electromagnetic repulsion between protons prevents most of their collisions from resulting in proton–proton fusion, this explaining how stars can burn so slowly: each second our sun generates thousands of times less energy per gram than the human body. The strength of electromagnetism by comparison with gravity is crucial here.

2.18 Let us look at some further details.

First, a star's surface temperature must be suitably related to the binding energies of chemical reactions used by organisms: it must be hot enough to encourage construction of new chemicals, as in photosynthesis, but also cool enough to limit destruction such as is produced by ultraviolet light. (One probably cannot compensate for changes in stellar temperature by placing the life-bearing planet nearer or further. The constructive or destructive power of individual, 'quantized' energy packets is crucial; compare how in a photographer's dark room no amount of red light affects the film as each individual photon packs too little punch.

Now, this power remains the same at any distance.) W. H. Press and A. P. Lightman show that an interestingly delicate balance between electromagnetism and gravity is involved.[47]

As in the cases of other such balances, further factors are involved as well: the masses of the proton and the electron are relevant. So even if electromagnetism and gravity stood in a different relationship the delicacy of balance might be imagined as maintained, could those masses be varied at will. But here our imaginations might run away with us. To guard against any one disaster by tinkering with these or those factors would be likely only to introduce some new disaster because each factor enters into so many vital relationships.[48] And even if disaster could in theory be avoided, actual avoidance of it – compensation for variations in one factor through appropriate changes elsewhere – could itself be a very impressive instance of fine tuning.

2.19 Next, B. Carter draws attention to how our sun's luminescence would fall sharply were electromagnetism stronger.[49] Solar surface temperatures lie close to those at which ionization occurs, at which point opacity increases markedly. Had electromagnetism been even very slightly stronger (for in Carter's formula its strength is raised to its twelfth power) then stars on the main sequence, a set of states characterized by steady nuclear burning, would all be red stars: stars which are unable to explode as the supernovae needed for spreading heavy elements (2.14) and which lose heat chiefly by convection and so are life-discouragingly cold. A planet near enough for warmth would presumably be swept by huge flares such as spring at intervals from the red dwarfs of our actual universe. And it would suffer tidal forces which reduced its rotation until it turned always the same face to its star, its liquids and even its gases then collecting in frozen masses on the far side.[50]

Had electromagnetism been very slightly *weaker*, on the other hand, then all main sequence stars would be blue: very hot, radiative, and short lived. Even as matters stand, stars of above 1.2 solar masses probably burn too briefly to support the evolution of intelligence on their planets,[51] if they have any, and hot blue giants remain stable for only a few million years.

Davies holds that Carter has shown that changes either in electromagnetism or in gravity 'by only one part in 10^{40} would spell catastrophe for stars like the sun'.[52]

2.20 Again, Rozental observes that all quarks – and hence all protons, essential to stars and even to individual atoms – could be transformed into leptons by superheavy bosons, whose mass is related to the electromagnetic force, were this force strengthened by as small a factor as 1.6; and further, that if this argument failed then a threefold increase in their electric charge would make protons repel one another sufficiently to prevent the existence, in stars or anywhere, of nuclei with atomic weights greater than three.[53]

With a tenfold increase there could be no stable atoms. The protons would pull the electrons into the nuclei.

2.21 Finally, remarks about how weakening the nuclear strong force would affect, e.g., protons – they could no longer be persuaded to come together in atomic nuclei, so hydrogen would be the only element – can be re-expressed as arguments for the disastrousness of electromagnetism's becoming slightly more powerful.

2.22 Similar points could next be made about *gravity*.

Some of them could be viewed as rephrasings of the statements of Carter and others about electromagnetism's needing to be appropriately powerful by comparison with gravity, or of the remark that the nuclear weak force must be very feeble if any hydrogen is to come out of the Bang.

Some, again, would be reworkings of the point that the cosmic expansion speed must be just right if galaxies are to form. Thus, gravity may need an appropriate strength if the cosmos is to inflate, or maybe Inflation is a false hypothesis and the speed had to be fine tuned from the very start by immensely accurate tuning of the gravitational constant. Again, gravity must be extremely weak for the universe to avoid recollapsing very quickly.

Others, however, are at least in part new.

2.23 These, for example:

(a) One reason stars live so long is that they are so huge (for besides providing a lot to burn, sheer size slows down the burning because radiation's random walk to the stellar surface takes millions of years) and yet are compressed so little by gravity. While the figure varies with whether we consider electron–electron or proton–proton interactions, we can say roughly that gravity is an astonishing 10^{39} times weaker than electromagnetism. Were it appreciably *stronger* than it is, stars would form from smaller amounts of gas; and/or they would blaze more fiercely (E. Teller calculated in 1948 that stellar radiation would increase as the seventh power of the gravitational constant,[54] and in 1957 Dicke linked this to how a change making gravity slightly nearer in strength to electromagnetism would mean that long ago 'all stars would be cold. This would preclude the existence of man'[55]); and/or they would collapse more easily to form white dwarfs, neutron stars, or black holes. Were it a million times stronger – which would leave it 10^{33} times weaker than electromagnetism, while we lack any well-developed theory saying that it had to be at all weaker – then stars would be a billion times less massive and burn a million times faster.[56] With even tenfold strengthening, a star with as much matter as our sun would burn only a million years.[57]

(b) What, on the other hand, if gravity were ten times *less strong*? It would now be doubtful whether stars and planets could form at all.[58] And any appreciable weakening could mean that 'all stars would be chemically homogeneous due to convective mixing and one would not get the onion-skin shell structure which characterizes pre-supernova models':[59] hence, it could seem, there would be no supernovae scattering heavy elements.

(c) With gravity at its actual strength, clouds the right size to form stable stars are just able to cool fast enough to avoid fragmentation.[60] Tinkering with the strength could destroy this happy phenomenon.

(d) If the protogalaxies formed by fragmentation of larger clouds then, J. Silk has argued, this required gravity's strength to be interestingly close to its actual value.[61]

(e) In many a galaxy, the galactic core – where gravity packs the stars closely, perhaps around a huge black hole – is very violent. In Cygnus A, for instance, the result is that the galaxy is bathed in 'hard, ionizing radiation hundreds of thousands of times more intense than on the surface of the Earth' and presumably fatal to all higher life forms.[62] Strengthening gravity might make every galaxy this nasty.

The Neutron–Proton Mass Difference

2.24 One last factor crucial to the stars and to much else is *the neutron–proton mass difference*. As S. W. Hawking says, if this 'were not about twice the mass of the electron, one would not obtain the couple of hundred or so stable nucleides that make up the elements and are the basis of chemistry and biology'.[63] Here are the reasons.[64] (i) The neutron is the more massive of the two particles, by about one part in a thousand. Less energy thus being tied up in a proton, decays of neutrons into protons threatened to yield a universe of protons only, with hydrogen the only possible element. (Neutrons are needed for making all the other elements because, being electrically neutral, they can add to the strong-force interaction which holds complex nuclei together without also adding enough electromagnetic repulsion to blow them to bits.) Fortunately, however, the Big Bang cooled just quickly enough to allow neutrons to become bound to protons inside atoms. Here the presence of electrons and the Pauli principle discourage their decay, but even that would not prevent it were the mass difference slightly greater. And were it *smaller* – one-third of what it is –then neutrons *outside* atoms would *not* decay. All protons would thus change irreversibly into neutrons during the Bang, whose violence produced frequent proton-to-neutron conversions. There could then be no atoms: the universe would be neutron stars and black holes. (ii) *The mass of the electron* enters the picture like this. If the neutron mass failed to exceed the proton mass by a little more than the electron mass then atoms would collapse, their electrons combining with their protons to yield neutrons. (Proton mass: 938.28 MeV. Electron: 0.51. Total: 938.79. And the neutron weighs in at 939.57.)

As things are, the neutron is just enough heavier to ensure that the Bang yielded only about one neutron to every seven protons. The excess protons were available for making the hydrogen of long-lived stable stars, water, and carbohydrates.

Notice, by the way, that hydrogen stars burn by producing neutrons. Despite the neutron's being heavier than the proton, it is *so little heavier* that a process whereby two protons fuse to form a deuteron – which, remember, is a combination of a proton and a neutron (2.16) – is energetically advantageous when the comparatively small binding energy is taken into account. (It could be added that an increase in Planck's constant by over 15 per cent would prevent the existence of the deuteron.)[65]

2.25 Another way of approaching the matter is to say that an increased electron mass would spell disaster. Rozental comments that the electron is astonishingly light: roughly two hundred times lighter than the next lightest particle, the muon, and some thousand times lighter than the average for the known particles.[66] The electron's being a lepton is not enough to explain this, for the tau lepton is actually heavier than the proton. Further, the neutron–proton mass difference is tiny compared with those found in almost all other cases of 'isotopic multiplets'.

2.26 Neutrons and protons differ in their quark content, so their fortunate mass difference can be explained as a reflection of the 'up' quark's being slightly lighter than the 'down'. Such an explanation, however, may succeed only in pushing one's puzzlement back a step: the question just becomes that of why the quark masses are so fortunate. Clearly, a theist *need not* think that each life-encouraging phenomenon is *directly* due to divine choice and lacks all further reasons. Newton took artistic and religious delight in how Nature was 'very conformable to herself, and very simple, performing all the great Motions of the heavenly bodies by the Attraction of Gravity, and almost all the small ones of their Particles by some other attractive and repelling Powers'.[67]

The seeming failure of the simplest Grand Unified Theory, 'minimal SU(5)', as evidenced by failure to see sufficiently many proton decays,[68] should however discourage the idea that some Principle of Simplicity is the only factor selecting Nature's laws. Hugely many alternative GUTs now compete for the physicist's attention. God, the theist could say, had a huge field from which to choose.

Material Particles, Hardness, Stable Space, etc.

2.27 To Newton, matter was made of 'hard, impenetrable, moveable Particles, of such Sizes and Figures, and with such other Properties' as best served desirable ends.[69] *Hardness* was crucial. The 'primitive particles' had to be 'even so very hard, as never to wear or break in pieces', else 'the Nature of Things depending on them would be changed. Water and Earth, composed of old worn Particles and Fragments of Particles, would not be of the same Nature and Texture now, with Water and Earth composed of entire Particles in the Beginning.'[70]

2.28 He was in part wrong. Atoms can be broken (ionized) by striking a match. And you cannot identify Newton's hard, unchanging particles with *subatomic* entities, because subatomic entities of one type often change into ones of some other type. The proton itself is now believed liable to decay – which can be viewed as beneficial, since the factors involved are probably responsible for *how matter came out of the Bang in any quantity instead of annihilating with antimatter to produce a universe of light*. The story runs like this. Superheavy bosons can transform quarks into leptons, with the result that protons – which are made of quarks – are not eternal. At present temperatures the superheavies are created rarely, proton decays being correspondingly rare; but early in the Bang superheavies were common, their own decays very fortunately producing *unequal* numbers of quarks (for making protons) and antiquarks (which make antiprotons).

Notice the following points, though.

(i) The story's details are uncertain. Even the 'sign' of the inequality – whether it would be more quarks or more antiquarks which were produced – can as yet be determined only by the verbal principle that we are sure to *call* the outcome 'matter' rather than 'antimatter'.[71] Hence claims that the story 'explains the matter excess' risk being seriously misleading.

(ii) For the story to be right, laws of charge and charge-parity conservation must fail, which means there must be two generations of quarks and leptons in addition to those of our everyday world of low energies.[72]

(iii) The story needs not only an expanding universe but also, probably, the very rapid expansion which Inflation provides.[73]

(iv) Further, something had to ensure that the excess of protons over antiprotons was paralleled by a precisely equal excess of electrons over positrons, to avoid *charge imbalance*. Charge imbalance would make condensations of matter hard to achieve if the universe were 'open'; while in a 'closed', finite universe the case would be if anything still worse, since lines of force would wind round and round, building up an infinite electric field.[74]

(v) As well as all that, neither too much nor too little matter was to be produced – an affair sensitive to fairly modest changes in the masses of the superheavies. Roughly, the actual excess was of one proton for every hundred million proton–antiproton pairs. Too many more protons, and the universe would quickly collapse, assuming that its expansion rate reflected the number of photons per proton; or it would become a collection of neutron stars and black holes; or at the very least there would be helium everywhere instead of hydrogen. Too many *fewer*, and there would be over-rapid expansion coupled with radiation pressures guaranteeing that protogalaxies and stars could not condense: any massive bound systems managing to form despite the expansion would trap radiation which stopped them fragmenting into the smaller bodies on whose existence Life depends.[75]

Proton decay, moreover, would need to be extremely slow. Proton lives of 10^{16} years, while about a million times the present age of the universe, would still mean, says M. Goldhaber, that the decays occurring *in you* would themselves kill you with their radiation.[76]

2.29 All this implies that the masses of the superheavy bosons must fall inside interestingly narrow limits. For instance, they must be at least one hundred million million times heavier than the proton if protons are to be stable enough.[77]

Again, making the electromagnetic fine structure constant larger than 1/85 would result in too many proton decays for there to be long-lived, stable stars, while 1/180 is a lower limit suggested by GUTs (Grand Unified Theories).[78] And if high levels of radiation were necessarily lethal then 1/85 would itself be too large, as the stability of living organisms would then be more sensitive than that of stars.

2.30 Newton's being partly wrong must therefore not blind us to how nearly he was right when writing that 'the Changes of corporeal things' are merely 'new Associations and Motions of permanent Particles'.[79] The average proton will live longer than 10^{31} years. Further, *particles do at least come in unchanging types*: a DNA molecule transmits information equivalent to ten thousand pages because atomic particles (and hence the atoms they compose) come in unvarying brands. Now, even in the 1970s Wheeler could write that 'the miraculous identity of particles of the same type must be regarded as a central mystery of physics'. Riemannian geometry was, he said, useful in physics only because of its suggestion – which 'exposes itself to destruction on a hundred fronts' – of a gauge symmetry without which 'electrons brought by different routes to the same iron atom at the center of the Earth would be expected to have different properties'. Failure of the symmetry would mean that 'the iron atom – and the center of the Earth – would collapse', since now the Pauli principle would fail.[80]

As V. F. Weisskopf explained, the Pauli principle 'in many ways replaces the classical concept of impenetrability and hardness'. By keeping apart all matter particles of the same type it prevents atomic collapse. But, he added, one would like to know why electrons and other matter particles (fermions) come *in specific types*. 'Very little can be said in regard to why the electron has the properties which we observe', things being made specially difficult by how Nature 'has provided us with a second kind of electron, the muon', which seemingly 'differs from the ordinary one by its mass only'.[81]

2.31 The Pauli principle's 'spreading out' of the atom by keeping electrons in a fixed hierarchy of orbits is decidedly fortunate. Could electrons take just any orbit then, (i) thermal buffetings would at once knock them into new orbits, so destroying the fixed properties which underlie the genetic code and the happy fact that atoms of different kinds behave very differently; and (ii) atoms would quickly collapse, their electrons spiralling inwards while radiating violently.

The 'wave-particle' natures of atomic particles could give us some insight into the principle. For consider sound waves. Air in an organ pipe likes to vibrate at a particular frequency or at simple multiples thereof. However, *bosons* also have wave-particle natures yet are *not* restricted by the Pauli principle. If electrons behaved like bosons then all could occupy the lowest possible orbit, and there could be no chemistry.

2.32 How does an electron in the lowest orbit escape being sucked into the oppositely charged atomic nucleus? Quantum theory answers that Heisenberg Uncertainty relating position and momentum makes the electron speed up as it nears the nucleus: hence atoms avoid collapsing. The obvious importance of this to the trees and rocks and cars of our everyday world – together with such affairs as the non-collapse of white dwarf and neutron stars, supported by similar 'Heisenberg agitation' – makes it implausible to attribute Heisenberg Uncertainty merely to how conscious beings cannot find out all the details of submicroscopic events. The Uncertainty must surely be 'out there' in Reality. And it is out there in a way whose fortunateness matches its strangeness. Electrons are not, thank heaven, for ever being sucked into nuclei.

2.33 Given 'hard, impenetrable' entities to use as bricks one could perhaps hope to build *rigid structures*. Yet as G. Wald said, 'if the proton had not so much greater mass than the electron, all matter would be fluid' since in that case 'all motions involving these particles would be mutual and nothing would stay put'.[82] It is only because their heavy nuclei are confined inside clouds of light electrons, clouds interacting complicatedly, that individual atoms can have fixed positions.

F. D. Kahn similarly pointed out that water molecules, benzene rings, DNA, etc. have structures that 'persist owing to the great difference between the mass of an electron and the mass of an atomic nucleus'.[83] At stake is 'the existence of chemistry (and also chemists)', since chemistry needs atoms 'full of open space with well-defined central nuclei'.[84] Electromagnetism's comparative weakness is involved too, as is the fact that electrons cannot feel the hundreds-of-times-more-powerful nuclear strong force. Kahn added that such reflections threw severe doubt on the possibility of non-chemical life based on the strong force rather than on electrons and electromagnetism. Protons and neutrons, the main particles governed by the strong force, have virtually equal masses, so 'no precision could be given to their locations'.

T. Regge argued that 'long chain molecules of the right kinds to make biological phenomena possible' could be threatened by 'the slightest variation' in the electron–proton mass difference.[85]

2.34 Important, too, is that *electron and proton have charges opposite but numerically equal*. Were things otherwise then the consequent charge imbalance would be fully as disastrous as the one discussed earlier (2.28). Wald commented that 'if a universe were started with charged hydrogen it could expand, but probably nothing more'. (R. A. Lyttleton and H. Bondi had dreamed in 1959 that proton and electron charges differed by about two parts in a billion billion, this tiny difference accounting for the cosmic expansion.) The actual charge equality seemed to him particularly mysterious because the proton had 'about 1840 times the rest mass of the electron'. There were other pairs of oppositely charged particles, proton and antiproton for instance, whose charges were exactly equal, but those 'can be generated as pairs of anti-particles out of photons', which are chargeless, so that there the equality was 'just an aspect of conservation of charge'. No such explanation was available here. True, protons might be made of quarks bearing charges one-third or two-thirds that of the electron; and this might be understood in terms of the possibility that quarks can change into leptons, the class to which electrons belong; but, said Wald, this would only push the need for an explanation to another level. For the charges on the various kinds of quark would now have to be 'equal or simple sub-multiples of each other' to enormous accuracy.[86]

Wald was writing prior to the very bold theories of the 1980s which might throw some light on this area. But as was said earlier (2.26), theists should not be too opposed to the idea of fundamental principles which dictate this or that fortunate phenomenon; for while such principles may be comparatively simple, they will still be impressively intricate and very far from being logically inevitable. Even the simplest modern GUT due to H. Georgi and S. Glashow, today thought to be too crude, involves twenty-four force fields.[87] Hugely many more complex theories now compete for the physicist's attention. And claims to have derived this or that quantity 'from basic principles' typically gloss over the fact that some other quantity, often the mass of a force-conveying 'messenger particle' like the pion, had first to be put in by hand.

2.35 Rozental estimates that an electron–proton charge difference of more than one part in ten billion would mean that no solid bodies could weigh above one gram.[88]

Again, he says, reduce the electron charge by two-thirds and even the low temperatures of interstellar space then disrupt all uncharged atoms.[89]

2.36 J. D. Barrow and F. J. Tipler remark that in any case *the difference between material things and waves* is maintained only thanks to the smallness of the electromagnetic fine structure constant: it has to be a small fraction – it is about 1/137 – to ensure 'the distinguishability of matter and radiation', for reasons centred on how an electron might be thought of as spending that same fraction of its time 'as an electromagnetic wave'. (There is a constant possibility that it will fuse with one of the short-lived positrons surrounding it; a short-lived electromagnetic wave then results. Charge Conservation is not violated, since a 'virtual' electron, born at the same time as that positron, becomes 'real', i.e. long-lived.) Had the fraction been much larger, atomic and molecular states would be very unstable.[90]

Might no: biology of some kind be based on waves instead of matter? More precisely, might it not be based on bosons, such as make up light waves, rather than on fermions (electrons, protons, neutrons, etc.)? Alas, the patterns which bosons weave lack properties of the kind which seem essential. Like the waves of the ocean, boson waves tend to pass through one another freely, and they could not provide the unchanging bricks, coming in unvarying brands and capable of precise positioning, with which genetic messages, for example, could be built up. True enough, they are in a complex sense composed of particles, particles which can interact. But when they do, it is in the way made familiar by laser light. They hurry to suppress their individualities, building up patterns of mass action.

2.37 Finally, *long-lasting material particles exist only because of space's topological and metrical properties.* For instance, it seems to be three dimensional, which was not a logical inevitability. Currently popular theories suggest that space-time has at least ten dimensions, all but four now being undetectable because each became very tightly rolled up, 'compactified'. Indeed, it is hard to see how the others managed to remain *uncompactified* in view of the enormous energy density of a 'vacuum' crammed with quantum fluctuations: see the discussion of the Flatness Problem (2.4–.5).

Were more than three spatial dimensions present in uncompactified form, atoms or elementary particles could be impossible, for reasons like these:

(a) Physicists' discussions of 'solitons' suggest that particles may be knots which persist in time because three-dimensional space is the one kind in which true knots can be tied.[91]

(b) Many have developed P. Ehrenfest's argument that the stability of atoms and of planetary orbits, the complexity of living organisms, and the ability of waves to propagate without distortion (perhaps crucial in nervous systems and elsewhere) are available only in three dimensions. S. W. Hawking adds to this that 'the sun' (i.e. its higher-dimensional analogue) 'would either fall apart or it would collapse to form a black hole' in any space whose dimensions exceeded three.[92]

(c) J. A. Wheeler has suggested that only three-dimensional space is complicated enough for Life's purposes while still simple enough to escape total break-up through quantum effects, effects making complete nonsense of a point's having 'a nearest neighbour'.[93]

2.38 Actually, it is sometimes held that space could have 'fractional dimensionality' and even that this might be essential to the complexities of Life and Mind. Fractals, infinitely complex curves, partially fill any higher-dimensional space in which they wriggle, so tending to take on *its* dimensionality. If our space might have been – or is – of some dimensionality like 2.99999998 or 3.00000001 then there could be much scope for fine tuning here.

2.39 Were the topology of space (the way in which its points are connected) a variable affair – and some have suggested that it does vary at each Big Squeeze of a perpetually oscillating cosmos – then whether there were *laws of parity conservation* could also vary: in their absence, heaven knows whether life forms of any kind would be possible.[94]

Again, P. C. W. Davies and S. D. Unwin argue that space's having a 'non-trivial' topology could dictate extremely slow variations in the cosmological constant. Twisted scalar fields would make the constant take different values in different regions. All that our telescopes can probe may be inside a single such region. Why do we discover it to be a region in which the constant seems exactly zero? Well, wherever the constant took measurably non-zero values, living beings could not exist.[95] But that last point could of course suggest an alternative, theistic account of why the constant's value is observed to be what it is.

2.40 A. D. Linde reasons that Life depends on space's having the right metric signature, A. D. Sakharov having shown that its coming out of the Bang with some other signature was possible. Reality might be split into domains with different signatures. The observed signature is $+++-$ (meaning that instead of the $d^2 = x^2 + y^2$ of Pythagoras's theorem we have $d^2 = x^2 + y^2 + z^2 - (ct)^2$, where t is time and c the velocity of light). Signature $++++$, for instance, would imply that 'life would be impossible due to the absence of particle-like states'.[96]

2.41 One should also mention the current idea that the space we inhabit is only metastable, like a statue balancing upright: it is filled with a field which might – with all the unpredictability of a quantum phenomenon – suddenly 'tunnel' to a lower value. The resulting bubble of stable space would expand at virtually the speed of light, destroying observers as it hit them. If the top quark has a mass as great as 125 GeV then we may be lucky that our world has lasted this long.[97] Equivalently, had its mass much exceeded 125 GeV then our world almost certainly would not have been so long-lasting.

Checks and Balances; Slow Changes; Complex Bonds

2.42 'Blind metaphysical necessity', said Newton, 'could produce no variety of things.'[98] Perhaps it could be found in matter's '*vis inertiae*', but God had supplied matter with 'certain active Principles' as well: the forces 'Gravity, Magnetism, and Electricity', and probably 'others which reach to so small distances as hitherto escape Observation'. Such facts as 'the cohering of two polished Marbles *in vacuo*' suggested that particles 'attract one another by some Force, which in immediate Contact is exceeding strong, at small distances performs chymical Operations'. 'The smallest Particles of Matter may cohere by the strongest Attractions, and compose bigger Particles of weaker Virtue; and many of these may cohere and compose bigger Particles whose Virtue is still weaker, and so on.' And 'as in Algebra, where affirmative Quantities vanish and cease, there negative ones begin; so in Mechanicks, where Attraction ceases, there a repulsive Virtue ought to succeed'.[99]

This was fine guesswork. Nature is governed by at least two main forces – the nuclear strong and weak forces – in addition to gravity and electromagnetism. All of these are essential to life forms based on heat, light, atoms, stars, and chemistry.[100] They do differ greatly in range and in power, the very short-range nuclear strong force being the strongest. And what seems like one and the same force can attract at one distance, repel at another.

2.43 Here are a few particulars:[101]

(i) Electrons are 'screened' by clouds of 'virtual' positrons, short-lasting entities conjured out of emptiness as quantum fluctuations. This stops an electron's influence from growing without limit as it is approached – which would make the electron immensely destructive yet was prima facie to be expected of so apparently pointlike a particle. The quarks in the atomic nucleus, on the other hand, maintain their separate identities thanks to 'antiscreening' by gluons which smear out the interquark 'colour force' so that it vanishes at short range, much as gravity does at the Earth's centre where it tugs equally from all directions.

(ii) The nuclear strong force, probably just the colour force in complicated guise, is repulsive at extremely short ranges, attractive at somewhat longer ones. By *repelling* it helps prevent the protons and neutrons in a complex atom from collapsing together, but by *attracting* it binds them tightly: this gives the atom a very precisely located centre, with the benefits mentioned earlier (2.33). And at ranges yet greater (but still very short) the force fortunately falls to zero: the messenger particles which convey it can travel no further as they must repay the energy they 'borrowed' in order to exist. As noted in 2.15, the force would rapidly collapse the universe were it long ranging.

(iii) Electromagnetism, in contrast, is conveyed by photons with zero rest mass. Not having to repay borrowed energy, photons can travel onwards indefinitely, but this is undisastrous because matter in bulk tends to exert no electric force. The positive charges are cancelled by the negative, so no cosmos-collapsing or cosmos-exploding field is built up.

(iv) The upshot is that the universe on large scales is ruled by the much feebler force of gravity. Planetary and galactic systems maintain themselves against its pull by the rotation to which Newton drew attention or, in the cases of some galaxies, just by random motions.

2.44 Result: a greatly complex dance of material particles. It obeys intriguing principles such as *Baryon Conservation* which might seem specially odd through not being associated with any force field as electromagnetism's Charge Conservation is. Without Baryon Conservation, 'the entire material contents of the universe would disappear in a fireball of gamma radiation, as the protons decayed to positrons and annihilated all the electrons'.[102]

Elaborate checks and balances keep the dance moving smoothly for billions of years: for instance, the balance in atomic nuclei between strong-force attraction and the electromagnetic repulsion which nearly blows apart any atom with two protons or more. Together with the Pauli principle, the small mass of the electron, the fact that electrons do not feel the strong force, and so on, this balance allows for a hundred or so markedly different kinds of atom: building-bricks whose electrons make them more useful than the solid spheres imagined by an early physics. As A. Szent-Györgyi commented, 'You will find it rather hard to build any mechanism out of marbles.'

2.45 Both in atomic nuclei and in whole atoms, such checks and balances lead to force-field 'hills' penetrable only with difficulty by particles trying to get in or others striving to get out. This makes for great stability. But the hills can be penetrated, for example in powerful collisions inside stars; so stars can burn.

Atoms are moreover very complexly sticky. The positively charged nucleus of one can attract the electrons of another; the two then approach until their electron clouds repel each other forcibly. This constitutes the feeble van der Waals bond, keeping liquids liquid. But the atoms may then exchange an electron, share electron pairs, or engage in intricate electron–electron and electron–proton interactions – maybe ones involving other atoms also, as in hydrogen bonding. Very many further physical and chemical ties can thus be built up. The weaker ones underlie *readily reversible reactions*. Life exploits these during photo-synthesis, during muscle movements (hydrogen bonds repeatedly formed and broken), when making or burning the cellular fuel ATP (phosphate bonds made and unmade), or when transporting new matter into cells. The latter are reminiscent of candle flames; their forms persist while their atoms are forever being replaced. Thus do men outlast their shoes.

2.46 On a larger scale we find stability of the kind to which F. Dyson drew attention, 'hang-ups' in the flow of energy.[103]

Dyson's 'thermonuclear hang-up' may be the most immediately impressive: it allowed our sun to support life's evolution for what Lord Kelvin thought impossibly much longer than any sun could burn. (As a star grows hot, heat movements of its particles fight further compression by gravity. The star remains spread out, its fusion processes slow.) When, however, we come to understand the Flatness Problem (2.4–.5) then the 'size hang-up', the fact that the galaxies and the cosmos are large enough to avoid immediate gravitational collapse and other life-excluding developments, can impress us still more.

Competing Interpretations

2.47 Much of the impressiveness of such affairs lies in the simplicity of their basic laws. (In 'Do we live in the simplest possible interesting world?' E. J. Squires argues that they could be the very most straightforward of those allowing anything as intricate as chemistry.)[104] Still, while we could join Newton in seeing in this sort of thing 'such principles as might work with considering men for the belief in a Deity',[105] might not an opposite reaction be better? 'In a mixed solid', says Wheeler, 'there are hundreds of distinct bonds, but all have their origin in something so fantastically simple as a system of positively and negatively charged masses moving in accordance with the laws of quantum mechanics'.[106] Rather than being evidence of divine ingenuity in selecting those laws, mightn't this show only that complex structures are sure to result wherever there are laws? See how readily flames, crystals, bubbles shaken by winds, reproduce themselves! Then read M. Eigen and R. Winkler. Besides repeating Darwin's point that, once reproduction is at work, intricate organisms can evolve from simpler ones by natural selection, these authors show how the simplest reproducers might originate.[107] Their examples include 'dissipative patterns' set up by energy flows, and the 'gliders' – oscillating, travelling, yet stable – evolved in J. H. Conway's game played with beads which reproduce or die in obedience to three short rules.

Well, we could consider such a style of reaction unappreciative of the near-incredible intricacy of living things: even the 'simple' cell has a microscopic structure about as complex as that of a whole man as viewed by the naked eye. We could also challenge its apparent assumption that there is bound to be an environment in which natural selection can proceed smoothly over long ages. Again, treating a world of living beings as unsurprising, a mere matter of a little more complexity, could strike us as turning a blind eye towards the immense qualitative difference between a universe's having or lacking such beings. However, reasonable people can disagree over these points. This chapter has therefore stressed that *quanti*tative considerations contribute strongly to a modern Design Argument. Very tiny changes in fundamental constants would have made living beings extremely unlikely.

Look again at that figure of one part in 10^{100}, representing how accurately gravity may have to be adjusted to the nuclear weak force for the cosmos not to suffer swift collapse or explosion (2.8). Recall the claim that changing by one part in 10^{40} the balance between gravity and electromagnetism could have made stars burn too fast or too slowly for Life's purposes (2.19). Think of the many other claims I reported.

2.48 True, few such claims involve figures as huge as 10^{100}; but they often compensate for this by being very firmly established. And my survey has been far from comprehensive. For instance, I did not mention how fast the cosmos would have collapsed if electron neutrinos, often thought to have a small mass, had weighed even a hundredth of what the electron does.[108] (The Bang produced some billion of them for every proton.) I was silent, too, about P. W. Atkins's calculation[109] that a 1 per cent increase in electromagnetism's strength could have doubled the years needed for intelligent life to evolve, while doubling it could have meant that 10^{62} years would be needed.

Atkins comments that were atoms more tightly knit then only 'prods like nuclear explosions' could have much probability of inducing changes in living structures made from them. He could have added that contemporary physics suggests that almost all protons would have decayed long before 10^{62} years had elapsed. Grand Unified Theories suggest a proton lifetime of 10^{33} years at most; and even if these theories are wrong, J. N. Islam observes, modern theories of gravity populate empty space with short-lasting ('virtual') black holes of all sizes, there being sufficiently many of the smaller ones to induce proton decay in perhaps 10^{45} or 10^{50} years.[110]

2.49 Argument on the above lines need not appeal to any need for an ozone layer to defend us against ultraviolet rays; or for ice to float so as to form a protective cover over ponds; or for there to be calcium, chlorine, magnesium, potassium, phosphorus, sodium, and sulphur, all of which are essential to the actual organisms on our planet. It need not even be assumed – though Wald and others give powerful grounds for assuming it[111] – that without carbon as a basis for complex chains and water's special properties there would be no living things in our universe. The big point is instead the one made by Rozental when he shows that small changes in fundamental constants – force strengths, particle masses, Planck's constant, etc. – would have meant the total absence of 'nuclei, atoms, stars and galaxies': not merely slight changes in the cosmic picture but rather 'the destruction of its foundations'.[112] Presumably this would imply the absence not just of observers made of carbon and water, but of absolutely all observers. There would be no fire, crystals, wind-shaken bubbles. And even if there were still things 'reproducing' much as fire does, that would be a long way from anything worth calling Life.

2.50 How about living beings based not on chemistry – which means on electromagnetism – but on *the nuclear strong force* or on *gravity*? Couldn't they flourish without fine tuning? No water or carbon can exist on a neutron star; its heat, gravity, and magnetism might destroy ordered structures in a quadrillionth of a second; yet couldn't the nuclear strong force work so fast that this would not matter? An entire neutron star civilization might last 'only a billionth of a second', while the evolution of intelligent life took 'one thirtieth of a second'.[113] Alternatively, might not 'gravitational life' – 'individual stars play the role of individual atoms or molecules in Earth life' – evolve 'after billions of billions of years, not the mere billions of years needed for life based on electromagnetic forces'?[114]

The reply must be, first, that these are speculations such as make the God hypothesis appear tame indeed; second, that neither 'nuclear-strong-force life' nor 'gravitational life' could have elements as precisely positioned as the electrons whose precise positioning is crucial to our genetic code (see 2.33: Wald, Kahn, etc.); and third, that one would not have the star-studded heavens of gravitational life or the neutron stars of nuclear-strong-force life, had basic constants been much altered. A trifling change, and the cosmos collapses in a thousandth of a second or flies to pieces so quickly that there is soon nothing but gas too dilute to become gravitationally bound. Another, and there is almost no excess of matter over antimatter: the universe is for practical purposes made of light alone. Another, and the first trillion years are too hot for stars to form, after which all is far too dilute. Another, and the Bang produces black holes only.

2.51 As was emphasized in Chapter 1, theists need not claim that *of all logically possible universes* only a small fraction would be life-containing. They need look only at universes in 'the local area' of possibilities, ones much like ours in their basic laws but differing in their force strengths, particle masses, expansion speeds, and so on. A bullet's hitting a fly can be remarkable when the area of wall near where the bullet lands is otherwise empty. There is no need to trouble one's head with how many flies there are in distant areas (1.24).

In cosmology our fly becomes a small 'window' inside which force strengths or other natural constants had to fall, for living beings to evolve. The local area becomes an area (or volume) of possibilities, measurable with the help of axes giving possible values for those constants. And the hitting of the window could be impressive even if the area contained one or two other small windows.

A pioneering paper by Rozental, I. Novikov, and A. Polnarev illustrates this. With axes showing various strengths of gravity and electromagnetism, they find a second tiny window of possible life-encouragingness in addition to 'our' window, the one surrounding the strengths as measured by us.[115] As they recognize, this certainly doesn't mean that there is nothing impressive in how our very small window has been hit. But in any case, more research could well reveal that the second window was illusory. For when we list ten grounds for thinking that a strength or mass or other constant must fall inside narrow limits if living beings are to evolve, we are not just guarding against error by giving ten arguments for a single conclusion. Rather we are offering ten grounds for saying that tinkering with this constant, or with a balance between it and others, will result in disaster for one reason or another.[116]

2.52 Notice that while changes of one part in a hundred – or maybe in 10^{100} – could ruin Life's prospects, Nature's forces have strengths so varied that the strongest is some trillion trillion quadrillion times stronger than the weakest; and remember, those claiming to calculate their strengths 'from theory' typically smuggle in, say, the observed characteristics of their messenger particles. Particle masses, furthermore, vary inside limits about as wide: masses as low as millionths of an eV have been suggested for neutrinos, which could weigh anything down to zero, while magnetic monopoles may be 10^{30} times as heavy. Are such masses predictable? Some have suggested reasons forcing photons to have zero rest mass, this removing all danger that these – they are as common as neutrinos, about a billion to each proton – would quickly collapse the universe. There is also an understandable tendency for 'higher generation' particles to have masses greater and closer together. But as with the force strengths, nobody can say that *just this* array of masses was inevitable. And as was touched on in connection with monopoles (2.6), a widely accepted story says the forces were originally all equal, mere aspects of a unified force, and that there was just a single species of particle: as the universe cooled this 'symmetry' was broken, force strengths and masses then taking values which were inherently unpredictable. (Compare how an electromagnetic symmetry breaks when a sphere of magnetic material cools below its Curie point. A magnetic field then appears. The field's direction, detectable by compass needles, cannot be known beforehand.)

Granted, the strengths and masses may be settled (1.7) by the strengths of scalar fields – fields characterized only by intensity, not direction, and thus hard to detect if they have the same intensities right across the visible universe. But any such field's strength was quite probably itself a chance affair.[117]

2.53 However, doesn't this all suggest that any fine tuning might be accounted for without bringing in God's creative choice?

Perhaps life-encouraging force strengths and particle masses are just what would be bound to occur somewhere in any sufficiently gigantic Reality.

Such a Reality could be split into immensely many huge domains: S. Weinberg compares them to the ice crystal domains which form when water freezes.[118] Perhaps almost all of them would be ones in which symmetries had broken in life-excluding ways. But obviously, we should find ourselves in a domain in which things were life-permitting. The attempt to see God behind this fact would show only our ignorance of the total situation. Indeed, Newton's own words can suggest this possibility.

2.54 'God', Newton speculated, 'is able to create Particles of Matter of several Sizes and figures, and in several Proportions to Space, and perhaps of different Densities and Forces, and thereby to vary the Laws of Nature, and make Worlds of several sorts in several Parts of the Universe.'[119] And something a bit like this could occur even without God's specifically so ordaining. Writing to Thomas Burnet, Newton remarked that 'saltpeter dissolved in water, though the solution be uniform, crystallizes not all over the vessel alike, but here and there in long bars of salt': crystal domains, in effect, with axes of symmetry set in different directions. Moreover he granted that Reality could include much more than telescopes detect. 'Many ancient philosophers', he wrote to Richard Bentley, 'have allowed that there may be worlds and parcels of matter innumerable or infinite.'[120]

It seems, then, that we could follow him without rejecting outright the today quite popular idea of a 'World Ensemble', a capital-U Universe with very many regions ('small-u universes', 'Worlds') which are largely or wholly separate and which vary widely (1.6–.7). But in that case, what reason would Nature's observed structure give us for believing in God? Although, as Newton recognized, God and World Ensemble are not flatly incompatible, mightn't we conclude that the God hypothesis had become considerably less attractive? Suppose an ensemble of tremendously many, tremendously varied Worlds: Worlds which perhaps contained between them all possible combinations of force strengths, particle masses, and so forth. Even in God's absence, things might be expected to be life-permitting in at least a few Worlds.

2.55 Were Newton alive today, how might he react to this? Perhaps as follows:

(a) World Ensemble theories are very speculative. The main evidence for them is the apparent fine tuning, but God could account for *that*.

(b) God might act through laws which produced an ensemble, relying on Chance to generate life-encouraging Worlds. Were the ensemble infinite, it could be sure to generate infinitely many of them. True, we should now be tempted to attribute life-encouraging properties to Chance alone, dismissing the God hypothesis as an unnecessary extra; yet the evidence for that hypothesis would not have been eroded entirely. For one thing, any World Ensemble explanation of fine tuning is in difficulties unless we assume Inflation – since how otherwise could there fail to be (2.6) a life-excluding chaos of domain walls, monopoles, etc.? Now, supposing Inflation of the right kind were dictated by the Unified Theory which applies to our cosmos, there would still be the question, more pressing now that 'minimal SU(5)' has failed (2.26), of why *just that* Theory applies.

(c) To answer this last question we might postulate an ensemble in which every possible Unified Theory is exemplified somewhere. (Atkins seems to do so.)[121] But might it not be simpler to introduce God to select the Theory appropriately and to answer why there is any world at all? As section 1.3 explained, we need not feel utterly stumped by the child's query, 'Then who created God?'

(d) Finally, we could list life-encouraging factors of a kind which could seem unable to vary from World to World as readily as a force strength or a particle mass.

Let us give a new chapter to listing them.

Chapter Three

Further Evidence

The fine tuning considered in Chapter 2 might be evidence of a World Ensemble rather than of divine creative action. The present chapter considers instead various fortunate affairs which could appear unable to vary from World to World with the randomness which might govern such things as force strengths. These affairs might be less ambiguous signs of God's reality. (i) Many of them concern principles that make the world both complex and understandable. (ii) The laws of quantum theory and of Relativity are counter-intuitive and bring interesting benefits. (iii) It can often seem that some fundamental constant needs tuning for several different reasons, all of which very fortunately demand that it be tuned in the same way. A slightly different Fundamental Theory might have made it impossible for there to be even a single life-permitting combination of constants.

Qualitative evidence

3.1 The evidence of fine tuning might at first look like a very strong indication of God's cosmos-creating activity. As we have seen, however, it could equally well point towards a multiplicity of Worlds, small-u universes, in which force strengths, particle masses, and other factors took very varied values, perhaps thanks to symmetry breakings (sections 1.7; 2.52) whose outcomes were random. Sooner or later, Chance could throw up life-permitting values, values which mimicked Design even to a hundred decimal places. And of course only Worlds which were life-permitting could ever be observed by living beings.

To help us to decide between God and Multiple Worlds, we might therefore ask whether there are any factors which seem strikingly fortunate and also unable to vary from World to World as easily as a force strength might. Such factors, we might think, could not be explained through any long, blind ringing of changes.

3.2 Any evidence provided by factors of this kind would be 'qualitative' rather than 'quantitative'. The theist who appealed to it would not be saying, 'Just look at this number! Had it been different even in its eighty-seventh decimal place, Life would almost certainly have been impossible.' The suggestion would instead be that the general form taken by physical laws, rather than particular constants entering into the equations which express those laws, is something which would be very odd unless God were real.

Just how odd? Inability to measure the oddity to so-and-so many decimal places could make the theist's argument dissatisfying to many people. And certainly, such an argument could appear rather weak if standing alone. But given the evidence of fine tuning, it does not stand alone. It is instead an argument to which we can turn when trying to choose between God and World Ensemble, two hypotheses which have already become attractive because of that evidence.

There is no need for it to be a decisive argument. It is enough if it can prove persuasive.

To what facts might it appeal?

Causal Orderliness; Understandable Complexity

3.3 The first fact might be *that there are causal regularities*. Events conform to something worth calling laws.

This point occupied a whole chapter in an earlier book of mine.[1] When developed in detail it can look more difficult than it really is. Here are a few of its simpler, more important aspects:

(a) Being impressed by the sheer presence of causal sequences need not be the same as claiming that it was 'a priori improbable' that events would fall into such sequences – i.e. that a being endowed with Thought but no Actual Experience of the World ought to think them unlikely to do so. Instead of declaring, so to speak, that none of this smoke was to be expected, theists could just say No Smoke without Fire; and they might say it on the basis of Actual Experience.

(b) Admittedly, Experience shows us that it is hard to generate purely random sequences. Roulette wheels have to be immensely well engineered if they are to generate reds exactly as often as blacks. But on the other hand it would be a very uncommon roulette wheel which generated, e.g., the sequence of prime numbers. What features each next event must have, for a physical law to be satisfied, is something which alters perpetually, yet events do conform to such ever-varying requirements.

(c) It is fashionable to laugh at Sir James Jeans's picture of God as a divine mathematician. No universe, his critics argue, could break mathematical laws – that seven plus five equals twelve, for example – without falling into contradictions. But what they forget is that a universe might well fail to *illustrate* mathematical laws as richly as ours does. Logic does not force events to fall into the mathematically elegant patterns which lead us to talk of Causation.

For us to comment that they fall into those patterns 'through their own powers' can seem only the giving of a name to a mystery. It is as if after finding atoms of the tidy varieties imagined in ancient Greece, perfect spheres, cubes, and regular polyhedra, we commented that this was because the universe had 'symmetromorphic proclivities'.

Here it could be useful to read E. P. Wigner's famous paper, 'The unreasonable effectiveness of mathematics in the natural sciences'.[2]

3.4 Next, our universe is complex. Even when it was at very high temperatures, any formula describing it must have had many terms, this being what made possible a complex hierarchy of forces when the Big Bang cooled. Yet at the same time it is simple enough to be understood.

Does this really call for explanation? Considered in an abstract way it could be found unimpressive. (a) Think, however, of how little we could understand were it not for *inertia*. Guaranteeing that particles do not shoot off at great speed in response to tiny forces, inertia is distinctly mysterious: Ernst Mach even blamed it on each object's being somehow attuned to every other object in the universe, an idea reminiscent of astrology but quite possibly essential to a fully developed General Relativity. A car's sluggish acceleration really may be in part due to the influence of the stars. (b) Or consider a point Bertrand Russell made in *Mysticism and Logic* (1918): that things are understandable only because the causal influences of distant objects are usually weak. This was far from inevitable. Forces between quarks *grow* with distance: it is as if these particles were connected by rubber bands. Again, any force associated with the cosmological constant may do the same, making our universe expand at an accelerating rate in the far future. (c) Objects do not change their properties markedly as they rotate and move around. This results from what physicists know as symmetry principles, including gauge principles which are not at all easily stated: cf. section 2.30 on Wheeler, Riemannian geometry, and the similar behaviour of electrons brought to the same iron atom by different routes. It seems entirely natural to us; and so it is, in the sense that it is very basic to Nature. But it is much less simple a matter than we might be inclined to think.

Quantum Theory

3.5 Much the same things could be said about the laws of Quantum Theory. Non-physicists are understandably surprised at the complex ways in which these underlie the apparent simplicity of everyday objects.

Basic to Quantum Theory are counter-intuitive facts such as the following. First, that even the particles of material bodies have wave-like properties. Second, that the wave-energy which is present here does not dissipate itself; it is instead concentrated in sudden bursts whose times and places cannot be predicted (which has led people to talk of 'waves of probability'). Third, that these bursts, instead of coming in a continuous range of magnitudes, must have ones which are definite multiples of basic units. Fourth, that there are mysterious restrictions on whether more than one particle can be in a given state at a given moment. (Here as in many other places, Quantum Theory suggests that the world's elements are much less separate in their existence than common sense tends to suppose.) And fifth, that efforts to locate particles with increased precision only make their energies increasingly uncertain.

Without facts like those, what would the world be like? For a start, photosynthesis could be in trouble since it involves sudden concentrations of light's wave-energy. Next, the genetic code would not work because atoms would no longer come in types with standardized properties: their electrons could now occupy any of infinitely many orbits, orbits changing constantly during thermal buffetings. Still worse, the orbits would shrink rapidly. Radiating violently, the electrons would spiral towards the nuclei and would then be swallowed by them (2.31–.32). *If*, that is to say, there could indeed still be anything so definite as a particle moving in a spiral. But quite probably there could not. In the seventeenth century, Huygens was intrigued by the seemingly straightforward truth that light travels in straight lines. He explained it by calculations showing that light waves taking other paths would cancel one another out. Similar calculations explain why light takes the swiftest route from point to point even when this means its acting like the intelligent lifeguard who, hurrying to save the non-swimmer, slants first in one direction across the sands and then in another through the water where progress is more difficult. Now, in our century Huygens's reasoning has been extended by R. P. Feynman to matter in general. The waves which 'interfere destructively', cancelling out, are now the probability waves which quantum mechanics describes as governing not just photons but absolutely every particle. It is quantum wave-interference, in effect, which keeps particles from wandering all over the place.

3.6 As already indicated (1.6[b]; 2.32), these strange matters cannot be dismissed as mere reflections of the trouble that macroscopic things – observers or their scientific apparatuses – have in keeping track of submicroscopic happenings. The failure of electrons to spiral into atomic nuclei, like the non-collapse of white dwarf stars thanks to how their electrons fight any increase in the precision with which they are located, is clearly 'out there' in the world. Again, the interference patterns found in double slit experiments, patterns which can suggest that each electron in some sense passes through two slits in a screen simultaneously, are much too queer to be shrugged off with the remark that people find it hard to know through which slit any given electron passed. Chapter 4 will return to this point (4.45 ff.).

3.7 There might seem to have been a severe risk that the advantages brought by the laws of quantum theory would be wiped out by something very disadvantageous coming in their train. Physics might have failed to be 'renormalizable'. *Renormalizability* means that quantum fluctuations, added to fluctuations-of-fluctuations, and so on – an endless succession of fleas with further fleas upon their backs to bite 'em – do not yield infinite results. Again, no infinities arrive through, e.g., 'virtual' point-particles fluctuating into existence indefinitely close to one another so that the forces between them become indefinitely strong. Only recently has anyone had much idea of how such infinities could be avoided. It turns out that many of the seemingly infinite terms can cancel one another. Further, point-particles may be replaced by 'superstrings'; or Space, instead of being infinitely divisible, may become 'foamy' at about 10^{-33} cm. All these complexities could be required for producing the seeming straightforwardness of the material world. Without it, that world probably could not develop the worthwhile complexities of Life.

It is of course possible to speculate that much the same beneficial effects might have been achieved without such complications, if only other phenomena of physics had been different. Yet there comes a stage where such a speculation, repeated in case after case, can get to look like the remark that of course a pencil can balance on a razor edge at any of a great many points along its length. All one needs is suitable lead weights attached at appropriate places.

Relativity; Baryon Conservation; Particle Spins; the 'Arrow of Time'

3.8 Relativity theory can inspire rather similar comments. Special Relativity tells us that Life can develop in different inertial systems no matter how fast they move towards or away from one another. Living beings in these systems could all of them see equally well in all directions. There would be no problem of finding it hard to see things to your left, for instance, because light rays coming from that direction found it difficult to catch you, while ones coming from your right all took the form of destructive gamma radiation owing to Doppler shifting (such as makes the horn of an approaching car sound shriller). Similarly, gravity and electromagnetism would not tug more forcefully in some particular direction, to the detriment of the beings whose planets would in that case undergo rotational break-up or whose genetic chemistry – based, like all chemistry, on electromagnetism – would suffer at the slightest sign of this sort of effect.

3.9 As I have argued in some detail elsewhere, these are again matters which must not be shrugged off.[3] They are not yielded by the truth of the age-old thesis that all motion is only of things relative to one another. Such relativity does not imply that a bullet could overtake a train just as rapidly no matter how fast that train moved relative to its track, nor does it imply that light rays would seem to perform this trick – and yet that is what they do seem to do.

Difficulties of understanding this are in no way tied to a belief in a jelly-like 'luminiferous ether'. Even without such an ether it is hard to understand why observers would find it convenient to assign the same speed, relative to themselves, to the same light ray, no matter how fast they moved relative to one another. An elaborate interplay of physical principles is involved here, as can be seen from how the mass–energy equivalence $e = mc^2$ can actually be derived from it. It depends on Space's having metric signature $+++-$ (see section 2.40) and on how light's speed enters into that signature. The notion that it could all have been predicted by using a little common sense is preposterous. Neither does analysis of our observational procedures establish it, as some philosophers have suggested. Such analysis could not tell us that we should see things with the aid of light rays which found it impossible to catch us, or with eyes fried by gamma radiation or unable to work thanks to disturbances in their chemistry.

3.10 The temptation is to continue like this for page after page.[4] However, let me limit myself to a quick mention of three further matters.

First, the Baryon Conservation to which section 2.44 referred. Mediated by no force field, this none the less manages to prevent the universe becoming a fireball of radiation.

Second, a fact commented on by I. L. Rozental: that if particles had no spin then there would be neither electromagnetism nor gravity, and that had all hadrons (particles which feel the nuclear strong force) lacked isotopic spin then complex stable nuclei would not exist.[5] Now, spins for elementary particles are odd enough to have been laughed at when first proposed. And for particles to spin in quite the way that tops do really would be laughable, an evident physical impossibility. The actual nature of their spinning is a subtle affair.

Third, the still perplexing fact that there is 'an arrow of time', a direction in which the world becomes more disorderly. (Life's processes, including mental processes, grow more orderly in a way parasitic on the general flow towards disorder, this being why we have – in what we call 'memory' – an intimate acquaintance with the past rather than with the future.)[6] The suggestion looked at in section 2.11, that our universe started off with low gravitational entropy, could give only a partial explanation for this; for why was such entropy ever low and why is there a dimension along which it could grow higher? As R. Penrose says, we are here 'groping at matters that are barely understood at all from the point of view of physics'.[7] Yet these matters are clearly essential to the possibility of Life.

Conclusions, and Some Final Arguments

3.11 The previous chapter made the point that the apparent failure of the simplest Grand Unified Theory, 'minimal SU(5)', leaves us with a wide field of somewhat more complex Fundamental Theories, any one of which God could be imagined as having chosen (2.26). One consequence is the difficulty physicists have in reaching any agreement about events early in the Big Bang. They cannot so much as agree on whether Inflation occurred (1.6[e]; 2.6). In other words, universes recognizably like ours in their physics could differ in something as important as whether their sizes grew by perhaps $10^{1,000,000}$ times at early instants. God would need to be careful which physics he chose.

Need God enter the picture, though, even if we grant that the affairs discussed in this chapter are strangely fortunate? Conceivably, a Fundamental Theory dictating such affairs could be arrived at through random variations across greatly many universes; for maybe very basic laws themselves differ from universe to universe, perhaps for no particular reason. Some have thought that 'Chaotic' or 'Stochastic' Gauge Theories smooth the path towards that idea.

According to the intuition behind these Gauge Theories, 'the natural thing' could be for many different sets of laws to operate side by side. It seems clear, however, that this intuition could not enjoy much scientific support if it implied that there exist many other universes with laws greatly unlike those we know. That would be flatly opposed to the respect for simplicity and continuity which underlies all science. And in fact the usual aim of Chaotic/Stochastic Gauge Theories is to show either (a) that Nature's actual laws are some kind of inevitable compromise between many different laws, or else (b) that they are at least typical of the various possibilities, rather as tossing about fifty heads is typical of all possible hundredfold tossings of a coin.

It can seem, then, that the idea of many universes ruled by different basic laws is a wild one. Unless, that is to say, God could be expected to have had reasons for producing them: for instance, a liking for Variety.

3.12 This chapter has argued in an imprecise, 'unquantifiable' way that mere fine tuning of physically and cosmologically important numbers could very well be insufficient. One could need careful selection of the world's most basic laws, as otherwise Life could be unlikely no matter what values were given to such numbers (corresponding to force strengths and suchlike). To end the chapter, let us look at what may be the strongest argument for saying this sort of thing. It is strong because it has at least a touch of quantifiability.

The argument runs like this. Those seeking evidence of fine tuning may appear to have embarrassingly much at which they can point. A force strength or a particle mass often seems to need to be more or less exactly what it is *not just for one reason, but for two or three or five*. Yet obviously it could not be tuned in first one way and then another, to satisfy several conflicting requirements. A force strength or a mass cannot take several different values at once! So, you might think, mustn't it be *inexplicable good fortune* that the requirements which have to be satisfied do not conflict? And yet if we are in this way compelled to accept many inexplicable facts which conspire to make Life possible then may not that mean that this book (which does try to suggest explanations) has gone badly wrong at some point?

One possible response would be that when factor A looks as if it needed fine tuning in order to bring it into life-generating harmony first with factor B, then with C, then with D, and so on, what really occurred was the reverse. It was factors B, C, and D which were all of them fine tuned so as to harmonize with A.

My hunch is that while such a response has some force, it is not by itself enough. After responding in that way in the case of factor A we would find ourselves under pressure to say the same kind of thing about factor B as well – but that would lead to inconsistency. So I suspect that we ought to be thinking in terms of hugely many possible Fundamental Theories. In most cases these Theories would make living beings impossible because, alas, the existence of such beings would demand that such-and-such factors be fine tuned in conflicting ways. Perhaps only extremely rarely would any Fundamental Theory – any Theory of Everything whose equations might be written on the back of an envelope or of an elephant – avoid this depressing result. But some small group of Theories would avoid it, and the Creator would be guided by that fact.

Or else, conceivably, at least one Theory from that small group would reign somewhere inside a huge field of universes, a field in which (despite what 3.11 said) basic laws differed from place to place for no reason whatever.

Chapter Four

Multiple Worlds

A multiplicity of Worlds, small-u universes, could help to make any fine tuning unmysterious. The chapter expands the earlier quick survey (section 1.6) of mechanisms by which multiple universes might be generated: oscillations, quantum World-splittings, quantum fluctuations, symmetry breakings which set up gigantic zones inside a perhaps infinitely large cosmos, and so on.

Such mechanisms could carve up Reality in many separate ways at once, making it hard to reach any agreement on how universes should be counted. However, the more marked the differences between any two gigantic regions, the stronger the excuse for calling them two universes. That makes it important to ask whether, e.g., force strengths and particle masses would be fixed randomly when symmetries broke. We must look also at philosophical arguments for and against widely varied universes.

Senses in Which There Might Be Many Universes

4.1 If by 'universe' you mean Everything That Exists then of course there is only the one universe. However, I have been calling this Everything 'the capital-U Universe', asking whether it is divided into many cosmic domains which could be named 'small-u universes' (or just 'universes'). Naming them in that way is common among cosmologists, although 'Worlds' is another label often used. People talk of a World Ensemble of perhaps infinitely many Worlds.

A small-u universe or World is hard to define satisfyingly. Proposed definitions sound quaintly tyrannical unless made fairly vague: compare the difficulties of specifying what 'bald headed' shall mean. Still, four factors are clearly worth bearing in mind when you ask whether two domains are to count as two universes rather than just as two large spatio-temporal regions.

4.2 *Absence of causal contact* or very limited causal contact is a first such factor. Consider for instance an expanding cosmos which stretches infinitely far. (It could do so even in its Big Bang's initial moments.[1] Even an infinite Space could be expanding in the sense that its individual regions were becoming ever more separated.) Regions beyond one another's 'particle horizons' – the limits to what light and other causal influences could have traversed since the Bang – might then be classified as separate universes. If one such region were *our universe as of now* then it might be expected to stretch some few billion light years, granted that the Bang which gave birth to everything now visible to us occurred some few billion years ago. This universe would be in contact with others at its edges, fusing with them as time went on because particle horizons widen at the speed of light. At any one time *points 1 and 2* could be in the same universe and so could *points 2 and 3*, while *1 and 3* were none the less in different universes – a fact which ought not to trouble you once you had grasped how the term 'universe' was being used.

Still, you might prefer to count as separate universes only those cosmic situations having no causal contact whatever, not even at their edges or in their far futures. Please yourself, but don't expect everyone to imitate you slavishly.

4.3 Second, cosmologists are specially inclined to count domains as separate universes *when their characters are greatly different*: for example, when they obey very different laws or at least ones which appear very different. We might talk of 'derived laws' which were different while 'fundamental laws' remained the same. This could be so when scalar fields of differing intensities had broken physical symmetries differently (1.7; 2.52–.53).

4.4 Third, something's chances of being called a universe are helped *when it is very large, or at least actually on its way to becoming very large*. This is not absolutely essential, however. It is often claimed that our universe would have recollapsed while still very tiny had its Bang expanded just marginally more slowly. We might reasonably speak of other universes which in fact expanded more slowly and so remained very tiny throughout their brief careers.

4.5 Perhaps most important is this fourth point: that universes apart from our own *should not be knowable by us in any direct way*.

Unknowability is not quite the same as lack of causal contact, please note. For suppose we believed in many cosmic oscillations – Big Bang, Big Squeeze, Big Bang, etc. – and suppose we thought that what would emerge from the knotholes separating successive oscillatory cycles was radically unpredictable. We could then feel encouraged to call cycles previous to the present cycle 'other universes' even if we thought of this cycle ('our universe') as in some fairly strong sense *caused* by its ancestors since in their absence it would never have come to exist. The other universes would be *other* just because information about their details would have been lost to us when they were squeezed.

Further ways in which information about other universes could be lost include extreme red-shifting of the light coming from them, red-shifting through their receding very fast. Or intervening galaxies and dust could hide their details.

4.6 Continuing absence of all causal contact is a clear theoretical possibility, though. (i) If the cosmos is infinitely large then there will always be regions beyond those from which light and other causal influences could have travelled to us. (ii) What is more, the special-relativistic principle that nothing can recede from us faster than light *may in an important sense fail* in the expanding spaces which General Relativity discusses.

While you will find cosmologists who deny that last point, their wrongness can be seen through considering the nowadays very popular 'inflationary' universe models. These are thought to solve various Horizon Problems: problems whose common theme is that the universe's parts could be expected to be poorly co-ordinated because faster-than-light signalling is impossible. Why, for instance, is the visible universe so smooth on large scales? Any two galaxies at opposite edges of it could seemingly have had insufficient time to interact, so how could they have come to any agreement on how to behave? Shouldn't we expect cosmic chaos? The nowadays popular answer is that the two groups of particles which developed into those two galaxies were in fact in causal contact during the Big Bang's earliest moments, later becoming pushed out of contact by a sudden accelerating expansion which may have inflated Space by a factor of $10^{1,000,000}$ in under 10^{-30} seconds. After this, everything returned to leisurely Big Bang expansion and deceleration – but the two groups would now find themselves immensely far apart. Light setting out from the one towards the other at the start of the inflationary period would take many billion years to complete a journey which would have terminated almost immediately had no Inflation occurred; hence the finishing post must for a while have receded from the starting post at a speed much faster than light. (Naturally this has to be given the sense, 'at a speed much faster than light would have receded had no Inflation occurred'. No particles in any area recede from us faster than light rays *in that same area* recede from us!) Now, in some versions of the inflationary story light *will never* complete various journeys, since on the largest scales Inflation will never end: our universe is simply a 'bubble' in which it has ended. Thus there exist regions whose details must remain for ever unknown to us.

Again, if Einstein's cosmological constant has a very tiny positive value then at late times the Space which we inhabit will embark on a never-ending inflationary career. Regions which had not interacted previously would then soon lose all chance of interacting. They would be separate universes throughout eternity.

Why Believe in Them?

4.7 Why believe in other universes when we cannot know of them directly? It could only be because we can *indirectly* know of them or at least gain good grounds for suspecting their existence.

If we could never gain such grounds, could we speak of other universes meaningfully? Yes. Admittedly the Verification Theory of Meaning – the theory that the only meaningful factual statements are the verifiable ones, the ones which could be checked sooner or later – would say otherwise; but that only helps show how fantastic this theory can be. Of course more may actually exist than we could ever have grounds to believe in and of course this *more* may include many systems of causally interacting objects, each such system as huge as all that we can see and containing trillions upon trillions of events whose details we could never know. Saying those things is nothing like a monkey's chattering. That there exists only a single huge causal system is not a truth of logic, sweet heaven! Yet all this should be plain enough. More interesting is that there are two fairly strong excuses for believing in universes in large numbers.

4.8 The first excuse is that Simplicity's demands may be satisfied only if there are many universes. Suppose, for instance, that various tidy reasons make us believe that the Big Bang out of which our atoms came was a quantum fluctuation in a Superspace. Bearing in mind what we know about more ordinary quantum fluctuations, mightn't it be absurdly complicated to think of this Bang as the only one ever to occur in that fashion? And couldn't it be every bit as complicated to add to our picture various *causal linkages* between all of a great many Bangs, so as to weld the lot into a single universe?

It would actually be scientifically outrageous, laughable, to suppose that Reality ended exactly at the limits of what is now visible to us. Simplicity dictates very firmly that *that*, at least, would be wrong unless there were strong evidence favouring it. But all the evidence points in the opposite direction. The visible universe is not nearly dense enough to end at precisely those limits if General Relativity is even approximately right, which it clearly is.

4.9 The second excuse we have met already: it formed the main topic of the first three chapters. The presence of vastly many universes very different in their characters might be our best explanation for why at least one universe has a life-permitting character. Cosmologists now often suggest that our universe is fine tuned to Life's needs. Had it expanded just a trifle more slowly at early times, for example, then it would have recollapsed in a fraction of a second and how then could living beings have evolved? And wouldn't matters have been equally life-discouraging had the early expansion speed been just a trifle greater? For in this case the speed would not have lessened anything like as rapidly as it did, so there would soon have been nothing but cold, enormously dilute gases. Yet if there existed many billion universes with varying early expansion speeds then at least a few might be expected to expand at speeds just right for Life's purposes. It would be no surprise that the universe in which we living beings found ourselves was one of those few. An observational selection effect would be operating here, as pointed out by B. Carter and many others. We should bear in mind what Carter calls 'the *anthropic principle* to the effect that what we can expect to observe must be restricted by the conditions necessary for our presence as observers' (see Chapter 6).

An Infinitely Extending Cosmos

4.10 Let us next look at various ways in which multiple universes might come to exist.

Consider, for a start, the Ellis–Brundrit Infinite Cosmos. G. F. R. Ellis and G. B. Brundrit remind us that the standardly accepted Friedmann–Robertson–Walker cosmic models, if combined with the low densities suggested by direct observations, give us a cosmos whose Space is 'open'.[2] (The surface of a sphere is in contrast 'closed' because it curves around and joins up with itself.) Unless it has a complex topology an open cosmos is infinitely large. If it is more or less the same everywhere – which is how our cosmos seems on the basis of our necessarily finite observations – then it contains infinitely many galaxies. Now, suppose we count its various regions as separate universes when they lie beyond one another's horizons. We then get infinitely many such universes.

4.11 Ellis and Brundrit comment that their infinitely extending scheme of things could very plausibly contain infinitely many planets with histories almost exactly like Earth's, with infinitely many beings named G. W. Leibniz, for instance.

This they find a bit disturbing, yet I cannot see why. (i) The birth of Leibniz must have been at least in part a chance matter (in the ordinary-language sense which allows for *chance matters* even in a perhaps fully deterministic universe); but so what? Given an infinite number of monkeys typing in chance ways, sonnets just like Shakespeare's would be typed infinitely often. (ii) Admittedly, running our day-to-day affairs in an Ellis–Brundrit cosmos would be possible only if there were a sense of 'more' in which those monkeys would type more nonsense than sense, and in which poets born in lands just like England could be expected to write more English than Chinese. Now, in number the pages of monkey-nonsense and monkey-sonnet would be equal; they would both be infinite; and mayn't that be a serious difficulty? Not at all. *In range* there would still be more of nonsense than of sonnet, much as one line's points can be greater in range than another's. (The first line can be the longer although strictly speaking it hasn't got *more points*.) This means that Chance could still be expected to rule to just the extent to which we have grown accustomed: neither more nor less. The notion of infinite repetitions even of improbable events need therefore be no stumbling-block.

4.12 In fact such a notion might offer explanatory advantages of a kind pointed out by M. H. Hart. If accepting it we could become readier to recognize that Life's chances of appearing as much as once in the whole visible universe may have been extremely low, in which case, says Hart, our failure to observe extraterrestrials would be explained. Only at very far scattered locations would molecular combinations happen to occur in ways leading to the evolution of living beings, yet in an infinitely large cosmos there could be infinitely many such unusual locations. And there would be nothing to surprise us in how it was at just such an unusual location that our first ancestors appeared.[3]

4.13 We can get much the same explanatory advantages, though, without journeying all the way to a cosmos open and infinite. *Great size* would be enough – and closed universes could have any size you cared to name. Elsewhere Ellis has stressed that any very immense universe might provide a rich field for observational selection effects.[4] Such a universe might be 'completely chaotic' in the large: 'vast regions would be expanding, vast regions contracting, some at very high and some at very low densities, some rotating at enormous speeds, and so on'. Observers could then view it only from 'very special places and times'. It should come as no surprise that their surroundings were life-permittingly unchaotic.

4.14 In an infinitely large universe there would be infinitely many distances at which 'Reality extends further than *this*' might

71

have been a false statement. Does that make infinite extension *infinitely unlikely*? Surely not. Matters could well be simplest if Reality extended for ever.

However, a seemingly much stronger objection to an infinite universe is this: that such a universe could appear to have no simple means of coming into existence in a Big Bang. From its earliest instants, its parts would have been separated by far more than the tiny distances at which the whole notion of 'separation' becomes ill defined in view of quantum uncertainties. How then could those parts have come to any measure of agreement on the time at which they would all spring into existence?

It might be thought that just anyone who accepts the huge universe shown us by our telescopes would face the same objection. But this is not so, as we shall see in a moment.

Inflation's Cosmos, with Symmetry Breaking

4.15 The currently popular Inflationary Cosmos can seem today's best bet to anyone hoping for multiple universes. A main source of its popularity is its claim to solve horizon problems. We have already met one: the Smoothness Problem (2.3; 4.6), the puzzle of why the visible universe is so unturbulent when galaxies at opposite points on our horizon could appear to have had insufficient time to interact.

You may ask: Wouldn't the Big Bang theory itself contain the solution to this puzzle? On this theory the entire visible scene came from a region which at early times was extremely small. At such times, wouldn't the region's parts have interacted readily? Well, in the absence of Inflation the answer turns out to be No. Space's expansion would too quickly have enlarged the tiny gaps across which those parts were trying to communicate. This difficulty could be overcome only if the region as a whole had been much smaller than calculations seemed to indicate. But recently many have come to think that it truly could have been much smaller. After a period of decelerating expansion, all may have started flying apart in swiftly *accelerated* fashion for long enough to make something of the size shown by the calculations from something very small indeed. This is the inflationary hypothesis. It could perhaps answer not only the Smoothness Problem but almost every other horizon problem: for instance, that of how the parts of the entire visible universe could have come to an agreement on just when they would jump into existence (4.14). Everything now visible to us might have grown from something measuring less than 10^{-33} cm – at which degree of smallness the concept of spatial separation begins to break down, say quantum theorists.

4.16 Central to the inflationary theory is the idea of *a false vacuum*. Quantum mechanics describes even apparently empty space as a ferment of fluctuations in which particles are for ever bursting into being and then vanishing: they 'borrow' the mass-energy needed for their existence and then pay it back before the accounts get more disordered than is allowed by the Heisenberg Uncertainty that connects *energy* with *time*. In the case of space in a 'false vacuum' state the energy density of the ferment would be enormous, leading to extremely fast expansion.

It would be gravitational forces which made the ferment so violent and which powered the expansion, gravity here behaving *repulsively*. But extreme tension would be present too. And by acting against the tension the gravitational forces would be doing so much work on the expanding space that its energy density could remain constant. After each increase in its size, its every cubic inch could have the same mass-energy as before. Its volume could double again and again, always in the same very brief interval, there being perhaps no limit to the number of doublings which could occur. As mentioned earlier, one suggestion – it comes from a leading developer of inflationary scenarios, A. D. Linde – is growth by a factor of $10^{1,000,000}$ before 10^{-30} seconds had passed. A region stretching perhaps 10^{-33} cm would in that case grow far greater than the entire visible universe, even before settling down to billions of years of leisurely Big Bang expansion.[5] (As is fairly standard practice, 'the entire visible universe' is here *not* taken to include everything inside the very wide horizon encompassing all material which could have interacted with us at pre-inflationary moments. Inflation, remember would mean that we had lost all contact with most of that material: see 4.6.)

4.17 Wouldn't the inflationary process amount to a magical violation of conservation laws? A getting of hugely much mass-energy for nothing? It is sometimes answered that energy is poorly defined in the case of an entire cosmos so that worries about its conservation lack clear meaning. However, in the presence of a mechanism for producing countless doublings this can look a feeble reply. Better, I think, is another approach. In physical calculations binding energy – for instance, the energy which ties electrons to their orbits around a nucleus – is standardly treated as *negative energy* (1.6[c]). This explains why, e.g., mass can actually be lost and stellar energy generated when a pair of protons fuse to form a deuteron, a proton–neutron combination which (since neutrons are slightly more massive than protons) one might at first expect to be more massive than the pair. Now, gravitational binding energy is no exception to the rule, and the new mass-energy continually appearing inside an inflating cosmos could be cancelled exactly by the gravitational binding energy of the particles in the quantum ferment.[6]

The position is reminiscent of the one described by the Steady State or Continuous Creation Theory perfected over the years by F. Hoyle and J. V. Narlikar. Here a perpetually expanding universe contains a negative-energy field. You might expect the field to be diluted by the expansion. The expansion, though, is accompanied by creation of atoms at an extremely slow rate. The positive mass-energy of the atoms is paid for by an increase in the negative energy of the field and, hey presto, neither the field's intensity nor the cosmic matter density alters over the years. Narlikar remarks that little divides this theme from an inflationary story mentioned earlier: one in which a supergigantic cosmos inflates eternally, our universe being just one of countless bubbles formed by local termination of the inflation. Alternatively one could use the theme to revive a Steady State in the way suggested recently by E. Gunzig, J. Geheniau, and I. Prigogine, whose cosmos undergoes bursts of creative activity whenever its expansion has spread out its matter sufficiently thinly.[7]

4.18 Early inflationary models were plagued by hugely many bubbles which appeared in the region now visible to us just as soon as its inflationary career ended. Collisions between the bubbles would have led to chaos. But in later models the entire visible scene was placed deep inside a single bubble. Linde has suggested that the bubble could extend 10^{800} cm at the time when it changed to comparatively sedate Big Bang expansion.[8] Contrast this with the mere 10^{28} cm at which our present horizon lies.

4.19 In a region so gigantic, and now grown still larger after expanding for another ten to twenty billion years,[9] there would be greatly many universes if by this you meant subregions each stretching as far as telescopes could probe. They would exist side by side in the greater 'bubble universe' which would be only a tiny fragment of a Space containing heaven knows how many more bubble universes. And this Space might in turn be only one among many Spaces, each of which could itself be called a universe. *There is no uniquely correct method of counting universes.*

Still, one method might be thought more interesting than others. An inflationary cosmos might divide into domains – either the bubbles just now considered or else smaller regions inside them – when Nature's four main forces 'froze out' from something more unified during successive phase transitions: radical changes of state comparable to steam's condensing. By occurring differently in different places, 'a domain' simply meaning a region throughout which they had occurred identically, the transitions could lead to great dissimilarities (1.7; 2.52–.53). These could give us particularly strong grounds for calling each domain a universe.

4.20 A possible first transition, widely presumed to have taken place only a little more than 10^{-43} seconds after the Big Bang started, involves gravity's separation from the rest of the forces. Any such transition would perhaps have happened too early to be of interest to us here, although the theory of 'primordial or supergravitational Inflation' proposed by D. V. Nanopoulos and others at CERN could suggest otherwise.[10] A later, 'grand unification' (GUT) transition, at 10^{-35} seconds, is often viewed as associated with an inflationary stage (which would of course be only a second such stage if the 'primordial inflation' idea were right). It is *loss of* grand unification which occurs here: the nuclear strong force breaks away from an electroweak one. A further transition took place at maybe 10^{-11} seconds, the electroweak force splitting into the nuclear weak force and electromagnetism. And, as T. W. B. Kibble has commented, the desert between those last two transitions might itself 'flower with multiple transitions'.[11]

Now, many are confident that at least the GUT transition would have resulted in domains of differently broken symmetries. A comparison is often made with domains which form when water loses its complete rotational symmetry (its property of looking the same in all directions) and takes on the more limited symmetries of ice crystals: the axes of symmetry of the different ice crystal domains are oriented randomly, and equally random effects might be expected through the breaking of GUT symmetries. At points of contact between domains of differently broken symmetry *magnetic monopoles* would be formed through 'misalignments', differences in the orientations of fields filling the various domains. The monopoles would be so heavy and so numerous that their gravity would recollapse the universe at once, had Inflation not spread them very far apart (2.6). But while its seeming ability to solve the Monopole Problem is one of Inflation's charms, of more direct interest to us is the point – Linde in particular insists on it – *that the domains of an inflated cosmos could differ in far more than how their fields were oriented.*

4.21 Why? Well, 'symmetries' can in this sort of case mean elegant likenesses between various forces and particles: forces and particles which, when the symmetries break, come to seem radically distinct or at best only distorted reflections of one another. Symmetries of the earliest times may actually have amounted to identities (compare how the photon 'is its own antiparticle') so that originally there was just a single force and a single particle kind. Domains produced by symmetry breaking might differ widely in the varieties of force and of particle which had come to exist in them, and in other respects also.[12]

4.22 As Linde emphasizes, we might get domains varying in any of a large number of features:

(i) *In their dimensionality* since in different places different numbers of dimensions could escape 'compactification' (2.37). The idea is that most dimensions of a perhaps ten-dimensional space-time would shrink. Thereafter each point of uncompactified space-time (in our domain it would of course be four-dimensional space-time) could be pictured as associated with a tiny sphere representing the compactified dimensions.

(ii) *In their metric signatures*, that of our domain being $+++-$ (meaning, as noted earlier, that in place of the $d^2 = x^2 + y^2$ of Pythagoras's theorem we have the $d^2 = x^2 + y^2 + z^2 - [ct]^2$ of Minkowski space-time, where t is time and c the velocity of light).

(iii) *In their vacuum energy densities* – which in many modern theories would fix the size of each domain's cosmological constant, a very important affair. In domains in which the constant was appreciably different from zero Life would almost certainly be impossible (2.8).

(iv) *In their gauge symmetries*. These would decide just how many types of force and of particle were to be found in each domain.

(v) And in further ways too: most plausibly, and very importantly, *in the strengths of each domain's forces and the masses of its particles*.[13]

4.23 Variations in force strengths and particle masses would be specially interesting in view of the evidence of fine tuning – the seeming fact that slight divergences from the observed strengths and masses would have ruled out living beings of any plausible kind.

Why might force strengths and particle masses vary? The story could run as follows. As the universe cooled, scalar fields appeared. An observer in a uniform *vector* field could easily detect this, maybe with a magnetic compass, but *scalar fields* have only intensities and not directions so that a scalar field uniform in intensity could seem sheer emptiness. (Think of how fish of the deep ocean are unaware of the water pressure.) However, the physicist's unified theories rely on these fields to break the symmetries believed to have been present at very high temperatures. When it interacts with a field a particle can gain mass by suffering drag – compare how a photon becomes massive on trying to penetrate a superconducting coil – or, as A. Salam puts it, by 'eating' the particles of which the field is made. And *force strength differences* may be caused largely or entirely by *differing masses*. The masses, for a start, of the messenger particles which convey the forces: if too massive these may even vanish before delivering their messages since their existence can be in part due to the energy borrowing which Heisenberg Uncertainty permits. The masses of the particles involved in 'screening' and 'antiscreening' which markedly affect how strongly each force acts at various ranges. And the masses, of course, of the particles which the forces are trying to push around or to transform into one another.

This sort of thing is basic to the Weinberg–Salam account of how the nuclear weak force broke away from electromagnetism: a scalar field gave large masses to the weak force's messenger particles while leaving electromagnetism's messenger massless. Much the same tale could be told, although more speculatively, in the cases of all or almost all symmetry breakings.[14]

4.24 Linde's idea is that several scalar fields switched on in succession as temperatures fell. Each affected different particles differently. And the potential energy of each had 'many minima of roughly equal depth, but corresponding to different values of the field',[15] minima into any of which it might settle as the Big Bang cooled. It might have chosen between them entirely randomly, the chances then being overwhelmingly against its choosing in the same way everywhere. The outcome would be immensely many domains distinguished by different combinations of force strengths and particle masses.

4.25 Speculative while this is, it cannot easily be shaken. Remember, Linde pictures our domain as inflated to such a size that other domains are invisible to us.

In effect, Inflation solves the horizon problem of how, so to speak, a randomly typing monkey (symmetry breaking) could type in the same way (produce the same force strengths and particle masses) throughout the visible universe: that is to say, throughout what might at first seem to be as many as 10^{83} regions which were causally separated when the symmetries broke.

Inflation takes just one region in which the monkey has typed in a particular way, puffing it up so that it extends far beyond everything now seen by us.

4.26 Probabilistic symmetry breaking provides, please note, a particularly plausible way – almost the only way which physicists have taken much beyond off-the-cuff remarks and hand-waving – of giving widely varying characters to different universes. (i) True enough, one might get wide variations in a manner which was instead fully deterministic. It may be recalled (from 2.39) that P. C. W. Davies and S. D. Unwin have imagined a huge cosmos whose topology is 'non-trivial', which forces the cosmological constant to vary from one gigantic region to another extremely slowly and deterministically. Combined with the strong presumption that living beings can exist only where the constant is pretty well exactly zero, that could throw light on why it seems zero when we measure it, they point out.[16] All this is very speculative and difficult, though. (ii) In contrast, a spectacularly large number of variations might be obtained with spectacular ease if Linde's probabilistic approach were right. Given many scalar fields each affecting different particles in different ways during symmetry breaking, and given that the intensities of those fields were settled randomly, we could have a mechanism making it likely that there would exist, somewhere or other within a huge set of universes, a universe whose force strengths and particle masses were tuned to Life's needs with enormous accuracy.

By far the greatest apparent difficulty with this suggestion is that of saying why strengths and masses, if indeed fixed randomly, should be fixed in the same way throughout the visible universe. Yet as we have just seen (4.25), *Inflation could get rid of that difficulty*.

One might therefore think that the inflationary hypothesis would be very obviously welcome to anyone trying to explain life-encouraging force strengths and particle masses 'anthropically', i.e. as the result of a combination of multiple universes with the kind of observational selection effect which Chapter 1 discussed. It would be welcome whether or not the many universes were themselves just domains of differently broken symmetry in a cosmos that had inflated. Even if those universes were instead obtained by one of the other mechanisms discussed in this present chapter – for instance, through cosmic oscillations or through quantum vacuum fluctuations – one could still need them to inflate, so as to get around the problem of why the randomly typing monkey had typed out the same strengths and masses wherever our telescopes probe.

How absurd, then, for people to claim – as they often do – that the inflationary hypothesis has somehow knocked the bottom out of 'anthropic' reasoning because, forsooth, it can explain observations of low turbulence and of a life-encouraging expansion speed without needing to appeal to such reasoning. As if degree of turbulence and expansion speed were the only things in apparent need of fine tuning! As if Inflation were not itself quite probably dependent on fine adjustments, including adjustments for degree of turbulence! And above all, as if it were easy to defend 'anthropic' reasoning *without* Inflation!

4.27 On the inflationary mechanism's difficulties, see sections 2.7–8. Those appealing to Inflation to solve this or that conundrum too often forget that it itself may require very accurate tuning if it is to occur appropriately. It may require it if it is to occur at all. Believers in multiple universes often picture it as occurring only in rare places, for example ones containing a field or fields in a state exceptionally far from the 'equilibrium' state of lowest energy.

Quantum–Fluctuational Universes

4.28 Next there is the idea that universes are born as quantum vacuum fluctuations.

The idea's many variants might all be looked on as stemming from a brief paper by E. P. Tryon.[17] He offers, he writes, the modest proposal that our universe 'is simply one of those things which happen from time to time'. Even what we call empty space is, he reminds us, a quantum ferment of fleetingly existing particles, their energies borrowed as is permitted by Heisenberg Uncertainty. The more energy tied up in the particles, the more rapidly must they disappear; but, says Tryon, our universe may have zero total energy when its gravitational binding energy (which, remember, is *negative energy*: 4.17) is taken into account. It could therefore be a fluctuation able to survive for indefinitely long. Vacuum fluctuations on this scale 'are probably quite rare', yet 'observers always find themselves in universes capable of generating life, and such universes are impressively large'.

4.29 Nowadays it is natural to combine this theme with the inflationary one, so removing the need for the fluctuation to be very extraordinarily gigantic. Inflation might quickly generate 10^{50} tons of universe from something weighing under 10^{-5} grams and measuring 10^{-33} cm or less. A fluctuation this tiny could have parts all causally connected, thereby escaping the horizon problem

79

which Tryon's 'impressively large' universe could have faced when its various areas tried to reach agreement on when to leap into being (4.14–.15).

Again, while Tryon's paper called for our universe to consist of equal amounts of matter and antimatter, which turned out to be in severe conflict with observations, this requirement could be abandoned. A universe originating without a matter excess could develop one at early times (2.28).

4.30 Tryon calls our universe 'a fluctuation of the vacuum, the vacuum of some larger space'. Might it not be objected that a multiplicity of such fluctuations would soon erode the space in question, making it 'all holes and no cheese', 'all bubbles and no champagne'? Perhaps; but replies are available. Maybe each bubble would stand a good chance of recollapsing before it made contact with others or maybe the champagne would be a space inflating so fast that its bubbles never made contact. Or possibly it would be so poorly structured that it would better be classified as 'space-time foam' rather than space, this perhaps making it not the sort of thing which bubbles could erode more and more as time progressed – for there might be no such thing as Progress of Time for the foam as a whole, and no well-ordered surrounding volume for any bubble to erode as it expanded. (Cosmologists feel little duty to imagine expansion as always movement into a surrounding void.) Writers developing Tryon's basic notion against the background of many different Spaces – open or closed, static or expanding at various speeds, foamy or otherwise – have therefore been happy to propose up to infinitely many universes.[18] While some of these would perhaps collide quickly, many others would not.

4.31 Are such background Spaces really needed, anyway? Some excitement has been generated by the idea that our universe may have 'quantum-tunnelled' *from nothing*.

Often – for example in A. Vilenkin's influential writings – 'nothing' appears to mean the space-time foam mentioned just a moment ago. In other cases it even means a fairly well-structured Space which is only misleadingly called 'a vacuum' since it is characterized by several different fields, albeit ones present each in its lowest energy state. J. B. Hartle and S. W. Hawking can however seem to do better when they calculate the probability that a four-dimensional system will originate from a three-dimensional geometry *of zero volume*.[19] Mayn't this be a major advance on theories which talk of universes as born inside a pre-existing something?

4.32 I think not. While we can calculate what could seem like probabilities for quantum-tunnelling from nothing at all, interpreting those probabilities is extremely difficult.[20] Hartle and Hawking reject an all-creating 'singularity', a point out of which the cosmos exploded. In their model, Time becomes more and more space-like as the analogue of a creation point is approached; and this analogue, like a needle's so-called point, is really only a rounded tip on which many points are more or less equally qualified for the role of 'being where it all began'. The zero volume out of which all supposedly tunnelled is not itself any identifiable one of those points, and it is hard to see how it should be treated. But even assuming it made clear sense to speak of tunnelling from a zero volume, could this truly mean that all creation's puzzles had at last been solved? Presumably not; for a zero volume *with three-dimensional geometry and sufficiently subject to the laws of quantum physics to allow for talk of 'tunnelling' from it* can look interestingly different from pure nothingness.

4.33 However, anyone in search of multiple universes need not oppose speculations of the Hartle–Hawking type, there being little reason to think that a Hartle–Hawking creation mechanism would operate *once only*. If a zero volume could give birth to a universe then what is there to prevent several such births?

Besides, as will be discussed below (4.59), a Hartle–Hawking scheme of things includes both *multiple branches* of a sort first imagined by H. Everett and *cosmic oscillations*. Now, these branches and oscillations could themselves count as separate universes.

4.34 Were some variety of quantum-fluctuational creation theory correct, where would that leave us?

First, we should presumably feel encouraged to believe in indefinitely many universes. Quantum-fluctuational talk is probabilistic talk and so presumably not about something guaranteed to occur only once.

Second, a universe originating as a quantum fluctuation might start off unsure of its properties, so to speak. Its earliest states could be expected to have the fuzziness typical of quantum happenings. While its scale would no doubt have to be finite, it could still be very uncertain about that scale until at least one interaction had occurred in it.[21] The same could apply to many or all of its other features.

Third, universes originating as quantum fluctuations might then each inflate and divide, Linde style, into many smaller universes in which symmetries had broken very differently.

Cosmic oscillations

4.35 Oscillatory models long provided the most popular means of getting multiple universes. Each oscillation could be spoken of as 'a new universe' in recognition of its being fairly sharply isolated from others. If successive oscillations differed greatly then this way of talking could sound all the more appropriate.

It was at first assumed that entropy ('disorder') would have to increase from each oscillatory cycle to the next, successive cycles therefore being both hotter and longer lasting. Calculations on these lines have suggested a maximum of about a hundred cycles, the hundred and first Bang being too violent for recollapse to occur;[22] but such estimates are far from sacred. For one thing, a last irreversible explosion would represent a change from a closed universe to one which was open, yet on the most straightforward models open universes contain infinitely much material whereas closed ones do not.

4.36 R. H. Dicke and P. J. E. Peebles have theorized that successive oscillations would contain progressively more matter: the energy for its creation is taken from gravity which weakens from oscillation to oscillation. This picture, like one in which entropy increases progressively without change in the amount of matter, shows how successive oscillations might work through a range of possibilities in a deterministic way.[23] A more widely admired scenario, however, is the one suggested by several writings of J. A. Wheeler.[24] Wheeler's notion is that whenever an oscillating cosmos underwent a Big Squeeze it would forget its earlier properties. While a deterministic working through of the possibilities would then be ruled out, the lack of memory would lead to 'probabilistic reprocessing' so that all possible combinations of properties would be realized sooner or later if nothing put an end to the oscillations.

4.37 Wheeler's reasoning is in part based on the idea that at about 10^{-33} cm, the 'Planck length', there may be an ever-fluctuating 'pregeometry' in which no point has fixed neighbours. So when squeezed down to the dimensions of a tiny black hole the cosmos may become unsure of its properties. Things could become so indefinite that a bounce could occur. Not knowing from just which state it was rebounding, each new Bang could decide on its properties in quantum-probabilistic fashion.

4.38 For a while oscillations were unfashionable because of the Hawking–Penrose singularity theorems. Falling towards a black hole, a spaceship would at a certain point become unable to escape: any energy fed into its motors could only increase the hole's gravitational pull on it. Hawking and Penrose were thought to have shown that for similar reasons a collapsing cosmos could not avoid a state of indefinitely high density from which no rebound would be possible. But their calculations assumed that gravity could never act repulsively – and as we saw (4.16) when considering Inflation, this is now widely rejected. Again, Hawking's subsequent proof that black holes are in a way misnamed since they can (in a complex sense) *radiate particles* encourages him to believe both that a black-hole-like collapsing cosmos could rebound and that what came out of the bounce could have only a very restricted memory of earlier conditions: amount of entropy, for instance.[25] (An interesting twist is added by his claim that in a sufficiently large collection of black holes 'a television set or the works of Proust' would be emitted from time to time, much as the occasional sonnet would be typed by any mighty enough army of monkeys.)[26] So people are once again willing to look at Wheeler's ideas.

4.39 To Wheeler, black holes are characterized solely by mass, charge, and angular momentum, and any closed cosmos would become black-hole-like during a Squeeze. He argues however that in such a cosmos total charge would automatically be zero while total mass and total angular momentum would be undefinable. There would thus be precious little it could remember of the previous cycle's properties if it rebounded. All kinds of very fundamental and important matters – for instance, whether the proton was *five* or *five million* times heavier than the electron – could be 'reprocessed' whenever a new oscillation began. What Wheeler rather misleadingly calls 'a biological selection of physical constants' could then ensure that every observing eye and brain saw an oscillation whose constants were such that biological eyes and brains could evolve.

Wheeler's argument may be in part faulty, not least through its 'positivistic', 'verificationist' decision that the only physically real properties of black holes are those detectable by observers stationed outside them. (Black holes have recently been shown to have high entropy, a high degree of 'disorder'; so mustn't they have complex internal structures, even if ones unknowable to such observers? Besides, an observer who had fallen inside the horizon of a very large black hole could for a while continue his observations without so much as being aware of having done so. And if it is 'closed' then our universe is in some sense itself 'a black hole' or black-hole-like even today: its light rays cannot go off to infinity.) Yet as Hawking's black hole radiation may help to show (4.38), the conclusion at which Wheeler arrives could still be a correct one. Again, recall Tryon's point that universes of very different sizes could all have zero total energy. This could suggest that the 'probabilistic reprocessing' of a universe's size would be easy.

Finally, notice that a modern advocate of such 'reprocessing' of fundamental properties need not join Wheeler in packing all interesting reprocessing into the instants when quantum fuzziness was coming to an end. Randomization of force strengths, of particle masses, and perhaps of other things also might be deferred until times which were considerably later on the logarithmic timescale which seems appropriate here. I mean times between 10^{-35} and 10^{-30} seconds after each bounce – a period during which random symmetry breaking and Inflation might occur.

4.40 Number of particles, proportion of matter particles to photons, period of expansion, particle masses, and force strengths all undergo reprocessing if Wheeler is right; and others have said that the topology of spacetime might change too.[27]

Many-Worlds Quantum Theory

4.41 Among further means of getting multiple universes, Many-Worlds quantum theory supplies the most startling. Reality in some sense splits into vastly many branches – 'Worlds', small-u universes. Every change whose possibility quantum theory recognizes is a change that actually occurs in some branch or other. Perhaps, then, there are infinitely many branches – because, e.g., the decay of each unstable particle may be possible at absolutely any moment, which might give us infinitely many infinitesimally different points at which it could decay. To the Many-Worlds theorist the so-called 'indeterminism' of particle decays and of all other quantum-probabilistic affairs is a matter just of our ignorance of a total picture in which all conceivable developments are in fact taking place somewhere. Not all of them take place in the cosmic branch which is *your World as of now*; but *you-now* are just one outcome of a multiple branching undergone by the you of just a moment ago.

4.42 Experience cannot refute this because interaction between the branches is strictly limited. It is not as if you could expect to be conscious of branches in which others bearing your name – 'other yous' we could perhaps call them, because their past histories are your past history, although if the word 'you' is to work normally then there is of course only one *you* just as there is (in a sense!) only one *now* and only one *here* – are faced with somewhat different situations. Yes, all the variants on you and all your friends and all their variants are equally conscious; there are no zombies among them; but no version of anybody (if we can speak like that) can be conscious of his or her other versions. No consciousness remains *unsplit* so as to be conscious of the many parts into which it *has split*.

In *your universe at this present instant* it is an incontrovertible truth that there is only one *you*. But, says the Many-Worlds quantum theorist, this is because the universe in question is a single twig of one of the very latest branches of a capital-U Universe. The twig will in turn split into countless more twigs, each a separate small-u universe, and in every one of them an observer bearing your name will again be able to contemplate the same incontrovertible truth. We here have a way of making some sense of the quantum physicist's typical but very odd claim that Reality is relative to the observer. For in the Many-Worlds picture just what you are going to observe a moment from now is of course relative to just which of the various yous – the ones into which you-now will have split – is in question.

4.43 What can be said for all this?

(i) If the entire visible universe can be thought to have exploded from something very simple – perhaps from an infinitely dense singularity, a mere point? – then I see no plain absurdity in its further exploding into vastly many branches which branch again at every instant.

(ii) The rare remaining defenders of 'hidden variable' theories deny any branching of quantum possibilities, let alone of actualities. But recent results (of Bell experiments: see 4.48) force such theories to take very complex forms. And their demand that Reality be deterministic is in any case satisfied by the Many-Worlds approach; for remember, this approach makes all so-called indeterminism a matter just of our lacking knowledge of other branches.

4.44 Couldn't our lack of knowledge come about more simply, though? Classical physics contains probabilistic expressions describing the location of an atom which has bounced off another and whose present whereabouts are unknown. When the atom is found, the expanding volume of its uncertain whereabouts collapses at once. Now, it could seem absurd to view the atom as having been itself smeared out over that expanding volume, then suddenly returning to atomic dimensions. It could be far better to treat the affair as an expansion and collapse *of human ignorance*. And wouldn't the same apply to any 'collapse of the wave-function', becoming-determinate of the indeterminate, which a quantum theorist described?

The answer is No. Quantum indeterminism defies all efforts to trivialize it. We cannot shrug it off with the quick comment that trying to find out about a submicroscopic particle such as a single electron must obviously disturb it so that human descriptions of its future behaviour can of course be probabilistic only. For a start, recent experiments – one of them involves a superconducting ring broken by a thin slice of insulating material – show that *as many as 10^{23} electrons* can join in producing a magnetic flux which slips from one intensity to another quantum-probabilistically.[28] Again, it is today clear that quantum alternatives truly are 'superposed' for interestingly long periods. They can even seem able to act on one another during those periods.

4.45 The double slit experiment illustrates this last point. A stream of particles – electrons, let's say – is fired at a slit in a screen. A smooth scatter-pattern appears on the photographic plate beyond the slit, much as if electrons were machine-gun bullets. A second slit is now opened. Behold, instead of two overlapping scatter-patterns we find bands suggestive of two sets of waves cancelling out at some places and reinforcing each other elsewhere. What is more, similar bands appear even when the electrons are emitted at such long intervals that only one is in flight at any moment.

How are we to interpret this? It might seem that each electron passes through both slits in wave-like form, undergoes wave-interference with itself, and then chooses its landing place through tossing dice weighted in accordance with the lights and shadows of the interference pattern. However, any attempt to detect a solitary electron as it passes through the screen never results in our seeing disturbances at both slits simultaneously. Should we then view the wave-interference as resulting from how *mere possibilities* interact? Should we instead imagine each electron as itself *actually spread out* over all the possible trajectories until such time as some trajectory hits a detector? The Many-Worlds picture shows a branching of trajectories each of which in fact carries an electron, and a corresponding branching of each detector so that only one electron is ever detected by any 'version' of it. Each well-correlated combination of an electron and a detector inhabits a different branch of an ever-branching cosmos, and anyone in any one branch will be tempted to dismiss the others as unrealized possibilities. But the other branches can make their reality felt in various ways. In particular, the branched totality of the electron trajectories forms two waves:

waves setting up interference patterns which determine, e.g., that no trajectory leads to where the interference shadows are deepest.

4.46 There is some dispute over how much of the cosmos would be forced to branch further whenever a range of quantum possibilities appeared. (Would each splitting extend instantaneously to enormous distances?) But instead of considering such niceties let us concentrate on the point that the Many-Worlds approach is not a crazy reaction to perfectly straightforward facts. You cannot dismiss the double slit experiment by talking of a human inability to predict things such as is present in the cases even of tossed coins and bullets buffeted by winds. A mind's ignorance of where a bullet would land could only be increased by supplying a second slit through which the winds might blow it, yet opening a second slit for an electron can in one respect *decrease* ignorance of what it will do because there are now interference shadows where we know it *will not* land. I. Prigogine's proposal that large-scale events are radically irreversible, and are so sensitive to minuscule differences that they are impossible to predict in detail, does nothing to explain this strange *decrease of ignorance*.[29]

4.47 Similarly bizarre effects are obtained with polarized light. A calcite crystal divides a beam of such light into two, the one polarized at a right angle to the other. When the two are recombined by a second calcite crystal the original polarization is restored even if the light is made so weak that only a single photon is in movement at any time. Any attempt to detect a photon during its passage results in its being found either wholly in the one beam path or else wholly in the other. Yet what happens when no such attempt is made? Answer: The polarization of each photon on ending its journey is suggestive of interaction between photons taking the two paths which it might have taken.

4.48 Again, consider experiments of sorts inspired by J. S. Bell. Pairs of particles are produced in ways making them subject to spin conservation laws. The particles of each pair move off in opposite directions, passing through detectors; now, when either one is found to be 'spin up' its partner turns out to be 'spin down' no matter what the axis with respect to which up-ness and down-ness are measured. But single particles of known spin *do not* interact always in the same way with a detector set at an angle to the spin axis. It appears, then, that we must take seriously the idea that the particles in any pair have 'superpositions', 'mixtures', of spins or possible spins. When they interact with detectors they choose their actual spins from those superpositions in ways that maintain spin conservation.

The Many-Worlds theorist looks on this as a case in which many different pairs of spins are *actual*, each pair in a different branch or World.

4.49 Despairing of placing Ignorance of an Unmysterious Kind at the basis of these strange results, some try to bring the Mental into the area by a quite other technique. It is Mind, they say, that triggers the collapse of quantum wave-functions or superpositions. But this looks to me very wrong. It suggests, for a start, that a computer print-out showing whether any atoms of a weakly radioactive substance have decayed will take on a specific form only when it is finally read by someone, perhaps years afterwards.

Worse yet, it makes Mind control the natural world on an immense scale.

4.50 Why? Well, quantum effects are of course not confined to laboratory experiments. (a) Quantum wave-interference helps explain (2.31–.32; 3.5) the non-collapse of atoms, the stability of chemical bonds, the fact that light rays take the fastest paths from point to point, and the more general fact that particles do not wander all over the place. (b) By creating the short-lived particles of force screening and antiscreening, by supplying much of the mass of many messenger particles, and by aiding particles to tunnel through force-field barriers as in the case of nuclear fission, the energy borrowings which quantum uncertainties make possible have major effects throughout the universe. (c) Individual events governed by quantum uncertainties can be made to trigger hydrogen bomb explosions. Will anyone pretend that whether a bomb has exploded depends on whether minds look for this? (d) Whether a region contains 'gross features such as a huge black hole' can be a matter of how the quantum dice happened to fall,[30] as can the existence of our entire universe if something like Tryon's approach is right (4.28).

All this forces us to see our minds as embedded in a cosmos whose character is at all stages and levels decided by phenomena of the curious kinds which encourage talk of real uncertainties, real superpositions, and real collapses of wave-functions. Now, even if minds were themselves immaterial whatnots, the fact would remain that their observations depend on material brains and bodies. And it can seem absurdly circular to imagine that observations collapse wave-functions *which must remain uncollapsed until observations occur* while at the same time the brains and bodies essential to those observations *themselves depend for the details of their evolution on how wave-functions collapse in particular ways* among all the ways possible during the many billion years before intelligent living beings come to exist!

Those looking for Mind at the foundations of quantum mechanics will be hard pressed to answer this difficulty. The Many-Worlds theorist, however, need not mention Mind at all.

4.51 Just what is wave-function collapse, anyhow? It is said to occur 'on measurement' – but to quantum theorists in general and Many-Worlds theorists in particular, *measurement* tends to be a term covering every measurement-like interaction regardless of whether minds or scientific instruments are involved. And when does an interaction become measurement-like? 'On irreversible amplification' runs the usual answer; yet just what could that mean? In actual experiments and in the elegant equations suggested by them there is no sign of a magic instant at which the amplification becomes irreversibly large. To H. Everett III, originator of the Many-Worlds approach, what this showed was that collapse never took place in a straightforward sense. Instead there was what he labelled 'splitting' but which I think might be better called *drifting apart*. Though it has a wave-function that never collapses, Reality streams into what could easily look like entirely separate branches. In each, collapses appear to have occurred.

4.52 Exactly how Many-Worlds Quantum Theory ought to run is hotly disputed.[31] Everett does not help matters when in a brief statement of his ideas he speaks of 'a cosmic superposition of all quantum possibilities' but also of 'total lack of effect of one branch on another'.[32] These last words – they occur in a 'Note added in proof', a reaction to people who had said that his approach conflicted with experience – are far too crude a summary of his position. A somewhat better statement of it is B. S. DeWitt's when he writes that each branch 'will (almost) never in the future interfere with any other'.[33] The notion of a perfectly sharp, indelible measurement marking the appearance of a new branch is widely considered to be an idealization only.[34] It would be the fact that the branches *did not* separate suddenly and totally – the fact that they were instead like tree branches which separate slowly and may even fuse together again after moving apart – which explained the outcome of the double slit experiment, the non-collapse of atoms, the stability of chemical bonds, etc. (4.45–.50). P. C. W. Davies talks of a 'jostling' of the multiple branches, alias Worlds. V. F. Mukhanov remarks that their multiplicity 'is just what accounts for interference effects' so that 'one can interpret quantum mechanics as a theory the very existence of which is due to the existence of many worlds'; while D. Deutsch asserts flatly, 'Quantum theory is a theory of parallel interfering universes.'[35]

4.53 Let me give the situation as I see it. It is standard quantum theory to look on various possible outcomes of interactions as *complexly active either as possibilities or as actualities* for significant periods succeeding those interactions. The lengths of the periods are not fixed by quantum-mechanical equations since these do not themselves identify any wave-function collapses. Now, Many-Worlds theorists take the equations at their face value. They prefer to treat *complex activity* as a sign of reality: the reality of happenings rather than of mere 'waves of probability'. In their eyes Simplicity is not much advanced by dismissing possible electron movements as 'unreal' when we are forced to admit in the same breath that those possible movements combine to set up wave-interference lights and shadows.

They might perhaps even hold that groups of physically possible later events branching off from any given event *never* become firmly split into separate branches, with one branch becoming 'our world' or 'the actual world' while others become 'absolutely non-actual' or 'totally unable to interact with our world's events': instead, apparently conflicting possibilities exist superposed and what could seem like the destruction of all but one of them is in point of fact a drifting apart that for ever remains compatible with 'jostling', i.e. the setting up of wave-interference patterns. There is even a continuing possibility – in typical cases it gets much fainter every microsecond – that two branches will suddenly jostle strongly enough to make it seem artificial to classify them as separate. The two may coalesce entirely.

4.54 D. Deutsch has suggested lately that an intelligent computer could perhaps say how it felt to have been in two branches which later coalesced.[36] In the experiment with the calcite crystals (4.47) we could well appear to have a case of controllable and complete coalescence of branches in which photons take different paths; but more controversial is whether coalescence can occur in varying degrees and in absolutely any case. Many seem to think (what Deutsch denies) that branches, apart from setting up wave-interference of the kind met with in double slit experiments, can interact only by 100 per cent coalescence with erasure of all traces of the fact that large-scale events had happened differently in each. But it might be better to say instead that the drifting apart hinted at by the double slit experiment is a matter always of degrees and of probabilities. Branches in which Napoleon's genius won Waterloo, quantum happenings in his brain having happened somewhat differently, would then be Worlds whose states of today had some continuing very, very faint possibility of 'jostling' our World.

4.55 I think we might say that sort of thing even if we viewed only the one branch as fully real, classifying the others merely as 'complexly active possibilities'. To the Many-Worlds theorist, however, *all* the possibilities which quantum theory recognizes – and it does recognize some very odd ones such as the possibility of your quantum-tunnelling through a brick wall – take on full reality. Each exists somewhere in the ever-branching cosmos. And if so then to call jostling of two branches 'only a very, very faint possibility' is not to say entirely straightforwardly that this jostling will almost certainly not happen. What it says is that its happening will be confined to a very, very small proportion of the sub-branches of those branches. Of the various *yous* into which you will split only vanishingly few – or if there are infinitely many of them then only a vanishingly tiny *range* (cf. 4.11) – will be detectably affected by branches containing Waterloo-winning Napoleons. Still fewer will be at all strongly affected.

Whether we are to speak of Many Worlds, or instead of many almost completely distinct 'parts' or 'aspects' of a single World, is then just a matter of verbal taste. The important point is simply that the Many-Worlds theory tells of a Reality whose many branches are only very loosely interwoven.

4.56 Now comes the big question. To what extent would the Worlds or 'parts' or 'aspects' be different?

Worlds branching apart at late times might differ with respect to whether particular bombs exploded or whether Napoleon won. Earlier branchings, however, could produce main branches whose differences were much more radical, all their sub-branches then inheriting those differences.

Thus, perhaps the first branchings would result in Worlds greatly different in scale (cf. 4.34). Later branchings might produce ones in which symmetries had been broken in all the varied fashions considered by Linde (4.22). And the greater the variations, the stronger would be our grounds for classifying the branches as multiple universes.

Yet More Universe-Making Mechanisms

4.57 There are several further ways in which many and varied universes might be generated. Here are a few:

(a) F. Hoyle and J. V. Narlikar describe a cosmos divided into huge cells, particle masses varying from place to place and becoming zero at cell boundaries.[37] Starlight from outside our cell reaches us in a form so scrambled that it looks like a Big Bang's black-body radiation. Its inability to give us detailed information about other cells reinforces our reasons for calling them other universes.

(b) K. Sato, H. Kodoma, M. Sasaki, and K. Maeda imagine 'child universes' – regions of an expanding false vacuum (4.16) which are pinched off after being surrounded by true vacuum.[38] These children continue to grow, regions of true vacuum forming inside them and pinching off further children; and so on, maybe *ad infinitum*. True vacuum regions might all evolve into universes somewhat like ours.

(c) A. D. Linde observes that a variant would have child universes created simply by quantum-tunnelling from their mothers.[39] The children would then never have been in any normal sense spatially connected to the mothers. (In contrast, in the case envisaged by Sato there would be umbilical cords which might however 'evaporate' so as to produce spatial disconnection.) To its inhabitants a child universe would seem to have burst into being from nothing at all. If it in turn produced further children then those inhabitants could easily know nothing of their births; for remember, the inflationary story suggests that the amount of material needed for the creation of a huge new universe is only very small.

(d) M. A. Markov paints a similar picture: 'daughter universes' give rise to 'granddaughters', 'great-granddaughters', etc.[40] Here, though, the births occur during Big Squeezes. Specially dense regions split off and then grow through oscillating as in the Dicke–Peebles model (4.36).

(e) 'Chaotic' or 'Stochastic' Gauge Theories allow universes to differ randomly in their laws. Very often (3.11) our universe is thought typical of the possibilities: compare how most tosses of a hundred pennies yield roughly fifty heads. But if universes existed in large numbers then a wide range of laws would be represented among them, a position V. F. Mukhanov has developed against the background of Many-Worlds quantum theory.[41] And if typical universes had laws hostile to Life then of course we should be in an atypical one.

4.58 Notice that Mukhanov might have chosen some quite other background: for instance, one in which universes appeared as quantum vacuum fluctuations.

In effect, *mechanisms for making universes very different* could be combined in any number of ways with *mechanisms for making what might well be called 'universes' (especially if they were very different).* Tryon's fluctuation universes might inflate, each becoming divided into many Linde-domain universes of differently broken symmetry; and/or they might oscillate, Wheeler fashion; and/or branch as suggested by Everett; and so on. Since many-universe theories need not compete with one another, Reality could be a cake sliced up in twenty different directions at once. Each gigantic realm, region, branch, among perhaps infinitely many, might itself be split into further realms, regions, or branches. And each of those might in turn be splintered into still more, etc.

4.59 This last point, together with the difficulty of knowing when any two realms, regions, or branches are separate enough and different enough to count as two universes, can make it a difficult and thankless task to divide multiple-universe scenarios into groups. G. Gale has proposed the categories 'spatially multiple', 'temporally multiple', and 'other-dimensionally multiple';[42] yet which of these would apply to a Hartle–Hawking scheme of things (4.31–.32), for example? Here some form of Many-Worlds quantum theory is accepted – the wave-function of the universe never collapses – but oscillations are accepted too. Further, Hartle and Hawking comment that the classical concept of Time becomes inapplicable between the oscillations. One therefore does not know whether to classify these as existing each as a continuation of another, or else as separate Everett-type branches.[43] One may not care.

Philosophical

4.60 Next, some mainly philosophical comments.

Can we be sure of the possibility, even, of universes much (or at all) different from our own? *That only the one kind of world is logically or mathematically or cognitively possible* has been suggested with varying degrees of clarity by various people. By various medieval Aristotelians, for instance. By N. Wilson among modern philosophers. Among scientists, by A. Einstein, P. A. M. Dirac, A. S. Eddington, J. A. Wheeler, G. F. Chew, V. Trimble, R. Penrose, J. D. Barrow, and F. J. Tipler – the last two finding support for the theme in the writings of B. S. DeWitt, J. B. Hartle, and S. W. Hawking.[44]

The Kantian notion of cognitive possibility strikes me as unhelpful here, however.[45] (For a start, must every real world indeed be graspable cognitively? And mayn't it be altogether too paradoxical to credit ourselves with cognitive mechanisms of the complexity required for 'filtering out' everything that departs in the slightest from a gigantic world-pattern whose intricacies physicists and astronomers and biologists are only just starting to understand?) And the doctrine that there is only one logically possible kind of world is if anything still worse, even when it softens its harshness somewhat by accepting Everett's continual branchings.

I can say this despite the trouble people have in constructing so much as a single self-consistent theory. Yes, symmetry principles and the conservation laws associated with them, plus the quantum-theoretic need for 'renormalizability' (3.7), keep dictating affairs which at first appeared entirely arbitrary. But let us not forget that symmetries and conservation laws have no intrinsic logical necessity: their denial involves no self-contradiction. Likewise, the infinities which renormalizability removes are contradictions not in themselves but only with the world as we find it.

4.61 In short, the results which physicists call logically required are only logically necessary consequences of non-logically neces-sary premisses.[46] It might conceivably be (a) that only the one kind of world was compatible with physical laws of the general sort which rule our world, and perhaps also (b) that a world would have to obey either precisely those laws or else ones markedly different, any attempt to vary the laws *just slightly* leading straight to self-contradiction. There would none the less be nothing contradictory in a world obeying markedly different laws or else no laws meriting the name. There could be worlds in which magic spells moved mountains or worlds so disorderly that there would be little point in stretching the word 'laws' until it fitted them.

4.62 Those still unconvinced might like to consider S. L. Jaki's remark that 'Gödel's incompleteness theorem, according to which no set of non-trivial arithmetical propositions can have its proof of consistency within itself, means that all scientific efforts which would show that the universe can only be what it is, are doomed to failure.'[47] (The import of Gödel's theorem is contro-versial and Jaki's point is expressed too quickly to inspire confidence. However, he seems to interpret the theorem as showing that alternative mathematics can be developed, all of them consistent and each specially suited to describing a different kind of universe. Even if our own universe were fully describable with a mathematics which could prove its own consistency, this would seem not to destroy the force of such reasoning.) To which we could add that there is no contradiction in *being* without *being perceived*, or in a cosmos from which consciousness is entirely absent.[48]

4.63 It can seem fairly clear, furthermore, that many different kinds of universe are 'physically conceivable' in some sense strong enough to be of interest to practising physicists. As has already been emphasized (2.26; 3.11), the simplest unified theory appears to have failed, leaving physicists with the task of sifting through greatly many other theories all just about equally complicated. Superstrings Theory, the most recently fashionable attempt at a Theory of Everything, can itself be developed in a multitude of ways. For one thing, it involves a 'compactification' of dimensions (2.37; 4.22) which seems able to take very varied forms.

4.64 Granted, though, that very different universes are in logical and other senses *possible*, mayn't Simplicity still demand that only one universe should actually exist or at least that all existing universes should look much the same?

Well, let us remind ourselves of arguments to the contrary. (i) Scientific theories might take their simplest forms when multiple universes existed. Virtually any mechanism able to generate a universe would look odd if bearing the label, THIS MECHA-NISM OPERATED ONCE ONLY. (ii) An infinitely large Reality could seem simpler than one which suddenly ended. And given such a Reality – or just a very large one – it could be simplest to *leave out* various links whose presence would connect it up into a unified whole. (iii) Even if universes all obeyed the same fundamental laws, derived laws might be greatly different thanks to how symmetry breaks had occurred differently.

4.65 Simplicity is measurable in many ways, however, and obviously Reality would be in some ways simpler if containing just the one universe or else just a small group of universes all much alike. And while I have done my best to present multiple-universe theories in the most generous of lights, all are very speculative and presumably destined to remain so. On any reasonable definition of *other universes* we could never have firm, direct evidence that other universes exist. Very poor or zero causal linkage with us is part of what their otherness means.

Moreover, the physics of universe creation and of such variation-producing affairs as GUT symmetry breaking is the physics of energies perhaps many trillion times beyond what could ever be achieved by particle accelerators. And efforts to achieve them could be horribly dangerous. One does not want to reproduce conditions such as gave rise to the Big Bang! (The space of our universe may be only metastable: 2.41. A close approach to Big Bang conditions could then create a bubble of fully stable space. One possibility, pointed out to me by D. Schramm, is that this would be the birth of a new universe which expanded enormously without affecting ours. But another is that the bubble would expand *through ours* at almost light speed, destroying every living thing.)[49]

4.66 The more nebulous a theory of multiple universes, the greater its immunity to detailed attack – but also the more dubious its claims to be scientific. One would like to see some clear advance on Hume's fantasy (in part XI of his *Natural History of Religion* (1757)) that 'the whole mythological system' of the heathen poets 'is so natural that, in the vast variety contained in this universe, it seems more than probable, that, somewhere or other, it is really carried into execution'; or on the vision of infinitely many, very varied universes developed in E. A. Poe's *Eureka* (1848) and called by him 'too beautiful' to be wrong; or on A. N. Whitehead's oddly confident contrasting (in *Process and Reality*, 1929) of 'our present cosmic epoch of electrons, protons, molecules and star-systems' with other cosmic epochs having laws so different that even shapes and dimensions are absent; or, for that matter, on the ancient theme that worlds appear as bubbles in Brahma's cosmic body. Yet everywhere we are confronted with the same plain difficulty: that the more radically other Worlds are separated from ours and the more their properties are different, the harder it is for scientific arguments to get any grip on them.

Even Linde's symmetry-breaking scalar fields, their intensities taking the same values right across the observable heavens, are strongly resistant to direct detection – rather like the medieval scientist's Music of the Spheres. And the claim that other values are taken in other regions well beyond our horizon is of course 100 per cent resistant to it.

4.67 Many-Worlds quantum theory could strike reasonable people as particularly speculative and unsimple. We could prefer to believe that events *suggestive of* wave-interference in a Many-Worlds Superspace do not in fact involve it. Mightn't it just be that Nature hesitates between alternatives when its laws give no reason for any one of them to be preferred, then arbitrarily plumping for one part of the pattern which they would have generated had they all existed together? Reality, we could say, just is ultimately probabilistic. Better that than the ontological extravagance, the 'deOckhamization' (multiplying of entities beyond what is strictly necessary), of continual branchings! While the point at which wave-function collapse occurred might in each case be settled randomly, it would occur very rapidly in almost every case. And it could be irreversible.

The same charge of deOckhamization could of course be brought against absolutely any theories of multiple universes. I would say that it is nowhere near conclusive against such theories – yet when you look at Many-Worlds quantum theory you can see why fairly sensible people often think it conclusive. The idea that all of us and all our surroundings are perpetually splitting can strike people as much too odd.

4.68 It is sometimes urged that two purely philosophical arguments favour multiple universes.

First, proper understanding of Causality involves respect for counterfactual statements such as, 'If the brick had hit it then the window would have broken.' Well, says D. Lewis, respect for them means taking them to correspond to other statements – e.g. 'The brick did hit the window and broke it' – which are true in other universes *real* and *existent* precisely as our universe is, Worlds whose 'non-actuality' is like the non-here-ness of Africa to someone in New York.[50]

Lewis extends this treatment not just to things which we tend to count as really possible – things like the simultaneous breaking of every window in Princeton – but to all logical possibilities. All the Greek gods, for instance, are really to be found in some universes. Curious though this is, it seems to him acceptable so long as they are not found in any universe at all close to ours in its properties. His treatment of the idea of *closeness* is thought important by many who refuse real existence to even the closest universes, but this Lewis sees as a case of their accepting the benefits of his position while rejecting the coins with which those benefits have to be purchased.

Second, while not joining Lewis in thinking that all possibles *must have* existence somewhere, other philosophers have suggested that arbitrariness is minimized if all of them exist in fact.[51]

4.69 What are we to make of these two positions? Contemptuous sniffs and incredulous stares are not enough to dismiss them, yet both face a difficulty I think decisive. If all possible Worlds exist then there truly are Worlds behaving like ours right up to this moment but which thereafter follow courses so disorderly that most inductive predictions fail in them. Frogs appear *ex nihilo*; stones move slowly upwards in tight spirals; pigs grow wings and cows explode; and so on. Now, maybe the number of orderly world-patterns could not be swamped by the number of disorderly ones, both numbers being infinite; but wouldn't the *range* of the disorderly ones be far the greater (cf. 4.11), given the real existence of all possible patterns? But if so then inductive predictions, instead of just being (as philosophers have long appreciated) somewhat hard to justify, would seem altogether untrustworthy – a conclusion horrid enough to force the rejection of any position which leads to it. The people whose predictions were reliable would fill a range tiny compared to that of those others – not 'merely equally possible' but equally really existing – whose predictions failed entirely.[52]

Besides, mightn't it be Lewis who was guilty of not taking *real possibilities* seriously enough when he supposed that the only way in which they could be real would be through their being *real existents* somewhere?

4.70 A still other philosophical argument which could help us to accept many and varied universes – or if that word is disliked, then many and varied huge regions of Reality – is defended by D. Goldstick.[53] Confidence in any natural law should continue to decrease, he reasons, with each increase in the territory the law is asked to govern. Suppose, now, that Reality extends much further than we can see. How much confidence should we have that any law holds universally? Goldstick replies that the confidence should be very small in the case of an immensely large Reality, declining to zero in that of an infinite one.

To me this is too reminiscent of W. S. Jevons's estimate that five thousand years of sunrise, while making it a safe bet that the sun will rise again at least once, yield only a half chance of its rising five thousand years in the future.[54] If we are to attach enough weight to the simplicity of unvarying laws then what we need, I think, is a perhaps infinitely prolonged decline towards *some lower limit*. Our confidence that cows will never jump over moons could get for ever smaller the wider the field over which it was asked to wander, while maybe never plunging below 99 per cent.

4.71 The conclusion suggested by all this (4.68–.70) is that – unless when influenced by theism or by something much like it, as when God is presumed to prefer multiplicity and variety – 'philosophy as such' supplies no really good grounds for accepting many and varied universes. Indeed, it might actually supply grounds for rejecting them even after all due attention had been paid to the arguments of physicists and cosmologists. *Simplicity* is fairly powerfully advanced the fewer the universes we believe in and the more we insist that any other universes must resemble ours. *Induction* – not at all clearly different from Respect for Simplicity – could scarcely be expected to give us firm grip on universes much different from the one we know. And there is even the threat that our confidence in inductive forecasts will fail entirely if we too quickly accept that Reality is greatly varied.

4.72 The threat to the forecasts can grow more vivid when we look at various actual scientific doctrines. As one possible solution to why our world is so low in entropy, so orderly, L. Boltzmann presented a cosmos extending indefinitely in time or in space and therefore containing many 'universes' in one of the senses we considered (4.2; 4.5): its far-separated regions have little or no information about one another. On the largest scales there is thermal equilibrium but this is of course compatible with entropy fluctuations, local departures from equilibrium of various sizes. Some very rare fluctuations are universe-sized, the universe which we observe being among them. No observers could exist outside departures from equilibrium because low entropy is Life's prerequisite.[55] But the trouble with this is that Boltzmann places me inside a fluctuation *much larger* than is needed to account for my awareness as of this moment. It would actually be far better to assume that the combination of my body and its immediate surroundings – or perhaps just my brain, well stocked with pseudo-observations of an outside world and pseudo-memories of happy years – is a very much smaller fluctuation in a desert of disorder, an oasis almost sure to extend no further than present experience.[56] As R. Penrose puts it, 'It is vastly "cheaper" (in terms of negative entropy) simply to produce a few conscious beings out of some carefully organized particle collisions.'[57]

4.73 Today, P. C. W. Davies might seem to repeat Boltzmann's mistake in the context of Many-Worlds quantum theory. He reasons that all quantum possibilities are represented in Everett's multiple branches: Life's prerequisites then dictate that we could find ourselves only in a branch whose entropy was exceptionally low.

Davies claims however that his position differs from Boltzmann's in that he can tie microcosmic entropy to macrocosmic. The visible universe is everywhere smooth on very large scales, as is shown by the evenness of the cosmic background radiation, and the local orderliness required by Life and Observership is most likely to occur inside such global orderliness.[58]

In general, to defend against the trap into which Boltzmann blundered you must imitate Davies by making your many universes satisfy the following restriction. The probability that a universe chosen randomly from among them will have the characteristics which you seem to see must exceed the probability that you don't really see what you seem to.

4.74 M. H. Hart, for instance, can defend himself in this style when he suggests (4.12) that the chances that living beings would evolve even once in the entire region now visible to us were extremely low but that in an infinitely large universe they would evolve in some such regions, these then being – obviously – the ones which observers would see. While the probability of Life's appearance even on an ideally suitable planet might easily be as slim as one in $10^{3,000}$ this would still be fat enough for avoidance of the trap.[59]

G. Steigman, in contrast, may be unable to mount any similar defence when he proposes that our universe has more matter than antimatter simply through the effects of Chance operating on immensely many universes; in most, observers cannot evolve because matter–antimatter annihilations sweep away the atoms needed for making them.[60] Will this survive close scrutiny? I think not. We observe roughly 10^{80} matter particles and 10^{89} photons such as result from matter–antimatter annihilations. Now, if tossing 2×10^{89} pennies your likelihood of getting 10^{80} more heads than tails is vanishingly tiny.

If, moreover, our universe contains even only marginally more matter than is strictly necessary for Life and Observership then Steigman's theory fails through its inability to account for this.

4.75 Suppose, though, that we ran no real risk of imitating Boltzmann's error. We ought still to be very cautious about ascribing our cosmological findings to Chance plus the observational selection effect with which Carter's 'Anthropic Principle' deals (1.26; 4.9). The grounds for caution are in part heuristic: we need to guard against human frailty. Realizing that our observations of various features might be explained 'anthropically' we could feel tempted to end all search for fundamental physical principles that dictate exactly those features. And then, of course, we might be missing the truth of the affair.

In fact, sheer laziness might occasionally underlie this or that argument for multiple universes. A cosmologist faces some life-encouraging phenomenon which on his present theories appears wildly improbable – so he invokes Worlds adequately numerous to ensure that the improbable will occur somewhere. What a way of practising science! It is specially tempting to say this when a new theory offers to explain what our cosmologist attributes to Chance. Thus, one tends to criticize Steigman (4.74) for not having taken Nature's hint and discovered the currently popular mechanisms for producing more matter than antimatter (2.28).

4.76 The other face of the coin, however, is that the cosmologist being damned as lazy may in fact have hit on the truth, any further search being both costly and doomed to lead nowhere.

Now, surely this should count for something heuristically. Surely our frailty is not so abysmal that in order to motivate prolonged searching we have to blind ourselves to the possibility of failure. ('I certainly wouldn't give up attempts to make the anthropic principle unnecessary by finding a theoretical basis for the value of all the constants. It's worth trying, *and we have to assume that we shall succeed, otherwise we surely shall fail*': S. Weinberg.[61] The point is a good one until you reach the words I've italicized.)

Observational Selection?

4.77 The evidence of the last few years makes it virtually certain that the main features of the visible universe *are not* all of them dictated by fundamental physical principles so much more elegant than their competitors that they just have to be right. The fact that physicists are confronted with so many different theories, all about equally complex (2.26; 3.11; 4.63), could be one reason for saying this. Yet the main reason lies elsewhere, in the natural constants – physically and cosmologically important numbers – which appear fine tuned to Life's needs. These form a list which has grown impressively long (1.4; Chapter 2). Further, there is the remarkable fact, very regularly overlooked, that one and the same constant often seems to need fine tuning in a certain way for several different reasons at once (3.12).

Such affairs are strong indications that some *selection effect* is at work. It chooses life-encouraging values of the constants, for a start. It quite probably ensures as well that the background physical theory should be of a very special kind: one which allows there to be *some* possible values of those constants which are life-encouraging, several different needs then all being satisfied harmoniously.

Just what kind of selection effect, though?

4.78 As we have seen, a fairly attractive possibility is that there exist many universes. They might be gigantic domains in a cosmos which once inflated enormously and underwent probabilistic symmetry breaking, or they might have come about in any of many other ways. Natural constants vary from universe to universe. Mankind finds itself in one of the very rare universes which permit observers to evolve. The selection effect is an observational one.

One of the problems with this scenario is that it can appear unable to account for the above-mentioned remarkable fact, very regularly overlooked, that one and the same constant often seems fine tuned in ways satisfying several different needs at once.

101

(Look again at the argument of 3.12.) In order that those needs should all be satisfied together in some universe or other, the many universes might well have to differ not just in their constants but also in the general forms of their fundamental laws. Now, it is hard to be sure how to reason in this area – yet differences in fundamental laws can seem rather implausible matters.

Notice, however, that if we accepted such differences then Weinberg's dichotomy (4.76) – *explanation by reference to fundamental laws*, on the one hand, and *anthropic explanation* on the other – suffers a breakdown. The 'anthropic' observational selection effect would now select universes with the right fundamental laws instead of just ensuring that the constants were tuned appropriately.

4.79 The alternative is that the selection is Divine Selection. God – either God-as-a-person or Neoplatonism's more abstract divine creative principle (1.3) – selects fundamental laws and natural constants in such a way as to make living beings able to evolve.

This would be compatible with there existing many universes with varied laws or constants. God could be very richly creative. Aware of all possible universes resulting from early symmetry breaks of a probabilistic kind, God may have chosen to give reality to all those in which observers would evolve. Or again, God could have considered all possible all-dictating laws, selecting ones which produced the desired result. Each of many possible sets of laws might serve and each might have been given a universe or group of universes to rule.

A divine person might conceivably create many entirely disconnected universes in which living beings *could not* exist, just to give completeness to a scheme of things containing a few which were more welcoming. However, it strikes me as somewhat strange to think of him as doing so. And if 'God' simply names the Neoplatonic principle that some ethical requirements *are themselves creatively effective* then I think God no more capable of this than of creating a thoroughly evil universe.

4.80 Science, remember, does not support the multiple-universes hypothesis *rather than* the God hypothesis. We do not have, independently of the delicate adjustments which – so science seems to say – were crucial to Life's possibility in this universe of ours, any strong evidence of a World Ensemble. It is not, for instance, as if Big Squeezes were known to occur and to involve a well-understood 'probabilistic reprocessing' of physical constants. We lack good independent grounds for believing in the existence of reams of nonsense, the output of a cosmic ran-domizer which was bound eventually to type something exciting.

4.81 Note the underlying assumption that Life truly is some-thing to get excited about: something *standing out* against a background of other possibilities like a fly in the centre of an otherwise empty area. The next chapter will discuss that point.

Chapter Five

The Need to Explain Life

A multiplicity of 'Worlds' or 'universes' could seem needed to explain why at least one universe includes observers, because Life apparently depends on fine tuning of natural constants. Yet why should a universe's life-permitting character require any more explanation than, say, the fact of its containing diamonds? Agreed, Life's intricate patterns do call for explanation – but are not Darwin's explanations enough? Why feel explanatory urges when faced by the sheer fact that our universe's properties made Darwinian evolution possible?

The answer lies in how needs for explanation are linked with the availability of tidy explanations (cf. sections 1.9–.11). When does a hand of cards cry out for explanation? When dishonest dealing is easy and brings huge benefits to the dealer. (This illustrates the common-sensical point, fundamental to science, that observations improve your reasons for accepting some hypothesis – e.g. that a dealt hand was not simply a chance affair – when its truth would have made those observations more likely.) Now, might observations of fine tuning be explained by Multiple Worlds plus Observational Selection? Or, indeed, by God? If so, then the need to explain our World's life-permitting character could appear fairly plain.

The chapter defends this conclusion against arguments which claim to show that being life-permitting must be unremarkable. Suppose, for instance, that we granted (very generously) that there could not be more than one universe. Some would then argue that basic cosmic properties could not be in any way 'improbable' because probabilities depend on the possibility of observing repetitions. But their argument would seem to require that even had our universe's properties been settled by a demon's dice tossing, they would still not have been settled probabilistically. Yet that seems very wrong – which is important because early symmetry breakings might have acted much like dice tossings.

Might Life Specially Need Explanation?

5.1 Chapter 4 suggested that physics, cosmology, and philosophy, if supplemented by nothing further, supply only rather weak grounds for believing in Multiple Worlds or small-u universes. To get stronger ones we have to add biology. We have to consider Life's 'delicacy': the apparent need for fine tuning of natural

104

constants and/or initial conditions if living beings are ever to evolve. The chief reason for belief in very many, very varied huge cosmic situations is that given sufficiently many of them conditions somewhere might be expected to be suitable for Life.

Suppose, for example, that altering the expansion speed of its Big Bang by one part in a million million would have made our universe fall to bits too fast or recollapse too quickly for living beings to stand a chance of evolving. Suppose this meant that implosive and explosive forces had to be adjusted more delicately than the two halves of a pencil balancing on a razor's edge. Our existence could then seem a near-incredible stroke of fortune – until we reflected that given vastly many universes with differing expansion speeds such a stroke of fortune could be expected somewhere or other.

5.2 Why, however, should Life be viewed as specially in need of explanation? Suppose it could be found in only one in every trillion quadrillion universes in 'the local area': the area of possible universes recognizably like ours in their basic laws but differing in the strengths of their forces, the masses of their particles, their degrees of turbulence, and so forth. So what? Why should Life's actual existence invite comparison with a bullet's hitting a fly placed in the middle of an otherwise empty area, which could suggest a machine-gun spraying bullets? Why not treat it instead as like a fly's being hit when other equally interesting insects – wasps, bees, beetles, moths, butterflies – are swarming all around it so that more or less any bullet could be expected to hit one of them? Why should *Life* be thought of as labelled 'bull's-eye'?

Imagine that, of the possible universes in question, only one in every trillion quadrillion would be like ours in containing fast-rotating neutron stars, carbon of a sort which can form both diamonds and graphite, or particles with masses of 493.67 MeV. Presumably none of this would be an immediate excuse for belief in God or in a World Ensemble, a collection of vastly many actually existing universes. So why react differently in Life's case?

5.3 What if we answered Yes to the question of whether there was something 'special' in a universe's having a life-permitting character? We should then face what could seem like a second, quite separate question of how being life-permitting could best be accounted for.

In fact, however, this second question is not easily separable from the first. Unless ways can be suggested in which an affair could plausibly be explained we may well hesitate to accept that it needs explanation. Consider typical modern attitudes towards the question, 'Why does anything at all have Actual Existence?' (Why is there any universe and not just a blank?) It is typically said that this could not possibly have an answer since existents can be explained only by other existents – and that therefore anyone who finds a puzzle in the Mere Existence of Something Rather than Nothing is being absurd.

Likewise, many people have thought that only God could conceivably be an answer to why our universe has life-permitting properties, and that the God hypothesis turns out to be foolish when looked at closely. Therefore, they reason, anyone asking why our universe has life-permitting properties is posing what turns out to be a silly question. The issue of what is a genuine problem is not so straightforward that we can settle it without troubling to enquire what answers might be had. Things do not bear labels saying whether they are problematic.

5.4 I shall argue that there is much to be said for such a line of reasoning. The main difficulty with it comes from over-hasty decisions about the impossibility of explaining this or that. (Even 'Why does anything at all have Actual Existence?' might be answered by a Neoplatonist: 1.3. Neoplatonism tries to explain the realm of Actual Existents by reference to unconditionally real ethical requirements: requirements which could be real even in the absence of all entities like atoms, tables, trees, and mental states. Now, it might be only entities of that general sort, and not anything as abstract as the reality *that two sets of two apples would make four apples* or the reality *that the absence of a universe of pure misery is ethically required in an unconditional way*, which we had in mind when speaking of Actual Existents.)

First, though, let us ask whether it could be prima facie plausible to see a problem in the sheer fact that a universe is life-permitting.

5.5 To begin with, let us destroy arguments to the effect that *no evidence whatever* of Life's delicacy – not even, say, absolute proof that a change by one quintillionth in the early cosmic expansion speed would have made living things impossible – could provide grounds for curiosity. Chief of the arguments are:

(A) That the universe contains living things cannot be remarkable since the very fact that we can ask whether to find it remarkable implies that we are alive.

(B) Basic laws of nature cannot be explained and therefore cannot need to be explained, and so cannot justify grand cosmogonic conclusions.

(C) The universe is unique; hence concepts of probability and improbability cannot apply to it; therefore we must not call it improbable that its laws should be, without any reason, of the sort which Life requires.

(D) Only experience can tell us what needs explanation, and we lack experience of other universes.

5.6 These arguments would seem to have little strength.

Consider (A). 'To wonder at the order of nature', says Baron d'Holbach in his *Good Sense* (1772), 'is to be surprised at one's own existence', which strikes him as absurd. 'The world's properties might have been such as to lead to no sensate beings', but in that case, remarks M. Scriven's *Primary Philosophy* (1966), 'there would be no one to discuss the teleological argument' – the implication being that, obviously, this makes that argument (otherwise known as the Design Argument for God's existence) merely stupid. And Design's supporters themselves find force in such a point. During the case of the Naval Treaty, Sherlock Holmes muses that 'our powers, our desires, our food, are really necessary for our existence in the first instance'; for evidence of Design we must therefore turn instead to the rose, which is 'an embellishment of life, not a condition of it'. But, I ask, can it really be true that our existence and its conditions ought never to arouse our curiosity?

What a superb means of banishing perplexities that would provide! Why does anything at all have actual existence? *Reply*: There must be something if we ourselves exist. Why do events fall into 'orderly' sequences, describable by fairly short mathematical equations? *Reply*: Were the world appreciably less orderly then we could not inhabit it. Again, is there a seeming difficulty in the theory that a human male and female came about without evolutionary preliminaries through chance migration of their atoms to the right positions, or does Arrhenius stagger us when he argues that self-propagating life forms have existed eternally and therefore do not call for explanation? Well, let us but reflect that Life, no matter how it came about (or, if eternal, failed to come about), cannot possibly be something to surprise us . . . .

Plainly the reasoning has gone wrong. When an artillery shell has exploded in your trench you can well find it curious that you live. Your living follows unsurprisingly from your ability to ask whether to be surprised, but this ability is itself a surprising one.

5.7 How are we to make Life unsurprising? (Because this must be our ultimate aim. We do not want our theories to tell us that what we see is *surprising in the last analysis*, i.e. surprising even when every explanation has been found; for that would just show that our theories were probably wrong. Our project must be one of showing instead that all this smoke, so to speak, could in the end be very much to be expected, were there a fire.)[1]

We might try arguing that more or less any world would be life-containing. By seeming to prove as much, Darwin severely weakened the Design Arguments of his century. His approach appeared to show that God was not needed in order to make Life into something other than a monstrous improbability. Yet it can today look as if Darwinian ideas are inadequate to show this. Not because they are wrong – for on the contrary they are known to be right. Granted that Nature's laws are in fact life-permitting, Darwinian accounts give (although usually only in very compressed form) the causal story of Life's evolution for which section 1.8 called. Still, not just any universe would be one in which Darwinian evolution would work. If a tiny reduction in the early cosmic expansion speed would have made everything recollapse within a fraction of a second while a tiny increase would quickly have yielded a universe far too dilute for stars to form, then such changes would (presumably) have been disastrous to Evolution's prospects. But how then are we to make Life unsurprising? Well, perhaps there exist so many universes with differing expansion speeds that Evolution will be bound to work somewhere – and of course, were that somewhere not *here* then we living beings wouldn't be discussing it *here*. Or perhaps we should say that God fine tuned the expansion speed. But to say simply, 'If the universe hadn't expanded at a speed compatible with Life's evolution then we shouldn't be able to discuss the affair', is to give no explanation whatever. One might as well have said straight out that the existence of living beings was fantastically improbable.

5.8 Compare the case of surviving a bite from a snake. It would be unreasonable to comment, 'If I hadn't survived then I shouldn't be here to consider the topic; hence I'll willingly accept that similar bites would prove fatal in all but one of a billion cases.'

Again, recall the Firing Squad Story (1.17). The fifty sharpshooters all miss the intended victim. Suspicion arises that those sharpshooters did not intend him to become a victim. And the condemned man can himself share the suspicion instead of commenting, 'If they hadn't all missed me then I shouldn't be contemplating the matter so I mustn't be surprised that they missed.'

Again, if the existence of all life on Earth depends on the non-explosion of hydrogen bombs connected to a randomizer, and the dials are set so that pressing a button ought to give 99.99999999 per cent probability that the bombs will explode, and the button is pressed and men find themselves still alive, then they ought to suspect that some fault has developed in the randomizer.

5.9 Notice that 'If things hadn't been fine tuned for Life then we shouldn't be here to contemplate them' is a comment which has just as much or as little power *no matter what* the supposed evidence of fine tuning is. But what if it had been proved that living things evolved only thanks to how two force strengths stood in exactly the ratio of 1 to 5735.67394521996246227, or what if it took a million figures to state the ratio? Few would then be tempted to make such a comment.

5.10 Now for argument (B), the objection that basic laws cannot be explained.

For a start, how on earth did we learn *that*? It may be tempting to reply that the right way of explaining any natural law is to reveal it as an instance of some more basic law, as when laws relating the temperature, pressure, and volume of a gas are explained first on dynamical lines – 'Gases are like collections of perfectly elastic billiard balls' – and later on electromagnetic ones (showing why those balls are perfectly elastic). Clearly the *most basic* laws, whatever they may be, cannot be explained in this fashion. But equally clearly, to imagine that this is the one and only right fashion is to beg the question against, for example, any theistic explanation of why those most basic laws are as they are. The question-begging would be obvious were electron microscopes to reveal that particles regularly formed long chains which spelled out GOD CREATED THE UNIVERSE, this then being shown to result inevitably from basic physics.

5.11 Next, *even if* Nature's basic laws were in some sense utterly inexplicable, it would not follow that evidence of fine tuning indicated nothing interesting; for the World Ensemble hypothesis could still throw light on how that evidence came to exist. The hypothesis, remember, is that laws and/or natural constants and/or initial conditions – distinctions which might no doubt be somewhat artificial – vary from universe to universe. Now, perhaps each universe just does *inexplicably* obey laws different from those obeyed by others; or perhaps there are some most basic laws which control how each universe differs from the next, but these laws *are themselves inexplicable*. But either way, talk of many universes provides an interesting *explanation* of why there exists at least one life-containing universe. (The explanation could take the form not of showing that there *had to exist* a life-permitting universe, but rather just of making it *unmysterious* that such a universe in fact existed.)

5.12 Look now at objection (C), which starts from the premiss that the universe is unique.

It definitely is unique if by 'universe' you mean Everything That Exists, but recall that for present purposes huge cosmic systems existing very largely or entirely in isolation from our own can count as 'other universes'. Still, mightn't it be protested that we could never get evidence of their existence? Well, fine tuning could be *evidence* – indirect evidence, ambiguous evidence (1.30–.31), but evidence none the less – for the reality of universes in large numbers. The question of whether any other universes had some very slight causal contact with ours, such as might eventually lead to their being detected *directly*, could seem as irrelevant to the strength of this evidence as it is (4.7) to the meaningfulness of 'other universes' talk. (As if the snapping of some last tiny causal link could send an entire other universe into the realm of unmeaning!)

There is, however, a widely accepted sense of 'universe' in which there is by definition only a single universe, a universe including all that is and was and ever will be. What if we for argument's sake hypothesize that its events form just a single system of causally interacting objects obeying always the same laws, with the same natural constants and so forth? The life-generating nature of that system is then no rarity among actualities since there just are no other actualities. Now, mightn't this ruin all attempts to argue for Design, since haven't we here bid goodbye to the statistical basis which would allow us to say that the universe, if undesigned, would be a monstrous improbability? And mightn't the World Ensemble theory be similarly embarrassed, since doesn't *its* statistical basis depend on begging the question against our present hypothesis that there is only the one World?

In fact, mightn't we be in much the same position even if the causal system into which we fit is not unique? For isn't it at least unique in our experience?

5.13 To this one might reply that probability statements can meaningfully be made even about single cases. Even if only one coin ever had been or ever would be tossed, it would not be nonsense to say that the coin had a half chance of landing heads. Again, repetitions seem inessential to *evidence of* probabilities. From a well-shaken urn containing a million balls you draw a single one, black. This is excellent evidence against the theory that all the rest of the balls are white. Yet the case of a universe could perhaps be objected to be radically different from these. Because whether or not you in fact toss your coin several times or draw several balls, you always *might*. But in dealing with a universe – it might be objected – there just is no possibility of 'repeating the experiment'. As D. H. Mellor puts it: 'The trouble with supposing the world to be the result of a chance process is that, not merely *has* the process only happened once, it *could* only happen once.'[2] Mellor concludes that probability talk has absolutely no sense in this area. Hence we mustn't think of the world's basic structure as *defying probability* in a way which might justify belief in God, for instance.

However, a seemingly crushing counter is (cf. 5.9) that any force had by objections on these lines would be had no matter what the supposed evidence was. They are not just calls for caution, sensible reminders that we are dealing with a very difficult field and must not be too confident in our conclusions. Instead they are purely logical objections. As such, they would supposedly succeed in the face of all logically possible scientific findings. So let us imagine that on measuring the strength ratio of two fundamental forces we find that the one is 11.2012100202100020000021102002100 times stronger. Intrigued – for when numbers are expressed decimally you expect something other than twos, ones and zeros – a scientist tests the idea that a Designer has here left a message in Morse code: zeros for dots, ones for dashes, and twos for spaces. The test yields MADE BY GOD. Whereupon philosophers comment that this is nowise 'contrary to chance', 'a defiance of probability', since the universe cannot happen more than once, etc.

Just where would they have gone wrong? At many places, probably.

5.14 Thus, it is often assumed (i) that there simply could not exist any universe additional to our own, in *any* helpful sense of 'universe'. Now, to this mistake may be added the thought met with in Mellor (ii) that anything which could happen only once couldn't be either probable or improbable – from which it is concluded that neither divine intervention nor anything else could be needed to 'bring it about despite its improbability'. But to see that this is unhelpful, consider cosmological speculations of the kind described in Chapter 4. A possibility treated with respect nowadays is that our universe underwent one or more phase transitions involving the splitting apart of Nature's four main forces. The forms, *themselves settled by Chance*, which these phase transitions took, could have fixed the relative strengths of those forces, the masses of various particles, and other affairs. If the universe started off small enough then these things could have been fixed in the same way everywhere. And the probability that the force strengths, particle masses, etc. would turn out to be life-permitting could very well have been extremely low. Now, it would be odd for philosophers to protest that talk of probabilities was out of place here because a universe *could undergo such phase transitions only once.* For physics might well demand that the transitions should take place in the non-deterministic fashion with which quantum physicists have made us familiar. It might actually have been quantum uncertainties which made the phase transitions non-deterministic. This would be reason enough for us to say, 'The chances that the phase transitions would yield just the results that they did were slim indeed.' It could be psychologically helpful to add that other universes might exist in large numbers so that phase transition probabilities could in point of fact be reflected by a statistical distribution of outcomes; yet this would be in no way essential to the meaningfulness of probability talk here. If philosophical theories of probability dispute this then let those theories be revised! Probabilistic physics mustn't be imperilled to suit philosophers. It mustn't be made to depend on the actual existence of many universes.

5.15 Philosophy of the kind I am attacking may be inspired in part by (iii) arguing as if an affair would have to be totally without parallel if it were in any way unique. The physicists would in contrast be influenced by how transitions in the early universe, even if occurring unrepeatably, could be interestingly similar to other transitions occurring later: phase transitions in magnetic material, for instance. (Magnetization destroyed by heating can recur on cooling, the direction of magnetization then being settled probabilistically.) If the Morse code MADE BY GOD were arrived at as described in section 5.13 then they would not say that the circumstances were novel so that nothing interesting could be concluded. They would instead be influenced by how the words produced in these circumstances were like messages familiar to all of us.[3]

Suppose, fantastically, that it could be proved both that ours was the only universe that there ever could be and that its characteristics had been settled by a demon's dice tossing. Would the fact that the universe had to be a one and only universe – that it had to be something unique *when considered under the description 'universe'* – imply that its characteristics HAD NOT been settled probabilistically? Clearly not. It would not be the one and only thing whose characteristics had been settled by dice; and all such things have characteristics settled probabilistically, don't they?

5.16 Perhaps, though, the main stumbling-block is the notion (iv) that mere possibilities are disreputable so that we drift on a sea of nonsense when considering universes *that there might have been*. This notion is a philosophical disaster. You cannot understand the language of ethics or even of causation without taking possibilities seriously. That an action was wrong implies that other possible actions would have been better. That event *A* caused event *B* states – except in cases of causal overkill – that in the purely possible case in which *A* failed to happen, *B* would not have happened. (There is no hope of translating statements about what would or would not have happened into statements about regularities among actually existing events – e.g. 'Immersed sugar always dissolves' – and about what would have needed to happen IF those regularities were to extend to events which didn't in fact occur – e.g. the immersion of John Smith's sugar. Such translations never capture the full boldness of saying what would have taken place elsewhere in the well-integrated structure of the world, had an alteration been made somewhere. Conceivably any such alteration would have brought about cosmic ruin instead of such things as some sugar's dissolving.) Now, once appreciating this we should find nothing too problematic in those causal statements which are *merely probabilistic*: statements about happenings *in such-and-such a percentage of the possible cases*. And the cases could include cases of possible early phase transitions. The fact, if it was one, that ours was the only universe ever, and that its early phase transitions could not be repeated without a miracle, would be irrelevant.

What is more, Experience allows us to discuss expertly even possible universes which are unlike ours in very significant respects. Take, for example, a universe whose phase transitions made gravity marginally stronger so that everything recollapsed after only ten seconds. That such a universe *would be lifeless* is far from being purest speculation. And each new physically plausible scenario yielding lifelessness strengthens the idea that living beings would be improbable unless either there existed many universes or else the God hypothesis was right.

5.17 Sometimes one meets (v) the view that improbabilities are really improbable only if they happen several times in a row 'because of course the improbable can be expected to occur occasionally, and if so, why not on the very first possible occasion?' (Struck by a bullet coming from a mile away our philosopher mutters, 'Very possibly yonder rifleman is an exceedingly poor shot. I should need to see him fire repeatedly before forming an opinion.') Inconsistently enough, this is often combined with the attitude (vi) that what happens several times in a row should be thought *probable* in a way removing all need to explain it. Thus even if believers in Design could see universe after universe leaping into being, each with its natural constants combining in a new fashion to allow Life to perform a very delicate balancing act, they would find themselves without an argument. Seemingly favourable evidence collected from a single universe would be rejected by their critics as 'jumping to conclusions from a single case', yet enthusiasm about similar evidence collected from a thousand cases would be dismissed as 'a finding of marvels in what has proved to be entirely natural'. In the background is (vii) the curious notion that since a universe *is only one universe* all its characteristics 'ought never to count more than once in any row'. So no scene which could conceivably meet our eyes – not even one in which GOD MADE ME was inscribed on every animal – ought ever to be thought contrary to Chance. To quote Scriven's *Primary Philosophy* once more: 'It is not contrary to the laws of chance that there should be intelligence in the Universe any more than it is puzzling that an unbiased die should throw the series 1, 2, 3, 4, 5, 6, 1, 2, 3, 4. It would be very puzzling if this happened many times in a row, but there are not several universes in a row: there is only one.'

One wonders how far a series running 1, 2, 3, 4, 5, 6, 1, 2, 3, 4, 5, 6, 1, 2, 3, 4, 5, 6, 1, 2, 3, 4, 5, 6, 1, 2, 3, 4, 5, 6 . . . would have to extend before Scriven noticed how arbitrary it was to dismiss it as 'just one series'. Compare the tale of the Telephathized Painting (1.25). And then consider the case where Life seemingly depends on a ratio between two force strengths, a ratio which must not be different by one part in 10^{50} or even 10^{100}. That is to say, the number expressing this ratio decimally must contain fifty-one or even one hundred and one figures, every single one of which must be just right. Is there any real force in the comment that such a ratio 'is just one number'?

5.18 Notice that in the course of answering objection (C) we in effect got – in section 5.15 – our reply to objection (D), the objection that only experience can tell us what needs explanation and that we lack experience of other universes. The reply is that although our universe is the one and only *universe* in our experience, its basic characteristics (e.g. its being large) need not be unique in our experience. It might therefore be suggestively similar to, say, products of Design.

What has still to be shown, however, is that a feature of this universe which might reasonably excite our curiosity is that it is life-containing.

How Might Life Stand Out Among the Possibilities?

5.19 As noted earlier, it is not enough to point out that life-containing universes *are rare* in the 'local area' of possibilities, the area generated by imagined slight changes in our universe's basic properties. Hitting a fly is unremarkable if the surrounding region is covered with equally interesting insects (5.2). A car number plate is not automatically remarkable because of being unique among millions. A set of four bridge hands does not become remarkable through the sheer fact that you would have to deal cards for many lifetimes before producing exactly such hands again, and your own existence is not rendered remarkable by how your parents' genes might have combined in billions of ways which did not yield *you*. But how then are we to make sense of the idea that Life 'is something special'?

5.20 Finding matters 'special' – specially in need of explanation – is not mere poetry. It is behind all science. Suppose that on throwing a die ten times you get ten 6s. Someone might comment that since this sequence was 'no more rare than any other' among the possible sequences of ten throws, the matter was not special in the least. (Scriven again: 'But if the world exists at all, it has to have *some properties*. What happened is just one of the possibilities. If we decide to toss a die ten times, it is then guaranteed that a particular one of the 6^{10} possible combinations of ten throws is going to occur. Each of them is equally likely. And each of them, if we study it closely, has interesting properties.') But how would you in fact react to the 6s, and how would any scientist react if the 6s continued for another hundred throws? Surely you would treat 6, 6, 6, 6, 6, 6, 6, 6, 6, 6 . . . as 'standing out' against the background of such patterns as 3, 6, 5, 2, 3, 4, 4, 1, 2, 5 . . . .

Thus, despite how 6, 6, 6, 6, 6, 6, 6, 6, 6, 6 might be the start of infinitely many different sequences, every one of them obeying some mathematical formula or other, you would tend to expect the sequence to continue as a simple sequence of 6s. Further, you would look for something explaining why it had continued in that way up to date. Simplicity suggests the constant operation of some one factor or small group of factors. Perhaps the face opposite to the 6-face is heavily weighted.

5.21 If unwilling to see sequences of various kinds as in special need of explanation, and explanations of various kinds as more to be favoured than others, we could learn nothing. There is an infinity of possible patterns which our sensations could be viewed as bearing – yet we in fact come to view them not as a blooming, buzzing confusion but as elements of a sort which would be generated inside a cosmic pattern obedient to fairly straightforward laws. Suppose, however, that after opening our eyes upon the world we set our fancies a-rambling, encouraging them to bring forward an endless variety of reports about what Causation's laws might be. Impressed at how those reports all had (equal) logical possibilities of being right, suppose that like the Philo of part II of Hume's *Dialogues* we saw no reason for preferring any one of them. We then very obviously could not do what this same Philo so inconsistently deems possible, namely, rely on experience to point out the true causes of phenomena. The infinity of possible patterns into which even a lifetime of phenomena might fall would be like the infinity of those which might begin with 6, 6, 6, 6, 6, 6, 6, 6, 6, 6, or with a billion 6s. It would be an infinity which for ever overwhelmed us.

Philosophers are at last coming to appreciate this 'Kantian' point – which is however to be found in Hume too. It has become less popular to urge that science is an affair simply of (a) 'seeing what goes on regularly and therefore needs no explanation', (b) identifying various matters as 'standing out in the only way possible', namely, through their apparent failure to blend into the general background of regularities, and then (c) explaining those matters 'in the only way possible' by finding laws which allow them to be, after all, true parts of that background. For we are today beginning to recognize that if unwilling to *see simple sequences as themselves standing out against a background of complex possibilities* we should never get as far as seeing any sequence *as regular* in any non-trivial way: any way, that is, which goes beyond the bare fact of conforming to some mathematical formula or other. (Every logically possible sequence does *that*, as was recognized in the seventeenth century.) We should be like the man who throws thirty or three hundred 6s and still treats this as the start of a sequence which could continue just as smoothly with 4, 5, 1, 2, 6, 2 as with anything else. Rather than perceiving the world as made up of straight lines, so to speak, we should perceive just the beginnings of what might very well be squiggles. (Instead of classifying grass as green, shouldn't we be equally ready to look on it as green-up-to-this-instant-but-destined-to-be-blue-ever-after? No doubt – if, that is, we could get as far as experiencing it *as grass*.)

5.22 Might we now try saying that Life 'stands out among possibilities' through being *a strange mixture of the simple and the complicated*? It has tremendous intricacy, an ordered complexity very different from mere complex messiness.

Alternatively, might we reflect that only conscious life can have any *intrinsic value*? Might this be enough to make a universe stand out against a background of universes from which such life was absent?

Or finally, might we see conscious life as specially associated with *explicability* – perhaps for reasons associated with its intrinsic value or perhaps because universes including such life are the only ones which could be observed?

Life's Intricacy

5.23 When a die falls 6 twenty times in a row, this uniformity is striking. When a straight black line runs across white paper we actually see the vastly many 'messy possibilities' so studiously avoided by the line, the white points which might have been black in the surrounding area; we at once conclude that the straightness did not come about by chance. Still more impressive, though, are cases where elements of many kinds – red points, blue points, green – fall into some fairly straightforward arrangement: for instance, the red and the blue forming concentric circles, the green a spiral linking the circles. We are impressed by what Leibniz called elegant richness generated by simple laws. Now, living beings surely provide the supreme examples of such richness.

On a definition useful at times, a gas evenly distributed through its container is in a 'simple' state. On another, this state is the reverse of simple. It is a hideously complex mess, a disorder so complete that we can call it 'random'. But the complexity-yet-simplicity of a living organism is unlike that of a gas. Life's complexity is not in the least disorderly. Nor is it quite enough to say that this is because it has a simple main theme in that it is all essentially directed towards success in the struggle for survival. For what is important for our purposes is that such success can be had only through very precise co-ordination between millions of very diverse subsystems. It is altogether different from the 'success' of a boulder whose bouncings were all 'directed towards' its arrival in the valley. In a living system vastly many and enormously varied elements are arranged in accordance with comparatively simple laws (the laws of physics, ultimately) to form a structure which is, at least in higher organisms, *markedly different* from non-living matter in how its parts co-operate.

5.24 Attempts have often been made to define this difference strictly and to quantify it. Although lacking a completely clear definition of entropy (physical disorder, patterning in accordance with Chance) we can say firmly that living things have remarkably low entropy obtained at the cost of much increased entropy elsewhere. We can point also to the 'improbable' way in which almost all the amino acids in Earth's organisms are 'left-handed'; to the 'improbable' DNA molecule, a million times longer than it is wide; to estimates that the information encoded in a single human chromosome is equivalent to several thousand volumes of small print, where 'information' may itself be best defined in terms of degree of deviation from chance ordering; and so on. Yet long before entering into all this it should be plain that plants and animals are markedly superior to stones in *ordered complexity*, *intricacy*, on any reasonable definition thereof. An ape can seem to be in this respect far superior to the entire sun, whose structure involves much mere repetition and is far better understood. Large changes in the positions of its individual atoms would leave the sun operating as before. Move around an ape's atoms, on the other hand . . . .

We must not just jot down in our notebooks that living things look and act somewhat otherwise than atomic particles, bubbles, and clouds. Whether or not medieval churchmen could do so, atheists must surely not say (with Arrhenius) that self-reproducing living things have always existed in the universe just as light rays have, and that even the problem of how intelligent beings first came to exist may be only a pseudo-problem. Life cries out to be explained instead of merely being put on a new page of one's stamp album.

5.25 However, Darwin's explanations showed that despite their 'improbability' very complex living structures were to be expected, probable, as the outcome of selection processes operating over billions of years. We therefore cannot move in any direct fashion from 'Living structures are in some sense very improbable' to 'A universe containing them is very improbable and so stands in special need of explanation.'

Mightn't we still run the following argument, though?

(1) A universe containing living organisms – and above all one of intelligent life, language, cultures, moon rockets, and so on – is on a much higher level of intricacy than any universe which just has such structures as stars, planets, mountains.

(2) The intricacy is something which scientists in general and biologists in particular must view as 'special' if they are to do much science.

(3) Darwinian theory is not by itself enough to explain why our universe has this intricacy, as is shown by the evidence of fine tuning. Very tiny changes in force strengths, particle masses, and so on would have made Darwinian evolution impossible.

(4) Hence the need to explain intricacy forces us to accept God or multiple universes.

5.26 In defence of this argument we could insist that whether living beings exist only in the solar system, or are instead widespread in Space and Time, is largely irrelevant. Fairly common though life forms may be in this actual universe, the big point is that they would seem to be rare in the local area of possible universes. (We mustn't say that if animalcules exist in every drop of water then that is evidence *against* Divine Design or Many Worlds!) Now, we may find it hard to swallow the idea that a one and only actually existing universe, ours, just chances to be vastly more intricate than the universes which would have been generated by slight changes in its basic properties. It is tempting to say: one might just as well take seriously the idea that a one and only draw from an urn of a million white balls and a single black just happens to yield the black. And from that it can be tempting to conclude: God, or a multiplicity of universes, must be real.

Such reasoning once seemed to me very powerful. Now, however, I am not at all sure of this. The difficulty is that it might seem guilty of 'double counting' the fact that Life's intricacy cries out for explanation. Yes, we could agree, the presence of this intricacy is 'special', like the hitting of a bull's-eye; it must not be left unexplained; but doesn't Darwinian theory give us the explanation we require? It may well be that Darwinian evolution could not have got moving had the universe's properties been marginally different; yet is the life-permitting mixture of properties *itself a further hitting of a bull's-eye*, a matter specially requiring explanation? Perhaps it is; but, it could be thought, this wouldn't be simply because of the point that Life's intricacy mustn't be left unexplained. For when we have reached the level of the universe's basic properties, to bring this point in once again could be to 'double count' the fact that the intricacy needs explaining.

The case could look rather unlike one in which a message such as MADE BY GOD appears in every rock, this then being shown to result from basic physics. *There* we should of course push our questions one stage further, asking why the physics was as it was. But it is less clear that we have a right to keep asking, 'Just why is the physics of our universe a physics which yields all this intricacy?'

5.27 Let us sum this up. Perhaps there is a reason why getting a life-permitting set of properties is like hitting a bull's-eye; but, one might think, any such reason would not lie in the bare fact that life of an advanced kind is an extraordinarily intricate affair, an affair crying out for explanation. The point that Life's intricacy cries out for explanation has been sufficiently taken into account, one might think, when Darwinian explanations are agreed to be needed. And if so, then people finding it remarkable that our universe is life-permitting *cannot* simply point to Life's intricacy in justification of their attitude. If they are to make the difference between Life and non-Life seem more cosmologically or theologically exciting than the difference between hitting a fly and hitting a wasp, bee, beetle, moth, or butterfly, then they must turn elsewhere.

Since the charge of 'double counting' does often seem to me forceful it is good to be able to report that there are other places to turn.

Life's Value

5.28 It might be held that a main way in which Life 'stands out' is in its having value, positive or negative. Universes devoid of consciousness could be neither good nor bad.

Here we might try arguing that since value is the basis of all *oughts* it follows that if anything ought to be treated as standing out then value should be. In his *Philosophers and Religious Truth* (1964), N. Smart writes: 'If there are no actual values without consciousness, and if the idea of significance includes that of importance, which is itself a value concept, then assuredly there must be a special significance in the birth of consciousness.' But I am unclear whether this point retains much strength when put to the use to which Smart puts it, namely, showing why *the universe's containing intelligent life* is in more need of a 'metaphysical explanation' than *so-and-so's having a wart on his nose* (which is Smart's example of an affair meriting a 'So what?'). Agreed, universes which contain living consciousness can stand out through being ethically significant, yet I doubt the success of Smart's argument for treating this as grounds for believing something metaphysically dramatic. A justifiable reaction might be, 'What good luck that this universe is one in which events can have ethical significance!' rather than, say, 'We ought to believe in universes sufficiently numerous to make it quite likely that such luck would be had somewhere.'

True enough, it isn't arbitrary to treat ethical significance as important. The case is unlike that of viewing our universe as 'markedly different' from other possible ones simply because it contains particles with masses of 493.67 MeV. But I am only really at ease when a marked difference which supposedly cries out for explanation *is a difference in explicability*. The next sections will develop this theme.

Life's Observability

5.29 Consider once more the case of bridge hands. Any hand of thirteen cards is in an important sense exactly as unlikely as any other, but our suspicions are aroused when we watch Smith winning a million dollars with the hand of thirteen spades which Smith has dealt to Smith. We do not just say 'Lucky Smith!', disregarding the explanation that stares at us. It is the fact that it is staring at us which makes the thirteen spades 'markedly different' from other possible hands.

Again, any car number plate will be in some sense 'improbable'. There are millions of number plates and only one CHT 4271, for instance; it was therefore unlikely that you would get that number plate on your birthday car; yet your getting of it has no special interest. But what if Bob, born on the eighth day of August (the eighth month), finds BOB 8893 on his birthday car in 1993? He would be obtuse if he commented, 'Nothing remarkable in that!'.

The moral to be drawn from such cases was drawn in section 1.11. *A chief reason for thinking that something stands in special need of explanation is that we actually glimpse some tidy way in which it might be explained.*

This is just one aspect of the point – fundamental to all science and formalized in Bayes's rule of the calculus of probabilities – that observations improve your reasons for accepting some hypothesis when its truth would have made those observations more likely. Yes, there is a slim chance that an honestly dealt bridge hand will consist of thirteen spades. But the chance that thirteen spades will come about by cheating is presumably a lot higher. And the same sort of thing can be said in the case of Bob's birthday car or in that of the collapsing arch or the silk merchant's thumb (1.10). In all such cases you prefer the hypothesis that more than Chance was involved. Why? Well, because this hypothesis gives so dramatic a boost to the probability that you would be seeing what you do. (That is to say, it gives this boost even if its own probability is rather low. It is no doubt true that few card sharpers would be so bold as to deal themselves hands of thirteen spades – but even bearing this in mind, thirteen spades can be a very suspicious hand.)

There is a feedback loop, a 'bootstrapping', connecting a tidy explanation with the need for a thing to be explained. After all, we were not born into the world with very much idea of what it is that needs explaining. Seeing the milk bottles falling off the wall, the philosophical baby might well treat it as an ultimate, inexplicable law that milk bottles do fall at intervals. It is the sight of a stick approaching each bottle in turn, just before it falls, which simultaneously suggests both *an explanation* and *the need for one*.

5.30 Dozing off during a train trip, a traveller observes emerald green everywhere when he wakes; does this need to be explained? Eyedrops which distort colour vision can be bought in joke shops and his travelling companion loves jokes. Besides giving an explanation, this confirms that there really is something here which needs one. Maybe some alternative explanation is correct. Maybe the military have test-sprayed Agent Emerald in vast amounts. But what simply won't do is to comment that there really is nothing calling for explanation – 'That emerald green is just how everything happens to be around here.'

Now consider the 'Anthropic Principle' point that if our universe had been hostile to Life then nobody would be observing it (1.26; 4.9). Observers could see only an extremely limited portion of the 'spectrum' of an ensemble of possible Worlds in which force strengths and particle masses differed from World to World. *Taken by itself* this cannot do much towards answering why a World which is life-containing is actually being observed; for remember the Firing Squad Story (1.17). But when the Worlds of the ensemble are believed to have actual existence then we do have a tidy answer, and this can sufficiently confirm that an answer is required. The answer is one into which *observability* enters in a crucial way.

5.31 We must tread carefully here because, I repeat, the availability of a tidy explanation does not mean that other explanations are wrong. The tidiness of an explanation can confirm only that some explanation or other is needed. Competing explanations may be even more tidy. So we might on reflection prefer to believe that our universe, and any others which actually exist, had to be life-containing since God wanted to produce living beings. I am saying only that it would be wrong to reject *all* explanations in this area, deciding that there was nothing to be explained. For this would be to imitate the man who fancies that his coloured spectacles and all objects in front of them simply chance to have the same colour; or that the one and only fish in the lake simply chanced to be of a length which his fishing apparatus could present to his delighted eyes, when this apparatus would reject any fish shorter than 23.25759 inches or longer than 23.25761.

Imagine that an experiment is proposed for detecting neutrinos if they have mass. It uses a crystal which could glow when hit by neutrinos, but only if their masses were almost exactly 6.75232 eV. The experimenters speculate that neutrinos may come in a continuous range of masses so that at least some will cause glowing. Glowing is observed. 'Seems to show the range is continuous', they comment. Now, would any philosopher protest that the only neutrino mass which the experiment could detect might very well simply chance to be the only neutrino mass that there was? Let's hope not! But notice that just as the theist could have special reasons for thinking that a divine being would create a universe of the only kind that could be observed (i.e. otherwise than by himself or by immaterial angels), a universe in which evolution could give rise to very complex living things, so also might our experimenters have special information – for instance, that neutrinos trapped inside the crystal could be important to the glowing – which suggested that if all neutrinos had the same mass then this could well be exactly the mass to which the crystal would respond. Indeed, they could suspect this while still lacking any special information on the subject. What would be foolish, however, would be to suggest that it was through chance alone that the crystal was tuned to the one and only mass which neutrinos ever had.

5.32 It has been emphasized that an ensemble of many *actual* Worlds is needed in order to make World Ensemble explanations work (1.17–.18; 5.7–.8; 5.30). It is not enough just to point out that *possible Worlds* much different from ours would be unobservable. That by itself could not remove our puzzlement as to why our World is so accurately tuned to Life's requirements. But the reverse of this coin, remember, is that a World Ensemble does not by itself supply a wondrous defence against all puzzlement. Unless harnessed to an observational selection effect it is not of much use for explaining anything (1.18–.19). A story of Ivan and the tzar can illustrate this. Ivan has sent his arrow two hundred yards to the very centre of the target, a feat demanded of this peasant, who had never before handled a bow, by a mad tzar promising to reward success with a ton of gold and failure by the deaths of him and all his village (I owe this interesting scene to Gerald Massey). Well, Ivan could perhaps thank the village priest for some well-phrased prayers, but what just won't serve is for him to say that there must have existed billions of parallel universes in which billions of mad tzars were demanding the same feat of billions of Ivans so that there was a fair chance that one or two arrows would succeed. It won't serve because it simply throws the difficulty back at our Ivan in a new form. Previously it had been the very odd occurrence of a prayed-for event *of a sort extremely rare among the possibilities*. And now, against the background of the new belief in billions of tzars, arrows, and Ivans, it merely becomes the equally great oddity that a prayed-for event *of a sort extremely rare among the actualities* has occurred *in the universe of this particular Ivan*. As he drew his bow our Ivan's need to ask for a priestly word in the divine ear was not in the slightest reduced by the billions of arrows which were about to fly along billions of different paths, for alas, only one of those arrows was in *his* universe.

The case of the World Ensemble explanation for Life is radically different. The Worlds/universes in which living beings are impossible *cannot be observed*. This point is absolutely crucial. If fish come in all lengths and in huge numbers then I have no excuse for puzzlement or praising God when I find that my apparatus, which can catch only fish of lengths falling inside very narrow limits, delights my eyes with one fitting its fussy requirements. Our Ivan, in contrast, is not in a tale featuring any similar limits to what can be detected. For the tale is not one in which this Ivan's *ever having become a conscious being* was magically tied to whether he was going to pass the tzar's severe test. Hence his case is in no relevant way analogous to ours when we contemplate the fact that our universe is one in which living things could evolve, a universe detectable by conscious beings. He is in no way helped by imagining billions of other Ivans, almost all of them watching executioners approaching ominously. Counting all the unfortunate Ivans and reflecting that they too are observers should only make him amazed that he does not find himself in the same sad situation.

5.33 A concession might however need to be made to those who have doubts about the World Ensemble hypothesis even when Observational Selection is added to it. A man's surprise at how his parents' genes yielded *just him* can be seen to be unwarranted – or at best to be *mere idle surprise* as distinct from surprise of the sort which motivates reasonable quests for explanation – when you appreciate that if those genes had combined differently then someone else would be there instead; someone who had, so to speak, started with very much the same probability of being born; someone whose birth would have provided him (or her) with precisely the same dubious excuse for being surprised. Precisely the same, that is to say, if we make the plausible assumption that no Controlling Powers were specially interested in whether our man – just he and no other – came into being. Now, it looks tempting to suppose that surprise at how *just our* universe was one of the life-containing ones would be equivalently idle. It looks tempting to comment: 'If *this* universe hadn't been suitable, others in the vast ensemble could still be serving as habitats for persons gasping in astonishment at how *their* universes were life-generating ones, persons paying insufficient attention to the truths (a) that life-generating conditions were pretty well bound to occur somewhere, and (b) that all intelligent beings evolving in any such somewhere would observe themselves to be in (Wow!) life-generating conditions.' However, perhaps this would be a case of forgetting that the difference between life-generating and non-life-generating conditions might indeed be 'of special interest to Controlling Powers'. After all, that's what theists typically believe.

In effect, a Multiple Worlds plus observational selection effect explanation for various fortunate facts might perhaps remain relatively unattractive even when one took seriously the idea of many Worlds and of wide variations in their properties. For a theistic explanation could give to each World *a far greater chance* of being life-generating.

Compare how the man who has survived the shots of a firing squad might attribute this to the squad's friendliness although convinced that so many squads were at work that even in the absence of all friendliness a few lucky individuals would still have survived through every bullet's just chancing to miss. He might argue that in each individual case of survival it was always much more likely that friendliness was responsible.

My suspicion is that this is no particularly good reason for favouring theistic explanations. (More about that later, in 6.35.) Still, maybe we should bear it in mind when we look at such explanations.

Life's Being What God Would Have Wanted

5.34 It was suggested earlier (5.28) that the sheer fact of intelligent life's having value might not be enough to make it 'stand out' as needing explanation. What we should really be looking for is factors which make things stand out *through themselves suggesting explanations*. There is a feedback loop between the need to explain a thing and the availability of some tidy explanation for that thing. However, a theist could protest that intelligent life's value could indeed enter into an explanation that was tidy. God would have had an understandable preference for universes that contained intelligent beings.

5.35 Much of Chapters 7 and 8 will be given to discussing this point. One aspect of it should be mentioned at once, though. The theist has a fairly strong obligation to show why God should be considered a tidy explanation of anything.

R. Swinburne is one contemporary philosopher who recognizes this obligation. He argues that an all-powerful, all-knowing God would be a supremely simple being. Also that a thing's *being willed* can itself be enough to explain it in a particularly tidy fashion, in the cases of human actions as well as in those of divine ones.

As indicated earlier (1.3; 1.32; 5.4), my account of God is different. If God is in fact a person then, I take it, this person exists because of the ethical requirement that he should exist.

And if his sheer will is causally or creatively effective, as Swinburne thinks, then that is because it is ethically required that it be effective.[4] Sitting in our armchairs and contemplating the Concept of Ethical Needs or Requirements, we get, I claim, absolutely no guidance about whether any such needs, alias requirements, are ever responsible for the actual existence of anything. It is not logical nonsense to believe that an ethical requirement accounts for the existence of a divine person. Again, there is no logical nonsense in understanding the name 'God' in the Neoplatonic way which I prefer: that is, as standing for the principle that the ethical need for a good universe or universes *is itself creatively responsible* for that universe or those universes.

5.36 Whether Neoplatonism could tidily explain the universe which we see is of course very controversial. Still, it would not be enough to protest that in this universe many ethical needs remain unsatisfied. Neoplatonists *are not* committed to the presumably absurd view that *absolutely all* ethical needs are creatively effective. The Problem of Evil – the problem of how belief in God can be reconciled with the world's disasters – is well known in theological circles. In responding to it, theists commonly claim that it was not even possible for all ethical needs to be satisfied simultaneously.

5.37 Discussing the world's goodness or badness, a major difficulty is that views about this often turn on What the World is Really Like; and views about *that* are often inextricably entangled with views about why there is any world at all. A world-model which looks only natural *when you think that the world exists reasonlessly* can seem altogether implausible when you instead attribute its existence to God – and vice versa. Which leads, unfortunately, into complexities too great for this book.[5]

Chapter Six

Anthropic Explanations

Fine tuning of our universe's properties to meet Life's needs might be made unmysterious by God – or else by a multiplicity of universes and an observational selection effect. This chapter examines B.Carter's Anthropic Principle that only life-containing cosmic situations can be observed.

The Principle risks being misunderstood in many ways. It has Strong and Weak versions, yet despite common claims they are not very importantly different: whether the Strong or the Weak applies to some cosmic situation can depend on how huge a situation has to be before you care to call it 'cosmic' (or 'a separate universe'). Both versions state logically necessary truths, yet they can enter into explanations: they point to possible observational selection effects, very ordinary components of science. 'Anthropic' explanations do not make the world a causal consequence of our existence. They are not specially concerned with mankind. They do not say that intelligent life was bound to come into existence in this universe. They need not say even that its coming to exist somewhere was highly likely, or that its coming to exist here was more likely because of a multiplicity of universes elsewhere. Again, they need not say that everything was fine tuned, or that all possible Worlds exist, or that intelligent life is rare in the realm of all possible Worlds, or that to exist is to be perceived, or that a thing's being a prerequisite of observations can by itself explain it. Further, it is quite wrong to maintain that they cannot encourage predictions.

Strong, Weak, and Superweak Anthropic Principles

6.1 Chapter 5's main theme was that we should hesitate to classify something as a chance matter when a tidy explanation thrusts itself upon us. Suppose every rock bore the letters MADE BY GOD. These should be viewed as forming a message rather than as what Nature's workings had just happened to produce. And similarly when we find that our universe's basic properties are fine tuned to Life's needs. It could now be very odd to believe that ours was a one and only actually existing universe, a universe which simply chanced to be life-containing – the very thing which God would have wanted, and just what would be needed *to make it observable*. For note that in the case of the fine tuning, unlike that of any messages in the rocks, an observational selection effect could help make matters unmysterious. Many Worlds could have been botched and bungled before symmetry-breaking phase transitions (1.7; 2.52; 4.20–.23) or other such factors struck out a system in which living beings could evolve. Only such a system could be observed by living beings. This is the basis of 'anthropic' explanations.

6.2 The Anthropic Principle could be stated as follows: *Any intelligent living beings that there are can find themselves only where intelligent life is possible.*

Clearly, this is just a logically necessary truth, on a par with the fact that any bachelors can find only that they are wifeless. Its implications could none the less be important. To see why, consider B. Carter's words introducing and baptizing the Principle: 'the *anthropic principle* to the effect that what we can expect to observe must be restricted by the conditions necessary for our presence as observers'.[1]

6.3 In Carter's formulation of it, the Principle has 'Weak' and 'Strong' forms. The Weak is 'that our location in the universe is *necessarily* privileged to the extent of being compatible with our existence as observers'; the Strong, that our universe 'must be such as to admit the creation of observers within it at some stage'.[2]

Care is needed in interpreting this.

(i) When the Weak Principle speaks of our being appropriately 'located', temporal as well as spatial location is in question. Following R. H. Dicke,[3] Carter points out that our universe must now be *old enough* for heavy elements – needed to build our bodies – to have been formed inside stars and then scattered by stellar explosions.

(ii) In Carter's 'our existence as observers' it is our *observership* which is important, not our being precisely *us*. While nearby galaxies may well contain many trillion little green men, they will be 'men' thanks to their intelligence and not to their having human form. For Carter's purposes brainy dinosaurs would be Big Green Men. 'Anthropic' considerations could not have much interest – they couldn't, for instance, give grounds for believing in a multiplicity of universes – if they concerned just our lovable warm-blooded humanhood. The non-appearance of the new plant which (so some have argued) made the dinosaurs die out from constipation might well have meant that no recognizably human-like bodies would ever have evolved anywhere.

All the same, anthropic considerations draw much of their interest from the idea that observers in general would be like us to the extent, for example, of having bodies unable to populate such exotic habitats as the sun's centre. (Or at least ones unable to have evolved there, while they might perhaps travel to there unharmed inside well-refrigerated spaceships.)

(iii) When Carter's Strong Principle says that our universe 'must be such as to admit the creation of observers' it is not meant that this universe's basic character *was forced to be such* that observership *was inevitable* in it. Instead it is being said that *its absence* cannot have been inevitable, else we shouldn't be observing it. The cosmic countryside is not one big minefield. It thus 'admits', i.e. is compatible with, renders possible, the existence of us wide-eyed rabbits. It may still fail to render rabbits necessary. Obviously. But cosmological and philosophical writings teem with misunderstandings of this obvious point. Carter himself adds to the confusion when he speaks of 'invocation of an extended (and hence rather questionable) "strong" anthropic principle'. What he ought to be saying is that *invoking the Principle* in one's explanations is questionable since it assumes (boldly, strongly) that some actually existing universes will never be observer-permitting, so that an observational selection effect underlies our seeing of one in which observers are permitted. *In themselves* both forms of the Principle are not in the least questionable, for of course the universe in which we observers exist now must be compatible with observership both *here and now* (Weak Principle) and *at some stage* (Strong Principle).

(iv) In this context, words like 'universe' or 'World' are not intended in senses making a contradiction out of any claim that there actually exist many Worlds, universes, among which the observational selection effect operates. Carter makes this clear enough when he states, first, that the Strong Principle could become the basis of an explanation if one thought 'in terms of a "world ensemble"' or 'ensemble of universes' in which initial conditions and fundamental constants varied from universe to universe, observers being possible only in 'an exceptional *cognizable* subset' of universes; and second, that a suitable background to such thinking would be Everett's Many-Worlds quantum theory (4.41 ff.) according to which a capital-U Universe continually divides into more and more branches of which all 'are equally "real"'.[4]

6.4 Let us now look at points like those in more detail.

Carter's Strong Principle tells us, remember, that our World or small-u universe is one in which observers can exist. Now, this might risk being dismissed as useless scientifically. We always have known – it might be yawned – that observership's prerequisites have been met. But yawns are mistakes here. Carter claims, for instance, that the Strong Principle can help explain a Large Number Coincidence used by A. S. Eddington to construct an entire physics in a manner later refined by P. A. M. Dirac: the Coincidence, namely, that the (large!) number of particles in the visible universe is roughly the inverse square of the gravitational coupling constant. Were gravity either marginally stronger or marginally weaker then stars like our sun could not exist and it is plausible that our universe would then be lifeless (2.19). So, given a belief in an ensemble of Worlds/universes, we can replace theories like those of Eddington and Dirac by an observational selection effect.

Admittedly, any such effect would be rather a strange one; we could not visit the other Worlds/universes in order to find out by personal experience that no living beings could experience them. But surely its strangeness would be no barrier to its importance. Surely it could be important to notice the truth (if it was one) that observers could never find themselves in universes which were much like ours but in which gravity was stronger or weaker. Measuring gravity's actual strength, a physicist unaware of this truth could be far more inclined to think that precisely this strength was dictated by basic physics in all physically possible universes. Compare how a fisherman unaware of the large hole in his net could well think that the first, exceptionally large fish that he netted had a size typical of its lake.

6.5 The Weak Principle too could be scientifically important. Carter comments that Dicke in effect used this Principle to show that a second Large Number Coincidence might suffer the same fate as the first. Why does the universe's present age stand to gravity's strength in a relationship into which large numbers enter? Dirac had suggested that this relationship held at all times, necessarily; therefore gravity had to be weakening very slowly over the years. Dicke, in contrast, saw Observational Selection here. Observers could exist only at times late enough for heavy elements to have been produced inside stars and early enough for stars not to have lost their life-giving heat and light. Calculations showed that at these times gravity's strength had to be very much as actually observed.

Compare the case of two competing explanations for why it looks as if distant stars are very hot: the first, that they really are all of them very hot; and the second, that only the hottest burn brightly enough to be seen by us.

6.6 Other Weak Principle explanations have been suggested by G. F. R. Ellis.[5] Observations, he notes, 'cannot distinguish a time variation of source properties in a spatially homogeneous universe from a change in source properties with spatial distance in a spatially inhomogeneous universe'. (Think of how a man on an island might be unable to decide whether distant islands only looked smaller, or were both more distant *and* smaller.) Hence we might exist at, say, one of the poles of a spindle-shaped cosmos – which would give us a very heretical explanation of why the cosmic background radiation comes at us evenly from all sides. Our being *just there* could be unpuzzling if this location alone were cool enough for observers. Yet suppose our surroundings were instead homogeneous out to vast distances. They might still form only an untypically orderly fragment of a 'completely chaotic' universe which was 'infinite (or very large)'. Observers could see such a universe only from the 'very special places and times' which were unchaotic enough to allow them to exist (cf. 4.13).

Why, then, are people so confident that they inhabit typical surroundings? Ellis answers: because of a blind trust in Principles of Mediocrity (sometimes called Copernican or Cosmological Principles) which assert that our dwelling place is nowhere special. A praiseworthy conviction 'that the creation of the universe was not centered on our presence' often leads us to the falsehood 'that we could equally well live at all places and all times'.

6.7 Consider, again, L. S. Marochnik's point that we are almost at that exact distance from the galactic centre at which a density wave orbits at the same speed as the stars. Marochnik comments that the coincidence of our being in such a very special location would have given our neighbourhood a very unusual history. It would have undergone prolonged compression such as might well be essential to the formation of planets – in which case, very plausibly, this distance from the galactic centre would be the only one at which observers could evolve.[6] The fact that such reasoning would so tidily explain the coincidence could help persuade us that it wasn't 'a mere coincidence'. (Cf. 5.29: feedback loop or bootstrapping connecting the presence of a tidy explanation with the need for a thing to be explained.)

6.8 Another variant of the Anthropic Principle I am tempted to call 'the Superweak'. What a Principle of Mediocrity would tell us would be that any planet vaguely similar to Earth would see the same slow evolution of a variety of life forms. People like M. H. Hart think, in contrast, that Life's emergence on Earth involved extremely improbable comings-together of complex molecules. Hart estimates that even on an ideally habitable planet the chance that living things would develop would probably be lower than 1 in $10^{3,000}$. This would explain why we see no sign of other intelligent beings in our galaxy, in which suitable planets number perhaps only ten million (a mere 10^7). Indeed, even the 10^{11} galaxies inside our horizon would almost certainly all be uninhabited. But mayn't this be very implausible, since wouldn't it have made it extremely unlikely that there would be *so much as one* inhabited planet in the universe? Not so, says Hart, because the universe could well be infinitely large. Intelligent observers would in that case be bound to evolve in countless places (4.12; 4.74). On each of perhaps infinitely many habitable planets Nature 'patiently tosses her tetrahedral dice for ten billion years, trying to line up 600 nucleotides in the proper sequence to make genesis DNA'. She fails almost everywhere – but the results of her efforts can be observed only where she has succeeded.[7]

While Hart's views about 'genesis DNA' could very easily be wrong, the ('Superweak') Principle which he is invoking is of obvious importance. *If intelligent life's emergence, NO MATTER HOW HOSPITABLE THE ENVIRONMENT, always involves very improbable happenings, then any intelligent living beings that there are evolved where such improbable happenings happened.* In a large enough universe it could be very likely that intelligent beings existed somewhere even if their existence could come about only in locations where very unlikely occurrences had occurred; and obviously it would be those locations which they observed when they crawled from the primeval slime. So, it seems, it could be scientifically unjustifiable to reject a theory simply because it said that Earth had once been a planet on which it was almost certain that intelligent life would never evolve.

Anthropic Principle Tautologies

6.9 In the forms I prefer to give to them, all varieties of Anthropic Principle – Strong, Weak, and Superweak – describe logically necessary links between observations and observation-permitting conditions. They are all of them tautologies, like statements about the marriedness of husbands. But tautologies can be important. Implicitly or explicitly they are always hypothetical, 'IFy–THENy'. (Bachelors are wifeless: i.e. If there are any bachelors then they are wifeless. Husbands are married: If a husband, then married.) Although *by themselves* they explain nothing, tautologies can provide frameworks which *enter into* explanations where IF-clauses are satisfied; and just as a partial cause can be called 'a cause', so something entering into an explanation may be called 'an explanation' or 'explanatory'. When, for instance, can it be explanatory that IF you have three groups of five objects THEN you have fifteen? Perhaps when, after putting three groups of five apples into a box, you ask why it contains more than fourteen apples.

6.10 The Strong Principle can be a tautology, a logically necessary truth, which points importantly towards a logically possible observational selection effect: a selection effect which operates IF there exists a capital-U Universe split into small-u universes with varied properties AND IF not all those universes are observable. Observable, that is to say, in view of the sorts of being that observers could in practice be. 'Cogito ergo mundus talis est', Carter writes. Since I am here to think things, my World has characteristics permitting the existence of intelligent beings. It is to that extent 'necessarily privileged'.

Admittedly, the extent of the privilege might be zero if there existed angels, pure observing minds without bodies, or if there were a World Ensemble in which every single World was hospitable even to non-angels. But this just admits that those IF clauses might perhaps not be satisfied. Now, their not being satisfied in any World containing angels would seem to have precious little scientific interest. Moreover they could be satisfied if even just one feature needed even just a little tuning to make Life and Observership possible, because it might well then be true that of a group of universes varying in this feature *not all* would be observable by living beings.

If there did exist very many universes widely varied in their features then it could be very strange if absolutely all of them – including universes recollapsing within a microsecond, universes in which temperatures remained above a million degrees until matter had become too dilute to condense into galaxies, universes consisting solely of light, universes of black holes only, and so forth – proved to be life-permitting. And it can well seem that extremely tiny changes to our universe would have led it to recollapse within a microsecond or to suffer some other fate quite as fatal to Life's prospects.

6.11 Similar remarks apply to the Weak Principle. It is no actual logical contradiction to imagine that absolutely all temporal and spatial locations are equally hospitable so that none is 'privileged'; but it would be fantastic to imagine it. The early instants of the Big Bang were surely inhospitable; so, presumably, is an exploding star; etc. And while it is nice to speculate that observers could migrate to the sun's centre in well-refrigerated spaceships, this cannot destroy the Weak Principle's importance. (We could if necessary rephrase it so that it spoke only of the temporal and spatial locations at which races of observers had first evolved. Or, in the cases of seeing-eye robots of human-like intelligence, those at which their designers had evolved.)

6.12 Many people, however, are disturbed by how tautologies can in themselves 'tell you nothing' (i.e. nothing beyond facts about the logically possible). Let these people turn if they wish to something with more content. Let them replace *IF P THEN Q* by *P, THEREFORE Q* when they state any Anthropic Principle. Instead of speaking of evidence for that Principle's *importance* they can then speak of evidence for the Principle itself.

Thus, frowning on the following tautological statement, a statement no more in need of evidence than the marriedness of husbands,

> *IF there were a gigantic Universe in which basic features varied from huge region to huge region, and in which only some of these huge regions had features compatible with Life, THEN any living observers in that Universe WOULD BE be viewing it from inside a huge region whose features were compatible with Life,*

let such people perform the manoeuvre of replacing it with a 'factual' statement such as this:

> *THERE IS a very large Universe in which basic features vary from huge region to huge region, and in which only some of the regions have features compatible with Life; and Yes, THERE ARE living observers in this Universe; THEREFORE those observers ARE viewing it from inside a huge region whose features are compatible with Life.*

There would be nothing wrong in manoeuvres of this type, apart from their being (a) none too important and (b) not in line with the writings of B. Carter who baptized the Anthropic Principle and thus has some right to decide what it says. And such manoeuvres do at least have the advantage that they get rid of the alleged stumbling-block that any Anthropic Principle, being tautologous, 'can say nothing'. It can be a nuisance to have to keep explaining that the wise need not stumble here.

6.13 An alternative would be to say, again 'factually', something like this:

> *The truth, in itself tautological, that living beings must be in life-permitting universes, IS INTERESTING because our universe's*

life-permitting nature DOES SEEM TO DEPEND ON FINE TUNING.

Quite a useful definition of a 'factual' Anthropic Principle on much these lines is given by J. C. Polkinghorne:[8]

> *anthropic principle* The collection of scientific insights which indicates that a universe capable of evolving systems as complicated as men must have a delicate balance in the structure of its fundamental forces and (perhaps) special initial conditions.

My main quarrel with Polkinghorne's definition is that his 'a universe' means 'absolutely any universe', so that in his hands the Anthropic Principle makes an unnecessarily bold claim. It could be better to present it as claiming only something about universes 'in the local area of possibilities', the ones produced by imagined small changes in our universe. Remember the tale of the Fly on the Wall (1.24).

In contrast, the fact that Polkinghorne's version of the Principle actually makes a claim, instead of just being a potentially interesting tautology such as Carter enunciated, is scarcely something to make a great fuss about. For even Carter thinks of his tautology as an *actually* very interesting tautology: a tautology which can have actual work to do because our universe is in fact fine tuned to Life's needs.

The Often Purely Verbal Difference Between the Strong and the Weak

6.14 Some, while agreeing that the Weak Anthropic Principle has obvious scientific importance, are none the less bitterly hostile to the Strong Principle. This is odd indeed since the two principles shade into one another. The Strong Principle concerns *our universe*; the Weak, *our region or location*; but as Chapter 4 made clear there just is no single correct way of counting universes and thus of distinguishing them from mere regions or locations. And when one speaker's universe is another's large spatio-temporal region, the first's Strong Principle matter can be the second's Weak Principle affair.

6.15 As an illustration, suppose you believe in a capital-U Universe (Absolutely Everything) which is split into many very largely separate systems – perhaps huge regions in which symmetry breakings have happened differently so that force strengths and particle masses are different. *Our being in surroundings suited to Life* could then be treated *either* as a Strong Principle matter, because we could count our huge region as a very largely separate system, a small-u universe, *or else* as food for the Weak Principle, because this region might instead be counted just as 'the right sort of location'.

6.16 Again, imagine an oscillating cosmos in which Big Bangs are always followed by Big Squeezes and then new Bangs. Suppose early cosmic expansion speeds were different in successive oscillatory cycles, only a very narrow range of speeds being life-permitting. It could be quite natural to speak of each new cycle as 'a new universe', *the Strong Principle* then telling us that the cycle in which we existed was a life-permitting universe. But equally, we might speak of each new cycle as 'a new temporal location' – in which case the *Weak* Principle would be telling us that the cycle in which we existed was a life-permitting temporal location. The distinction is a purely verbal one.

Misunderstandings of Anthropic Reasoning

6.17 The ways in which 'anthropic' reasoning can be misunderstood form a long and dreary list.

For a start, numerous critics have seized on the word 'anthropic', crying that what is involved here is sheer anthropocentrism, obsession with *anthropos*, *homo sapiens*, mankind. But Carter intended nothing of the sort by this word. He now kicks himself for ever having used it, naïvely relying on people to read his surrounding sentences. 'Psychocentric Principle' could have been better; or 'Cognizability Principle', to bring out the fact that *being observable by intelligent beings* is what is in question. True, it can be virtuous to show caution when deciding that such-and-such conditions are a prerequisite of all intelligent observership; yet we also want to avoid making our Principle into one which just states the triviality that small changes would have meant that mankind never evolved.

It even seems to me doubtful whether there is much interest in the sheer fact that this or that is a prerequisite of observers *who breathe oxygen* or of observers *with bodies based on chemistry*. Having discovered that we breathe oxygen, it is no surprise that we are on a planet with oxygen in its atmosphere; having found that our bodies are based on chemistry we can conclude that we aren't at the sun's centre or in a universe whose temperatures never fall below ten billion degrees; yet such conclusions are hardly new and exciting. (Seeing the fit produced by Darwinian evolution between an oxygen-producing universe and oxygen-breathing observers, we could be tempted to compare it to that between a fish and a fishing apparatus whose properties were automatically adjusted to allow it to catch more or less any fish which swam by. If such adjustments were possible almost always then, obviously, the catching of a fish with that apparatus would be little reason for excitement.) But if, on the other hand, oxygen or chemistry were prerequisites of all intelligent life in universes recognizably like ours, then anthropic reasoning might use that fact excitingly. It could become a ground for believing in multiple universes.

One needs also to avoid the opposite extreme, the dismissal of everything human as so irrelevant that even intelligence and consciousness are disregarded. The Anthropic Principle must not be replaced by a Carbonic Principle (1.28–.29), Planetary Principle, Galactic Principle, or anything else which has nothing to do with observational selection effects.

Just how brainy must an organism be, to count as 'an observer' or 'an intelligent observer'? There can be no clear-cut answer. Dogs, frogs, maybe even ants might be called observers, and every observer has at least some slight intelligence. But when we ask whether various possible observational selection effects mightn't give scientific weight to the Anthropic Principle in its various versions, what we ought chiefly to have in mind is observers intelligent enough to be scientists.

6.18 Another common objection is that anthropic reasoning 'is back to front'; it makes the universe's properties into a result of the existence of intelligent observers, whereas any child can see that it is instead the properties which led to the observers. Yet such an objection is wildly unfair. What we observe can indeed be 'in a sense . . . a consequence of our existence', as S. W. Hawking said, but this is not like saying that being a wife is a consequence, often, of being a woman: that is to say, a *causal* consequence. Instead it is like saying that being a woman is a *logical* consequence of being a wife. Hawking was trying to account for how our universe was so smooth. He held that immensely accurate tuning of the early expansion speed would do the trick – and he then argued that any universe in which the speed failed to be tuned in the right way would be expanding too fast or too slowly for observers to come into existence.[9] Now, this points towards a possible observational selection effect: one which operates if there actually exist many universes expanding at different speeds. Nothing back to front in that!

Agreed, you do need the actual existence of the other universes in order to get a selection-effect explanation. Otherwise, as the Firing Squad Story illustrates (1.17), you get either nothing or else something back to front. Yet why imagine that users of anthropic reasoning must always be unaware of this? And if they were sometimes unaware of it, wouldn't that show only that their reasoning needed some patching up before it could work?

You certainly mustn't just assume that everybody who says that a universe with us in it *must have* life-permitting properties is *ipso facto* defending the seemingly preposterous idea that *we gave the universe its properties*. It is much more natural to suppose that an *ex-post-facto* or consequential 'must' is meant, as in 'Since the passport photo is labelled WIFE it must be of a woman' or 'The silverware has vanished so a burglar must have called.'

6.19 Next, notice that observational selection effects can operate long before the field to be selected from has grown to include all physically possible situations. They could operate if there existed *just two* situations, the one observable and the other not. And even supposing that observable situations were extremely rare in the field of possibilities, it of course wouldn't follow that every single possibility would have to become actual before there were any observable situations. The car number plate LOOK 1234 WOW might be expected to exist long before all possible combinations of letters and numbers had appeared on cars. So let people please stop writing that the Strong Anthropic Principle could have work to do only if all possible universes existed! When Carter speaks of 'thinking in terms of' an ensemble of universes 'characterized by all conceivable combinations of initial conditions and fundamental constants' you may be tempted to understand him as saying something like that; but Charity demands that you resist the temptation.

6.20 Likewise, you mustn't attack anthropic reasoning by saying that it involves making claims about the rarity of Life and Intelligence in the field of all possible universes. Yes, any such claims might indeed go too far beyond our evidence; but the user of anthropic reasoning need not make them, as is shown by the tale of the Fly (1.24). If a tiny group of flies is surrounded by a largish fly-free wall area then whether a bullet hits a fly in the group will be very sensitive to the direction in which the firer's rifle points, even if other very different areas of the wall are thick with flies. So it is sufficient to consider *a local area of possible universes*, e.g. those produced by slight changes in gravity's strength, or in the early cosmic expansion speed which reflects that strength. It certainly needn't be claimed that Life and Intelligence could exist *only if* certain force strengths, particle masses, etc. fell within certain narrow ranges. For all we know, it might well be that universes could be life-permitting even if *none of* the forces and particles known to us were present in them. All that need be claimed is that a lifeless universe would have resulted from *fairly minor changes* in the forces etc. with which we are familiar.

When imagining such changes we limit our thought-experiments to a local area of possibilities which cosmologists can and do discuss with some confidence. Like it or not, they have actual scientific grounds for saying, e.g., that a slight increase or decrease in the early cosmic density would have spelt disaster.

6.21 Similarly, users of anthropic reasoning need not claim that absolutely every force strength and particle mass is tuned to Life's needs with enormous accuracy, or that there are no physical laws apart from ones which we can regard as being observationally selected. Why not? Because (cf. 6.10) observational selection effects might well operate even if as little as *just one force strength* (or mass, or whatever) varied from universe to universe, and even if this needed only *very rough* tuning. (But of course apparent fine tuning gives a greater excuse for believing in multiple universes, the greater the number of features involved and the more accurate the tuning which they seem to have needed.)

Compare the case of the claim that God designed our universe so that living beings would evolve in it. The theist need not be claiming that God has fine tuned absolutely everything with enormous accuracy or that, of all possible law-controlled types of universe, *only one* is life-permitting. Again, the God hypothesis does not fail whenever we meet any physical law or constant or cosmic initial condition which seems inessential to Life's presence. It does not come crashing to the ground if, say, there are more varieties of quark and lepton than seem strictly needed.

6.22 Pressing further with our insight that 'anthropic' reasoning could well be useful just as soon as anthropic observational selection effects got a field in which they could well operate, we can see that no users of such reasoning need claim (i) that Life and Intelligence *were inevitable*, or even (ii) that they were *extremely likely*, either (a) in *this* universe or spatio-temporal locality or (b) in *at least one* universe or locality. Wherever Life appeared, its appearance could have depended on symmetry breakings which just chanced to occur in exceptionally fortunate ways; or it might have depended on tremendous luck with molecular combinations in some primeval soup; and if so, then perhaps there are too few universes to have made it likely even that lowly life forms (let alone intelligent beings) would exist as much as once. Why, it needn't even be claimed (iii) that it was inevitable or extremely likely that at least one universe or locality would be *life-permitting*. For when might our existence be made unpuzzling through a multiplicity of universes and an observational selection effect? Answer: Just as soon as the multiplicity and the variety of those universes *were great enough to give a fair chance* that at least one universe would contain intelligent observers.

If the move from being *life-permitting* to being *life-containing* is a difficult one, and if it is also difficult for Evolution to bring about the change from mere bacteria to intelligent observership, then a greater number of universes will be needed in order to provide the fair chance in question. (But remember, believing in more and more universes cannot solve every possible problem because there is the risk of joining Boltzmann in the trap into which he fell: 4.72. There might come a stage at which it would be preferable to believe that one's brain, well stocked with pseudo-memories, had come about merely by a random migration of atoms.)

Just how large must a chance grow to be for it to become a fair one? A 25 per cent chance? A 10 per cent chance? Reasonable people could disagree widely here. To each of them, however, a chance would tend to be uninteresting (or 'not a fair chance') when it seemed small enough to make an anthropic explanation appreciably less likely than some competing explanation, e.g. a theistic explanation. A chance of only 1 per cent could still strike you as a fair chance if it seemed to you the basis of the best explanation available.

6.23 Particularly bizarre is the view that anthropic reasoning must be 'cozy',[10] presenting our cosmic situation as warm and loving. Isn't calling a situation *life-permitting* plainly different from saying that life is easy in it? Sadists too like their victims to be alive.

The Difference Between Making Unmysterious and Making Less Lucky

6.24 How could anthropic explanations throw any light on the fact of our observing Life's presence and the presence of Life's prerequisites? As was stressed in section 1.8, they would not serve as substitutes for scientifically very ordinary causal accounts of Life's evolution; neither (as we have just now seen) would they have to demonstrate that its evolution had been very likely to occur somewhere or other in our universe. They need not destroy our feeling of how lucky we are to be alive (1.12; 1.15). Their explanatory task is instead that of making our luck *less mysterious*. They can reduce or remove the puzzlement which we might very naturally feel when faced by the evidence of fine tuning. They can give us a right to feel less amazed.

Isn't reduction of puzzlement or amazement what explanation is all about? Perhaps not quite. Correctly to explain some situation is to give a correct account of how it came about, and sometimes the process of coming to accept such an account could make us more amazed than before. Still, how are we to judge whether an account is correct? Well, a fairly reliable sign of correctness is ability to reduce amazement, or at any rate to lead to as little amazement as is possible when all the apparent facts are viewed. It might be that the cards of a pack, all perfectly ordered by suit and by rank, had got that way by a solitary shuffle rather than by one of vastly many shuffles which were subjected to a selection effect. As D. Lewis has pointed out, coming to know that this was the correct explanation of their perfect order could only increase our feeling that the world was an amazing place. But, I ask, how could we come to know it? What right could we have to believe in such an explanation's correctness? There would have to be exceptionally strong evidence for it! Although at the risk of error, a risk involved in all arguments from probabilities, we ought to reject the evidence in question unless the chance of its being false evidence was even slimmer than the chance of the pack's having that perfect order after a single shuffle – so that it would actually be more amazing that the evidence should be faulty than that just one shuffle was responsible.

6.25 How might anthropic explanations reduce our amazement? It would not be that they told us, say, that the existence of other universes implied that the universe which in fact became ours, perhaps thanks to symmetry breakings which took a fortunate turn, *had from its first moments been specially likely to become* 'ours' to living beings (1.19). Rather, they would show such things as that there had been a fair chance (or better) that some universe or other would become 'ours' to such beings; and then they could remind us that any universe which any such beings were calling 'ours' would be a life-permitting universe.

The points to bear in mind are (1) that the existence of other universes *would in no way reduce the luck that we had had* if, say, our universe's early symmetries had just chanced to break life-permittingly, and (2) that their existence *could none the less reduce our amazement* by providing a field large enough to give a fair chance that life-permitting conditions would be being observed somewhere – the beings who observed them then having little right to be puzzled at how that somewhere was their 'here'.

6.26 Consider in this connection various arguments by I. Hacking.[11] Hacking judges that our existence would be adequately explained 'if all logically possible universes consistent with classical big-bang cosmology actually coexist'. However, he detects a fallacy in efforts – he cites mine and those of P. C. W. Davies – to do similar explanatory work with J. A. Wheeler's oscillating cosmos whose many cycles are characterized by different force strengths etc., perhaps thanks to early symmetry breakings whose outcomes are random. Hacking's idea is that Davies and I are like a dim-witted gambler trying to account for a roll of double six. The gambler

> enters the room as a roll is about to be made. The kibitzer asks, 'Is this the first roll of the dice . . . or have we made many a one earlier tonight?' The gambler . . . says, 'Can I wait until I see how this roll comes out . . .?' The roll is double six. The gambler foolishly says, 'Ha, that makes a difference – I think there have been quite a few rolls.'

In Hacking's eyes the proposed excuse for believing in quite a few previous cycles of an oscillating cosmos – namely, that here we are in a cycle in which all the force strengths etc. are just right – is equally foolish.

Now, the first thing to notice here is that Hacking's story involves no observational selection effect. His gambler is not forced to wait outside the room until a double six (Life, or life-permitting conditions) has been rolled for him to observe. Instead he 'enters the room as a roll is about to be made'. So the story would seem to be irrelevant.

6.27 Next, let us suppose that the dice-roller's policy was to make a thousand rolls of two dice. It is then almost certain that double six would have been rolled sooner or later. But it is also almost certain that it would not have been rolled on the first roll. Therefore it is very likely that *it would have been on a roll later than the first that the roller first rolled it*. (No foolishness there.)

Now, suppose instead that the two dice were to be rolled just once or else a thousand times. A gambler was to be created in the room, *ex nihilo*, just whenever double six was rolled, and annihilated before the next roll. (We can now feel encouraged to talk of Observational Selection. No gambler will ever observe anything but a double six.) Well, you are one such gambler. Why are you alive and observing a double six? Have you any reason for thinking that a thousand rolls were to be made?

Whatever reason you had could of course be overruled; you could, e.g., have special grounds for believing that the roller hated gamblers and hence had been immensely likely to roll once only. But *some* reason for favouring the Many Rolls hypothesis could be the following. On this hypothesis it could be very likely that, sooner or later, at least one gambler would be observing double six, as you are, whereas if the dice were to be rolled only then it would be very likely that there would be no such gambler.

Are you therefore more likely to have been created on, say, a ninety-third roll rather than on a first? Of course not. Any ninety-third roll would have had no increased likelihood of being a double six. Yet it can remain very likely that *even a first* gambler to have been created would have been created *on a roll later than the first* if there were many rolls.

Imagine that you are put into suspended animation, knowing that you will awake if and only if a particular monkey (who can keep typing for vastly many years) manages to type a sonnet. Here waking would give you fairly forceful grounds for thinking that the monkey had engaged in more than one sonnet-length bout of typing.

6.28 Let us vary our story, though. Let's say that gamblers were to be created just whenever the dice were rolled, but unless *his or her* roll was a double six each gambler would be kept in an unconscious condition. You are a conscious gambler. You ask yourself whether there have been many other gamblers. You exclaim, 'Ha! How on earth could the existence of other dice rolls and other gamblers have increased *my* chance of being a conscious gambler?' – and you feel yourself tugged strongly in Hacking's direction.

I protest, however, that Davies and I would never argue that the existence of many other universes or cosmic cycles had in any way *increased the chance* that *this* universe or cosmic cycle would develop life-permitting properties when it underwent early symmetry breakings. During the first instants of its Big Bang it may well have been immensely unlikely that this universe of ours would become 'ours' to any observers. As was indicated above, the excuse for believing in many universes/cosmic cycles is not that these would make our observership less lucky, *less improbable*. Rather it is that they would make it *less amazing*.

Is this a dizzying paradox? Not at all. The distinction between the improbable and the amazing is widely recognized. A lottery has a thousand million tickets. Mr Jones wins, immensely luckily: the improbability of his winning had been enormous. Had he instead won three lotteries in a row, each of a thousand tickets, this would be exactly as improbable but much more amazing: much more in apparent need of an explanation – e.g. Jones cheated – which would reduce our amazement. Because if most of the tickets were sold then it could be very much to be expected that somebody or other would win the lottery of the thousand million tickets. But it isn't to be expected that one and the same person would win all three lotteries of a thousand.

6.29 Elsewhere, Hacking and I have pursued this dispute in ways bringing in Bayes's rule of probabilities.[12] My claim is that if you are to use this rule then you must distinguish between (a) the case where the dice-roller's policy is to roll a thousand times, say, then inviting the gambler into the room if and only if double six appears on *exactly* the thousandth roll, and (b) the one where the policy is to roll *up to* a thousand times, inviting the gambler in just as soon as double six appears. Thus, suppose the second policy is followed. The chance that double six would lie on the table when the roller had rolled once *and then stopped rolling* would now be not 1/36, as one might think; it would instead be 1, i.e. certainty; for if anything other than double six had been rolled then the rolling would have continued. But, given that the second policy is being followed, it is crucial that any roll whose result the gambler saw would be a roll *which stopped the rolling* until he had been invited into the room to inspect that result. Instead of being a roll taken at random, it would be a selected roll. An observational selection effect would be involved.

Bayes's rule encourages you to modify your theories as a result of new experiences. Observing a double six, a gambler should be readier than before to believe that the dice-roller's policy was to roll up to a thousand times and not just once; for then, if the experiment is repeated many times and he is again and again invited into the room to observe double sixes, his belief that the roller isn't always rolling just once can grow nearer and nearer to a certainty. (When you are again and again awakened from suspended animation to see a typed sonnet, you mustn't remain as convinced as ever that the monkey is being given always just the one chance to type it correctly.)

A 'Must' Neither Teleological nor Idealistic

6.30 Some, seeing that the Strong Principle states that our universe *must* be one in which observers can exist, have treated this as expressing some deep metaphysical necessity which forces all actual universes to be life-permitting. One popular line is then the teleological or theistic one. Universes, it is said, must serve purposes – perhaps divine purposes. The 'must' may then be cashed as that of 'God *must* have wanted observers to evolve.'

Sympathetic though I am towards theistic explanations, this seems to me a pointless muddying of the waters. What is the use of a Principle which can mean just whatever you wish it to mean? How is anyone to understand anyone else if Strong Anthropic Principle talk can be *either* observational selection effect talk *or else* teleological/theistic talk *or else* some mixture of the two and perhaps of other things as well? You will find nothing teleological or theistic in Carter's anthropic-principle-baptizing article; and surely this article has a strong right to be consulted. Carter's 'must be such as to admit the creation of observers' is not telling us that a Creator compels the cosmos to contain observers. If you want to speak about that kind of compulsion, please say something like 'Teleological Principle'! Carter's point is just that *since we are alive* it *follows necessarily* that our universe is in fact a life-permitting one (6.18).

Still, it may already be too late to make a major fuss about this. Too many physicists and cosmologists have given teleological overtones to the words 'Strong Anthropic Principle'. Among them are such experts as P. C. W. Davies and J. D. Barrow. The latter even has a let's-bring-order-to-all-this-mess paper, 'Anthropic definitions',[13] in which the very first of four competing 'interpretations' of the Strong Principle is that our universe was 'designed with the goal of generating and sustaining observers'. Barrow and F. J. Tipler go so far as to suggest that it is scientifically useful to work with a Principle open to any number of different interpretations.

6.31 Similar things can be said about making the Strong Principle's 'must' into an Idealistic one, an expression of the notion that *to be* is *to be perceived* or that a universe without consciousness is a logical contradiction or lacks intelligibility or 'meaning' (in one or other of that word's various meanings). Although much liking some varieties of Idealism[14] I see no excuse for muddying the distinction between observational-selection-effect reasoning and idealistic reasoning – particularly when the notion that *to be* could only be *to be perceived* receives no support from quantum physics (4.49–.50) and has been proved wrong by generations of philosophers (4.62). But once again it might be too late to make much fuss about this large departure from the text of Carter's paper.[15]

Anthropic Predictions

6.32 Let us now look at a charge levelled by H. R. Pagels among many others.[16] The Anthropic Principle, he says, 'never predicts anything', since, for one thing, 'there is no way we can actually go to an imaginary universe and check for life'.

This is very odd. We cannot visit the early Big Bang, either, yet physicists and cosmologists are able to know quite a lot about it, including that it was hot enough to be inhospitable to all plausible life forms. *Thought experiments* can tell us, perhaps not infallibly but surely plausibly, that intelligent beings would never have evolved if the universe had recollapsed within a microsecond through expanding marginally more slowly, or if it had quickly developed into nothing but cold, immensely dilute gases, because of expanding marginally faster. Do we really need trips to other universes which did recollapse within a microsecond, to assure ourselves that no life could develop there?

Besides, the claim that the early Big Bang was too hot to be hospitable is itself clearly associated with a prediction: namely, that very hot situations will never be found to contain intelligent life forms. When Pagels tells us that anthropic reasoning is 'anthropocentrism' because it assumes that living organisms everywhere must be much like those on Earth, our comment must be (i) that such reasoning can operate just so long as it can be stated that all intelligent living beings will be *somewhat like* those on Earth, for instance in having bodies unable to survive at billion degree temperatures, and (ii) that if such a statement is mistaken, then what is it but *a mistaken prediction*?

Again, when Pagels tells us first that anthropic reasoning 'is not testable' and next that recent scientific developments have proved its unprofitability by supplying alternative explanations for various observed facts on which it tries to throw light, for instance the observed excess of matter over antimatter or the observed cosmic smoothness, then he has contradicted himself. For in effect he has said that recent scientific developments have indeed tested such reasoning and that it has failed the test. (But actually it has failed the test only if we can assume that the excess of matter over antimatter, and the Inflation which supposedly produces cosmic smoothness, are not themselves in need of 'fine tuning': see 2.7–.8; 2.28. And even if it has failed here, that doesn't mean failure everywhere.)

6.33 In point of fact, anthropic reasoning encourages numerous predictions – although there are perhaps hardly any of which you could say, 'Every user of such reasoning will want to accept this one.' Here are some of them:

- Intelligent life won't be found just about anywhere. It will not be found in frozen hydrogen, or in the molten depths of our planet, or near neutron star surfaces, or in the outer regions of red giant stars, or in the high interiors of ordinary stars, or inside white dwarf stars, or at the core of the sun, or in interstellar gas clouds. It is difficult to achieve, in ways helping to justify the talk of 'fine tuning'.
- Intelligent life will be found only rarely even in places ideally suited to its evolution. (You will recognize this as a prediction made by users of the Superweak Principle: see section 6.8. It gives, by the way, an exceptionally good reason for not risking nuclear war. It suggests that nuclear war could wipe out the only intelligent beings that there ever would be in our universe, anywhere, even if it is a universe containing billions of suitable planets.)
- Developments in physics and astronomy will strengthen the idea that Reality is split up into very many, very varied parts which might reasonably be called 'universes'. They will quite probably confirm that Inflation occurred, producing a gigantic Universe; and further, that symmetry breakings could very well have taken place in largely random ways, dividing that Universe into huge domains – domains very different in their force strengths and particle masses yet each (thanks to Inflation) forming a region in which the randomly typing monkey had typed in the same way for as far as telescopes could probe. They will very probably confirm the plausibility of at least one of the mechanisms for creating multiple universes which Chapter 4 discussed. People refusing to countenance anthropic reasoning will get to look more and more parochial in their world-view. Such people will come to be thought of as 'inhabitants of Little Puddle'. (Contrast section 1.26, where it was the users of such reasoning who found themselves accused of being Littlepuddlians.)
- Claims that our universe is 'fine tuned for Life' in various respects, i.e. that small changes in its basic properties would have made it very unlikely that any life forms would appear in it, will tend to be borne out by developments in cosmology, physics, and biology. And many new cases of such seeming fine tuning will probably be discovered.
- Today's attempts to explain all of our universe's basic properties with the help of some physical theory 'so simple that it just has to be right' will fail, just as Eddington's did (6.4). Hostility towards a probabilistic fixing of such properties will come to seem as antiquated as opposition to a probabilistic quantum

mechanics. The notion that the visible universe must be typical of Reality as a whole, and that no observational selection effect could possibly be involved here, will be laughed at in introductory courses in philosophy of science. Hume and Kant, philosophers now usually read as opposing the kinds of thing said in this book, will be re-read and found to say much that supports them. (The notion that many worlds were botched and bungled before this one is very definitely Humian. Kant, too, was firmly against taking the visible world as necessarily typical.)

6.34 Yes, it would be absurd for a user of anthropic reasoning to claim that if he or she had been endowed with Pure Intelligence but no Actual Experience then, simply on the basis of the need for it to be observable, he or she could have predicted just what an observable world would be like. However, no users of such reasoning have ever claimed this.

Are Theistic Explanations at an Advantage Through Having Made It More Likely That THIS Universe Would Be Life-Containing?

6.35 To end the chapter, let us look more closely at a point raised in section 5.33. When theistic explanations are compared with anthropic ones, i.e. with ones proposing a World Ensemble and an observational selection effect, then may not the theist be at a definite advantage? For a theistic account could give any particular World a far greater chance of being life-generating.

Look at the Firing Squad case. The fifty bullets of the sharpshooters all miss you. You reflect (a) that there may have been greatly many squads at work, making it quite likely that somewhere some lucky person would be asking, 'How did they all manage to miss?' But isn't there a more attractive hypothesis (b) that you are popular with the sharpshooters? Wouldn't the correctness of this have made it far more likely that you yourself would be alive to ask questions?

Here one's intuitions can tug in conflicting directions.

Other things being equal, shouldn't the Popularity hypothesis (which of course corresponds to the God hypothesis) be preferred for the reason just stated? Isn't it important that this hypothesis could have given *you personally* a greater probability of being alive? Yes, I at first feel tugged to say. For consider the case of a million-ticket lottery. Someone or other was bound to win; yet shouldn't the actual winner suspect that his girlfriend who works at lottery company headquarters has secretly ensured his win? For that would explain why he in particular is able to say, 'The winner is standing *here*, in *my* shoes.'

On the other hand I consider the apparent evidence that we are the only intelligent beings in our galaxy. (If there were many others then surely some of their spaceships would have reached here by now.) Query: Do such beings inhabit many other galaxies among the perhaps several hundred billion in the visible universe? Ought one to argue (b_1) that if each galaxy stood a fair chance (say, 30 per cent) of containing intelligent beings then, just as it could occasion no surprise that someone with an appropriately placed girlfriend should win a lottery or that a man popular with the sharpshooters should be missed by a firing squad, so also it was quite to be expected that intelligent life would evolve *in this galaxy*; and that this scenario ought to be preferred to one in which the chances of its evolving here had been only one in many hundred billion? Or should one instead be content with the idea (a_1) that there was a fair chance (let's again say 30 per cent) of intelligent life's evolving at least once in the history of our universe, in some galaxy or other? Ought one to argue that provided there was that fair chance it could be absurd to keep puzzling over why it had evolved *just here*, since whichever galaxy intelligent life evolved in would be 'here' to the intelligent beings who lived there?

In fact it is in the second way (a_1) that I feel inclined to argue. But this means that my intuitions now tug otherwise than they did in the girlfriend case. So my tentative conclusion is that God has no clear advantage over World Ensemble plus Observational Selection.

6.36 If the tentative conclusion is correct then it could be very hard to choose between theistic and observational-selection explanations. Even in a distant future in which far more scientific knowledge had been gathered, the two explanations could be expected to remain in vigorous competition. After all, they do both involve selection of life-containing universes from a wider field of possible universes. In the one case the possible universes are imagined as all of them actually existing, but no living being could ever hope to observe anything but a life-containing one. In the other, they are universes among which God would select, the assumption being that neither good cause nor sheer creative exuberance would lead to the creation of absolutely all of them; but here again, the idea is that the universe or universes selected would be selected from among the life-containing ones. So how could we ever decide firmly whether God did the selecting, or whether it was instead done by the fact that being alive is a prerequisite of making observations?

Chapter Seven

The Design Argument

Looking at a succession of very influential objections against the Design Argument for God's reality, the chapter argues that every one of them is weak. Had they been powerful then they would have shown that fine tuning of natural constants or cosmic initial conditions to suit Life's needs could not be a sign of anything interesting – not even of the existence of multiple universes.

In fact, such arguments would actually have risked proving the absurdity that an infinitely powerful Creator could do nothing whatever to indicate his existence when choosing the properties of any universe he created. Leaving messages in the rocks or in molecular structures would be ineffectual.

Some Alleged Weaknesses of Design Arguments

7.1 The Argument from Design tries to prove God's reality by examining our universe. In the form given to it today by those naming themselves 'creation scientists' it earns the fury of genuine scientists. Most reputable thinkers consider it long dead and buried, in this and every other form.

Creation scientists try to keep the Argument alive by giving it a second childhood. The Earth, they say, was created only a few thousand years ago. God's hand moulded all living things, as we can see just by looking at them. The eye, for instance, must be a product of divine workmanship rather than of Darwinian natural selection because the latter, an affair of blind chance, could create nothing intricate and useful.

I call this a second childhood because it reverts to many detailed beliefs about God's activities which every rational, educated adult knows to be wrong.

In its first childhood, in contrast, the Argument was wondrously vague. Plato thanks Anaxagoras for suggesting that Mind governs all things but chides him for not going on to argue that it governs them in good ways – so perhaps even the notion that Design *was beneficent* was absent during the Argument's early infancy. Later we find Aquinas torn between the view that God directs the world's activities and the Aristotelian picture of things as instead directing themselves towards the divine like bees struggling to reach honey. Only in the seventeenth and eighteenth centuries do we repeatedly meet with claims that living organisms have a complexity which proves God to have designed each individually.

Such claims have suffered drastically at the hands of Darwin. Darwin's theory of course *does not* rely simply on the workings of Blind Chance, since Natural Selection is a wind separating the wheat from the vast quantities of chaff to which chance gives rise. Life's evolutionary development from simple beginnings is today an established fact; and neo-Darwinism's ability to explain it, suggesting even how the business could have got started at a pre-biological, chemical level, is almost equally well proven. And while the hypothesis that God occasionally intervenes with a helpful shove would be immensely difficult to disprove, it lacks the charms of simplicity.

The upshot is that many of the ablest modern defenders of Design limit themselves to suggesting that *looking on* Nature *as* an expression of the divine should come easily to the believer somewhat as looking on a squiggle as a drawing of a duck rather than of a rabbit should come easily to the duck-loving rabbit-hater.

7.2 What reduced them to so humble a state? A tale now fairly standard among philosophers runs as follows. The Design Argument is *an argument from analogy*, and all such arguments are insecure. This one, though, is far worse than most because its analogy is ludicrously weak. God is conceived on the model of a watch designer. Yet the realm of stars and planets does not much resemble a watch, and neither does a living organism. Put watches, electric motors, windmills, in among earthworms, birds, and cabbages, and any child can tell the difference.

At the opening of the nineteenth century a clever man like William Paley could comment that this only went to show the skill of a designer who could, as it were, make watches which crawled or flew around, grew larger, and even gave birth to further watches. But the trouble with such a comment is that watch-like things able to manufacture others of their own kind might have started off as comparatively simple affairs, growing to be vastly complex only after billions of years of trial, error, and competition for survival.

Besides, it is said, the rules of analogy tell us *not to jump from the finite to the infinite.* Hence instead of introducing an omniscient, omnipotent Designer it would be better to believe in a bungling committee of demigods laboriously developing ever more sophisticated plans.

7.3 Faced with such problems (the standard tale continues), defenders of Design often retreat to the claim that God planned not whole organisms but only the natural laws and materials which allow Evolution by Natural Selection to work. How immense, they exclaim, was the skill that this demanded! But what facts could there possibly be to support their way of viewing things? There is no doubt an excellent fit between *life as we know it* and Nature's actual laws and materials, but to praise God for this could be like praising him for causing great rivers to flow through Europe's principal cities. Mightn't it be that just as more or less any sizeable river attracts a largish town, so more or less any universe would have given birth to life forms of some sort or to something else quite as complexly interesting?

It can often seem that Design's supporters try to have things both ways. When they see obstacles which Life only barely succeeds in overcoming they applaud the divine intelligence which supplied just the means needed for overcoming them. When on the other hand all runs easily, they again glorify that same intelligence for making easy running possible. Moreover they pick and choose their evidence shamelessly. The frozen desert of the Antarctic is forgotten in favour of a few ponds whose depths are protected by the ice above, ice described as having very providentially expanded as it formed, so that it floats. (The marvellous result is that plant and animal cells down below are protected from the damage which so unprovidentially results when water expands into ice inside plant and animal cells.) The sun's controlled nuclear fusion is admired; the fact that the principles behind it can lead to fusion of the hydrogen-bomb kind is conveniently ignored. The billions of wasted years before complex life evolved are dismissed as unimportant. The creation of a few human beings is seized upon, scant attention being paid to the Creator's apparent preference for beetles or for life-threatening germs. The vast emptiness of interstellar space, the inferno inside the stars, the uninhabited planets, are disregarded so that our minds may concentrate on the single tiny habitat that we know.

7.4 Underlying all the Argument's idiocies (so the standard story runs) are two horrendous blunders.

First, patterns of evidence collected in Nature are treated as indicating the presence of something supernatural. Yet Nature cannot possibly give evidence of anything beyond herself! One reason for this is that the natural world, the universe, is by definition a one and only affair. There cannot be two universes. But a central principle of probability theory is *that probabilities cannot govern necessarily unique cases*. To judge that the natural world would be 'improbable' unless God had chosen it in preference to other, 'more probable' worlds is therefore mathematical lunacy.

Second, the supporter of Design overlooks the fact that if the world had been one in which intelligent life could never evolve *then we shouldn't be here to discuss the matter.* We are invited to feel surprise and awe at how natural laws are such as can give rise to complex organisms over billions of years. But how could we even have wondered whether to be surprised, if complex organisms such as ourselves had not arisen?

These two simple, logical considerations are decisive. There is no need to probe all the other holes with which the Design Argument is riddled: for example, its failure to explain anything when it points to God, the Reasonlessly Existing Magician.

Why Cosmologists Could Well Deny That the Weaknesses Are Real

7.5 For reasons suggested by earlier chapters, these standard objections against the Design Argument are a threat to the development of science.

Let us agree that sensible defenders of Design are not 'creation scientists' and do not wish to get much mileage out of how ice protects the depths of ponds. Instead they argue that there is something crying out for explanation in the sheer fact that our cosmos has basic properties making Darwinian evolution possible. Now, proofs that there could be nothing remarkable in such a fact – that its unremarkableness is guaranteed by probability theory, by the very simplest of logic, by the need to distrust feeble analogies, or by sound common sense – would do more than just destroy all alleged evidence of Design. They would mean as well that there could be no such thing as 'fine tuning' evidence for multiple universes.

7.6 When we consider such evidence and how modern cosmologists might well handle it, we find for a start that the objection *that there is by definition just a single universe* is unimpressive. Certainly you can settle this by a definition if you want, but the question then merely becomes one of whether there are many *gigantic cosmic regions* each perhaps much greater than everything inside our horizon (which lies, remember, at a distance of some ten to twenty billion light years).

Why might we want to believe in a multiplicity of such regions, 'small-u universes'? Well, it is not at all obvious that you could alter the details of a universe very much and still leave it as a place in which intelligent organisms could evolve. An impressive sign that ours was only one universe among many could be this: that actual investigations suggested that very tiny alterations in it would have made it uninhabitable and hence unobservable. For in that case we could very reasonably ask how the universe observed by us managed to balance on such a razor edge. We could reasonably ask it because a tidy answer would be available. If there existed many universes and if they varied in their properties then it would be unsurprising that at least one of them was inhabitable; and obviously it could only be in an inhabitable universe that people could be asking, 'How came we to be so fortunate? Why are our universe's observed details of the very special sort which seem required if there is to be anyone to observe it?'

For reasons like those listed in Chapter 2, many scientists do think we are observing a universe which would have been made uninhabitable by very marginal alterations, for instance in its early expansion rate. To many of them it then seems altogether natural to believe in, say, a billion universes with differing expansion rates; they are willing to see a problem in the fact that our universe is 'just right'. Now, willingness to see a problem here is central to the Argument from Design.

To put this in another way: a cosmologist who says there is 'no difficulty' in how the expansion rate and other features were all just right, because if there were greatly many universes with varied properties 'then it would be fairly sure that one or two of them would be life-permitting and of course only those could be observed', is in effect saying that there *is* a difficulty here but that it would be very neatly resolved by postulating greatly many universes with varied properties. The neatness of the solution is as fine an indication as you could wish that there really is something which needs to be explained (5.29: feedback loop). Catching a 23.2576 inch fish and then finding that your fishing apparatus can catch only ones of more or less exactly this length, you do not simply shrug your shoulders and say that just any fish must have some length or other. Not when you see how tidily the affair could be accounted for if there were many differently lengthed fish in the lake.

7.7 Remember however that an account in terms of multiple universes may well not be the only tidy one available. The believer in God, too, could claim to have a tidy account making it to be expected that a universe should be life-permitting. And the question of which account is right is not trivial scientifically. It could be very important to know whether the basic laws of physics encourage the existence of multiple universes with varied properties. It would be nice, for instance, to know whether there was some randomness in how force strengths and particle masses were settled when a unified force split into many during our universe's early instants. One doesn't want to surrender at once to a suggestion that God must have guaranteed life-permitting strengths and masses – but neither should one want some ill-considered philosophical objections against the Design Argument served up as an excuse for shrugging off all possible evidence that our universe is startlingly well suited to Life's requirements.

7.8 Is it true that any supposed special need to explain our universe's life-generating nature *must be derived from a hopelessly weak argument from analogy*?

For a start, must we accept that 'argument from analogy' is a particularly useful description here?

Agreed, those who suppose the special need are using scientific findings, and Induction, central to science, depends on viewing various situations as interestingly analogous. But must it therefore be helpful to call, say, a fine tuning argument for God or for multiple universes 'an Argument from Analogy'? Surely not. Surely it would be better called *an argument from probabilities*.[1] If – which does not in itself seem at all obviously unlikely – there were very many universes, universes which differed greatly, then it could seem altogether probable that at least a few of them should be just right for Life, and it would be unsurprising that we observers found ourselves in one which was just right. There would be nothing to startle us in a discovery that very tiny changes in our universe's basic features would have prevented the evolution of complex living things. We should have our explanation for any such discovery. But if on the other hand ours were a one and only universe, so that this explanation failed, and if an explanation by reference to God failed also, then the discovery could be very startling indeed. It could seem highly improbable that a one and only universe *should just chance to have features fine tuned for suggesting such explanations.*

The conclusion to this argument from probabilities could be that it is altogether likely that *either* there exist many universes *or* God has ensured that our universe is just right for Life, *or both*. For note that probabilistic arguments often do a better job of showing that some explanation is needed than of actually picking out the right explanation. Scientists whose theories make seemingly improbable events very probable, and who then, when these events are observed, congratulate themselves on being right, are often dismayed to find that other theories predict the same events and have the advantage of actually being right. (Yet remember that it is possible for evidence to support a theory despite also giving support to a competing theory: see section 1.30's tale of the Empty Treasure Chest.)

Note also that probabilistic arguments could add force to the God hypothesis even if it somehow managed to be uncertain that God would prefer a life-containing to a non-life-containing universe.[2] For the most that the arguments require is that a universe should be more likely to be life-containing if God-created than if non-God-created.

7.9 If, however, you do want Arguments from Analogy here, then they can be supplied.

The tale of the Fly on the Wall (1.24) could be one of them. When a bullet would need very careful positioning in order to hit a fly it can be natural to believe either in many bullets (cf. Multiple Worlds) or else in a marksman (cf. God).

The Fishing Story (1.9) might be another. Before shrugging your shoulders and saying in response to section 7.8 that you see no special reason to explain why our universe has such-and-such basic features, even if they are indeed features *very finely tuned for allowing a tidy explanation or explanations to become available*, please ask how you would react to the man who, catching a fish, next discovered that his fishing apparatus would accept only fish of exactly that length, to one part in a million, and who still saw absolutely no ground for believing in a fish-creating benefactor or in multiple fish.

All I am claiming is that this is not an area where arguments from analogy have to be used.

Their main use, in fact, is to remind people about common-sensical ways of reasoning (e.g. probabilistic ones) which they ought never to have forgotten yet which they have managed to forget because the situation is an unusual one. It is depressing when the reminder is then resisted with an, 'Oh, but you're employing a very weak analogy. Can't you see that this is an unusual situation?'

Take an extreme example. Suppose it could be very firmly established that our universe's expansion speed at early instants had to be just right, to within one part in a trillion trillion trillion trillion trillion trillion trillion trillion trillion, for there to have been any chance that observers would evolve in it; and suppose also that it could be proved that fundamental physics gave absolutely no preference to the speed in question. It would now be just common sense to suppose that something dramatic such as God or multiple universes would be needed to explain the actual existence of observers. 'But where is the analogy?' a philosopher protests. 'How dissimilar this all is from your cases of catching a fish or hitting a fly with a bullet! Surely you can see that observing a universe is in countless respects different from shooting and fishing!' Well, indeed, it is very different, but not different in any obviously relevant way. For in all these cases we should be guided by the Principle that the neatness of an explanation can help show that an explanation is needed. Besides being a special case of applying Bayes's rule of probabilities (5.29), this Principle is wired into the human brain in a way that makes it 'just common sense'. There is no need for us actually to go fishing with an apparatus of a particularly fussy kind, or to experiment with flies and bullets, so as to learn by experience what ways of reasoning work well in such situations, then at last getting into a position to make a desperate leap into the in many respects *dis*analogous situation of observing a universe.

Even William Paley insisted that his celebrated argument about finding a watch on a heath did not rely on actual experiences of watches and watchmakers.

7.10 Still, isn't it utterly obvious that users of the Design Argument should be bothered by *their leap from a finite world to an infinite God*?

No, it is not in the least obvious, for reasons suggested in section 1.32. Our explanations should be simple ones. Introducing an infinity often increases simplicity – as can perhaps be seen by looking at the theories, first, that there exist seven hundred and fifty-seven universes, and next, that there exist infinitely many. And it mustn't merely be assumed (in blissful disregard of such writers as Spinoza, A. Farrer, and R. Swinburne) that God would be *more complex* if infinite. It cannot even be assumed that an infinitely powerful God – one able to do anything that was truly possible – would have to be *an infinitely complex person*, or any kind of person. (More on that subject later.) But an infinitely powerful, omniscient person might in any case be a good deal simpler than a committee of (let's say) seven hundred and fifty-seven blundering demigods complete with hands and heads and stomach ulcers.

7.11 But (to continue down the list of Standard Objections) doesn't the Design Argument *wrongly concentrate on life as we know it*? Mightn't more or less any universe generate living beings of some sort or, failing that, then at least something else equally interesting?

Several matters are raised by this question. Let us take the last one first. I find it hard to imagine anything which could begin to compete in its organized intricacy with the products of Darwinian evolution. The idea that a lifeless galaxy could be as complexly interesting as an amoeba, let alone a human being, seems to me all wrong. But even if something other than Life could be 'equally interesting' (which is hard to rule out, given the vagueness of those words) it is difficult to see why that should harm the Design hypothesis. For, like the many-universes hypothesis, this does not just offer to explain how there comes to be a world in which complexly organized patterns develop. It offers as well a reason why there exists anyone to observe any patterns. For our purposes the most striking thing about Life is that it is a prerequisite of Observation. It would be extremely odd if a one and only actually existing universe simply chanced to have such features as an early expansion rate which was (to enormous accuracy) precisely right for giving birth to conscious beings, so that the two explanations we are considering – the theistic one and the one which introduces many universes and an observational selection effect – should suggest themselves. This would be equally odd whether or not lifeless universes could be expected to contain other things as fascinating as conscious beings are. *Situations must be assumed NOT simply to happen to be fine tuned in ways which make tidy explanations available.* That moral comes from the Fishing Story, the Story of the Collapsing Arch, the Story of the Silk Merchant's Thumb, the Message in Granite Story, the Story of the Firing Squad, the Story of the Hand of Thirteen Spades, etc. (1.9–.11; 1.17; 1.21; 5.29; 7.8). It is (7.9) a moral given to us by Bayes's rule and by common sense. Without it we might as well give up on trying to practise science or to survive in a world harsh towards idiots.

7.12 Still, mightn't life and consciousness of kinds unfamiliar to us be found *in universes very unlike our own*? (A second matter raised by the above question.)

Need one repeat that, as is shown by the tale of the unfortunate fly, we have no need to consider universes very unlike our own (1.24)? What we have to explain is how this universe of ours manages to be fine tuned to Life's requirements. The fine tuning exhibited by our universe can be just as impressive whether or not there could be other *very different* life-containing universes, universes whose fundamental laws were of kinds completely unfamiliar to us, *which were not* fine tuned (i.e. which were such that all or most universes in their 'local areas' inside the realm of possibilities were like them in being life-containing).

Part of the reason for telling the Fly on the Wall Story is that a universe could be much like ours in its basic physics, so that our scientific arguments could get a grip on it, while still being unlike it with respect, say, to whether it recollapsed very quickly.

7.13 But may not *our own universe* contain *life forms of unfamiliar kinds*, ones not dependent on fine tuning? (A third matter that the question raises.)

This has been answered in 1.27 and 2.50. Suppose we grant – much too generously? – that living organisms might well be based on something other than chemistry and so could occur inside neutron stars or at the sun's centre or in other such seemingly hostile locations. It can still appear plain enough that our universe would need to be tuned in many ways and with considerable accuracy for there to be suns or neutron stars, or any other even just conceivably favourable environments. It is for instance very hard to take seriously the idea that any life forms, let alone intelligent observers, could have evolved if the universe had expanded very marginally more slowly in its first instants so that it recollapsed in a thousandth of a second.

7.14 The issue here is not the rarity or otherwise of living beings in our universe. It is instead whether living beings ever could evolve in a universe just slightly different in its basic characteristics. The main evidence for multiple universes or for God is the seeming fact that tiny changes would have made our universe permanently lifeless. How curious to argue that *the frozen desert of the Antarctic, the emptiness of interstellar space, and the inferno inside the stars are strong evidence against Design!*[3] As if the only acceptable sign of a universe's being God-created would be that it was crammed with living beings from end to end and from start to finish! As if God could create only a single universe so that he would need to ensure that it was well packed! (As if, indeed, it were completely obvious that our universe doesn't extend infinitely, which – 4.12 – would mean that even very sparsely scattered living beings could exist in infinite number.) As if, moreover, it were plain that the natural laws of a well-designed universe would be compatible with its being well supplied with living beings from its earliest instants; or as though (despite centuries of discussing the Problem of Evil, especially as presented by earthquakes and other such natural disasters) theists could only be utterly baffled by how Nature works by laws rather than by magic!

7.15 How curious it can again seem, against the background of the modern debate over multiple universes, when people attack the Design Argument by declaring that our universe *is obviously a one and only universe, and therefore not something to which words like 'probable' or 'improbable' could be applied!*[4] Were their reasoning forceful then of course the theist would be confused when saying that only a 'very improbable' universe would take a life-permitting form unless God had designed it. But the weaknesses of such reasoning were exposed earlier (5.13 ff.). If, for instance, it is reasoned that there is by definition only one universe then we can just restate the point with the words 'huge system of causally interacting things' replacing the word 'universe'. If it is reasoned that probability statements cannot be applied to *unique cases* then it can be answered, first, that this is not at all obvious; second, that anyway there may exist many a universe (in the sense of 'huge system of causally interacting things'); and third, that a universe could be unique *under the description 'universe'* (i.e. could be the one and only universe) while still not being unique under other descriptions (so that it could be one of many spatially extended things, very large things, things looking as if designed, and so forth). Thus even the fact that our universe is, obviously, unique in being the one and only universe directly known to us is unimpressive. It is not the one and only thing known to us that obeys the laws of physics, and physics we know to be very often probabilistic.

Finally, crushingly, it can be asked whether every conceivable piece of seeming evidence of divine creative activity, including, say, messages written in the structures of naturally occurring chain molecules or encoded as section 5.13 described, would be shrugged off with the comment, 'Nothing improbable in *that*!' Consistently developed, such a comment would lead to the conclusion that whereas the banknote forger has immense difficulty in hiding his creative acts, an omnipotent Creator would find it logically impossible to produce a world which looked as if it were *probably God-made* or even *more likely to be God-made* than, say, some utterly evil, irretrievably disgusting world. But that is a grotesque conclusion. If the message MADE BY GOD were written everywhere thanks to the action of Nature's forces then we shouldn't need to travel to other universes which lacked such messages before concluding that the forces had quite probably been carefully selected, if not by God then at least by some immensely powerful person or persons, with this effect in mind.

In point of fact, those who run the above argument against calling our universe 'probably God-designed' are often also heard to declare that a universe with as many evils as ours would be 'a highly improbable' product of divine power.

7.16 How strange it can again sound to people who know of recent developments in cosmology when an opponent of the Design Argument remarks that *if the universe weren't life-containing then we shouldn't be here to discuss it*! For the Anthropic Principle which formed the subject-matter of Chapter 6 – namely, that intelligent observers necessarily find themselves in situations in which intelligent observers can exist – is not simply left to stand on its own. On its own it is as unhelpful as the reflection that if the bullets of an entire firing squad hadn't missed then you wouldn't be alive to consider the affair. What one needs is (1.12; 1.17; 6.18) either the actual existence of many universes (corresponding to many firing squad situations, or to many fish in the lake whose waters you are probing with an exceptionally fussy fishing apparatus) or else a universe-creating deity (corresponding to a friendly firing squad or a fish-creating being who wants you to have a fish supper).

The Design Hypothesis

7.17 It might be thought, however, that my various counters to the Standard Objections manage only to do the wrong job. They may succeed in showing that our universe's life-permitting character could be something in special need of explanation; but, a protest could run, their successes should be counted always as successes for many-universe theories. For when multiple universes are so well able to account for any facts of fine tuning, who needs the antiquated and silly hypothesis of Design?

This protest deserves an answer despite the fact that Design and multiple universes are compatible. God might very well have had reasons for creating more than one universe – but it remains true that the way in which multiple and varied universes might lead to Life without God's aid can make belief in God less attractive since it means that we are not forced to choose between that belief and simply shrugging off all evidence of fine tuning. So I need to say why the God hypothesis strikes me as non-silly, and even as every bit as plausible as the many-universes hypothesis.

7.18 For a start, I am not much bothered by two surprisingly influential objections to it: that it *could not by itself generate any detailed predictions* about the world's nature and that *it is in itself somewhat vague*, for instance with respect to how God should be pictured. I am unbothered because very similar things could be said of the many-universes approach without damaging it.

Thus, the hypothesis of many universes and of an observational selection effect could be scientifically important in the ways listed in 6.33 – e.g. in encouraging us to reject any physics which would make all universes so much alike that postulating greatly many of them could do little to explain how there managed to be an observer-permitting universe – even though *Pure Reason could not have predicted* that an observer-permitting universe would have just the mixture of physical laws and constants and initial conditions which we actually discover. Yes, the actually discovered laws, constants, and initial conditions seem such that very minor variations in them would have yielded lifelessness; but supporters of many universes need not claim that so delicately balanced a situation was predictable. Instead they can offer to explain it when they have actually come across it. A bullet that hits a fly may be seen as needing to be explained when the local area of the wall is blank, but the person offering the explanation that many bullets are hitting the wall need not be taken as having been willing to predict that the area around the fly would be blank. The main point of the Fly on Wall Story (1.24) is that any need for an explanation is fully compatible with supposing that most flies on the wall are in areas thickly covered with flies – and *that* is equivalent to saying that, for all one knows or cares, it could be that in almost all possible life-containing universes Life *would not* depend on any 'delicate balancing' or 'fine tuning'. All we need know or care about is the fact that *our universe* is one in which Life depends on fine tuning. *Our* fly, so to speak, could be hit only by a bullet travelling just rightly: hence (at least plausibly) Multiple Bullets or Marksman.

All this should have been obvious. When Sherlock Holmes offers to explain a murder-by-accurately-aimed-airgun you cannot declare that he could therefore have predicted the murder and thus shares in the guilt, neither can he be taken as denying that the murderer might equally well have used some instrument not requiring accuracy, perhaps an axe. And similarly, people can see force in the Design Argument while thinking that God might equally well have created conscious beings (angels?) in a vacuum instead of through fine adjustments leading to stars, planets, carbon, water, and intelligent life evolving in obedience to physical laws. It is ludicrous to declare that we could have suggestive evidence of divine activity only if able to form in our armchairs a detailed picture of what a God-created universe would look like, then going out into the world to check whether the picture corresponded to the facts. For any such declaration leads straight to the following conclusion: that if Pure Reason could not tell us to expect that divinely selected natural laws would generate a voice in the clouds, wonderfully melodious and conveying some instruction altogether worthy of a benevolent and omniscient being, then actually finding that they did generate it could not provide any indication of such a being's existence. (The example is a variant on one in Hume's *Dialogues*.)

7.19 Granted, it is doubtful whether the God hypothesis is consistent with as many evils as there are; but as Hume noted, it could be far easier to detect something worth calling Design than to find convincing evidence of its goodness or badness. Now, what exactly is the force of Hume's point? Must we say that Design's goodness, if it could not be known directly, could not be known at all, so that the Design Argument would be useless for proving a deity rather than a devil? Surely not. Design's goodness might be concluded from how this alone would fit into a plausible account of how Design operated. It is hard to imagine anything more absurd than that there just happens to exist a devil of immense creative power and intelligence who planned life's evolution so as to have opportunities for devilry. But – as I hope to illustrate in the next chapter – belief in God might take a form which saved it from sharing in this kind of absurdity.

If so, then one consequence would be that any Design Argument would not have to wait until we had *discovered that our universe was very markedly good*. Which is just as well, for otherwise the argument might be unable to get started. Even if we rather oddly supposed that goodness could often be detected directly just as redness is – so that one could *know*, say, that the pleasures of skiing were better than the pains of struggling with philosophy, instead of just believing them better – it could still be the sign of a foolish, callous mind if a man were to look around a bit and then declare that despite snakebite, plague, earthquake, war, and inevitable death, the universe was so visibly good that God had to be behind its existence. But what can none the less be said is that it might be almost as foolish to claim to be able to see that our universe has no great goodness; second, that only a universe containing living consciousness could at all plausibly be considered either good or bad, and that this universe of ours appears to steer an impressively careful path between possibilities which threatened to make it lifeless; and third, that its taking of this path – i.e. its being fine tuned in the ways earlier chapters discussed – might well be rather tidily explained by a properly developed theism.

True, no evidence of Design supplied by fine tuning could be as conclusive as hearing a voice from the clouds (7.18) or witnessing scenes of a sort suggested by a straightforward reading of the Book of Genesis or finding that book itself inscribed on every suitably large rock face. My suspicion, though, is that while such experiences would banish once and for all the curious idea that nothing whatever could be 'odd', 'remarkable', 'improbable' in ways suggesting Design, what they would tend to prove would be the reality of a deity whose power was matched only by his vulgarity. At any rate, defences against the Problem of Evil have to rely heavily on such a suspicion: in other words, on the

Leibnizian suggestion that the world's goodness may lie largely in its obedience to natural laws.

7.20 Again, the many-universes hypothesis could be defended even if nobody could say quite how the universes were generated. (All of the universe-generating mechanisms described in Chapter 4 could be wrong, some as yet undiscovered physical principle bearing responsibility for our universe and for countless others.) Its being *a somewhat vague hypothesis*, an incomplete one, would not ruin it. And similarly with the Design hypothesis. Arguments in favour of Design could be forceful and interesting through tending to establish that a combination of creative power and goodness was behind the universe, even if nobody knew quite how the power and the goodness came to be combined. Such arguments might be among many elements supporting faith in some particular religion despite their failure to point towards this religion rather than towards that one or towards some world-view (e.g. mine) which may be too abstract to be called religious. Arguments can help support a theory when they make it more likely that some theory *of that general type* is correct. It is bizarre to suppose that the Design Argument could be an aid to Christianity, for example, only if it itself said things about Christ.

Equally bizarre is the widespread opinion that it could be an aid only to someone already believing in Christ. As if the Argument could have considerable ability to reinforce belief while being entirely useless for persuading someone who was hesitating on the threshold of becoming a believer for the first time, or who had once believed but then developed doubts just sufficient to produce unbelief!

7.21 On the other hand, not just any picture of God and God's creative activity could be acceptable. If forced to choose between a multiplicity of universes and God the Reasonlessly Existing, Universe-Designing Person with Ultimately Inexplicable Powers, then I choose the first without hesitation.

However, as the next chapter will discuss, there is no need to think of God as a person who exists reasonlessly.

Chapter Eight

God

The chapter asks how divine action could be explanatory. There is little force in the protest that a divine Designer's mind would have to be at least as complex as the world it supposedly explained. God might not even have a mind in any straightforward sense. Theologians encourage us to use caution when describing the Creator in everyday terms, and Neoplatonism's God is just the creative ethical requiredness of the scheme of things.

The world's evils provide fairly strong arguments against such a God or any other God combining great power and goodness. The arguments are far from being conclusively strong, however. For one thing, ethical requirements may sometimes remain unsatisfied because they have entered into conflict with stronger ethical requirements. (This is basic to the well-known Free Will Defence against the Problem of Evil.) Again, Reality may be much more varied than people tend to think; variety may be a great good; and it is by no means clear that the universe which we see could contribute nothing worthwhile to a richly varied capital-U Universe.

The chapter ends with a discussion of whether all God-created universes would have basic laws guaranteeing Life's coming to exist.

Avoiding Belief in a Reasonlessly Existing Person

8.1 There is no need to think of God as a person who exists reasonlessly. God may not be a person at all (1.3; 1.32; 5.4; 5.35). The reason why there exists something rather than nothing could be as follows: that *ethical needs for the existence of things are in some cases creatively effective*. This, Neoplatonist theology suggests, could be what is best meant by *God*.

Thus, examining in the light of Pure Reason the quite ordinary concept of an ethical need, alias an ethical necessity or requirement for the existence of this or that, a concept well entrenched in everyday thought and language, you get (as J. L. Mackie concedes in a chapter discussing my Neoplatonism)[1] no guidance at all on whether ethical needs, necessities, requirements, grounds for the existence of this or that, are or are not able to create a universe. What you find is just that they might conceivably create one: that there is no actual logical absurdity in such a suggestion.

Contrast the logically absurd suggestions that the number 17, or redness, or the truth that any bachelor must be unmarried while any Immensely Evil Being must be a Being, could act creatively.

Consider now the facts (i) that a universe exists, (ii) that it is patterned in the ways we call 'causal', (iii) that the laws governing its patterning can well seem to have been cunningly selected (Chapter 3) so that being alive would be possible if various natural constants took appropriate values, and finally (iv) that these constants do take those values: values such that tiny deviations from them would seemingly have led to a lifeless universe (Chapter 2). You might reasonably consider these to be four affairs which call for explanation. And in that case you could come to believe that a supreme ethical requirement – or, which is just another way of saying the same thing, a set of ethical requirements that come together consistently (which mayn't be so simple a matter as people tend to think) – does have creative power, producing our life-containing universe and perhaps also many another universe. And if that is what is meant by *God* and by *Design*, as has been suggested by a long succession of Neoplatonist writers culminating in such modern theologians as P. Tillich, then God and Design may enter into a simple and unmysterious world-picture.

Alternatively, God may be an all-powerful person, an omniscient Designer who owes his existence, knowledge, and power to the fact that these are ethically required.

8.2 Belief that ethical requirements can themselves be creatively powerful *sometimes* – at times, that is, when they come together in consistent sets which are not overruled by stronger consistent sets of ethical requirements – immediately raises the Problem of Evil. Why do so many things happen in ways which seem anything but good?

Any attempt at an answer must I think include these elements:

(1) *An insistence that it is no easy matter to bring ethical requirements together in consistent sets.* For instance, one well-known defence against the Problem of Evil is that it may be impossible to have *both* the good of freedom exercised at a high level *and* the good of a guaranteed absence of wicked decisions. As this illustrates, defending against the Problem of Evil is not the same as suggesting that there are no real evils.

(2) *An insistence that Reality may be considerably richer than people tend to suppose.* As was said in 5.37, a world-model which looks only natural when your belief is that the world exists reasonlessly can seem altogether implausible when you instead

think that it owes its existence to God. It is not the making of arbitrary suppositions, silly fantasizing, to adjust your world-model to your beliefs about how the world's patterns come to be generated. Scientists do it all the time. (A classic example was provided when W. Pauli postulated the neutrino so as to save the principle of Conservation of Energy. At the time, neutrinos were totally undetectable.)

8.3 I cannot go into Neoplatonism or the Problem of Evil in much detail without repeating an earlier book.[2] But the next pages will give rough outlines of a few points.

Neoplatonism: Ethical Requirements as Themselves Universe-Creating

8.4 Neoplatonism is today often expressed in such formulae as that God 'is not a being but the Power of Being'. On my interpretation, what such dark sayings say is that God *is the world's creative ethical requiredness* or, equivalently, that God *is the creatively effective ethical need that there should exist a (good) world.*

The suggestion is that the ethical need for a universe or set of universes itself bears creative responsibility for that universe or set of universes.

Where does this need have its source? In the nature, of course, which such a universe or set of universes would have if it existed. Compare how the eternally existing, unconditionally real ethical need for the *non-existence* of a world crammed with unalleviated misery has *its* source in the fact that such a world would be such a loathsome one if it existed.

8.5 Neoplatonism's creative principle can only very controversially be classified as 'a replacement for God'. It itself *is* God to a great many Catholic, Protestant, and Greek Orthodox thinkers, and many others are at least willing to grant that God may be like this. Neoplatonism has been a strong element in Christian theology since its beginnings.

Still, it is possible to defend this creative principle without being a Christian. The notion that an ethical requirement or set of requirements *could itself be creatively effective* may supply a philosophically tidy answer to the question of 'why there is something rather than nothing', i.e. why any person or thing is ever more than merely possible. And this question has no other answers which are in the least plausible, I think. Either something or other – a divine person creatively responsible for all things outside himself, or a universe or universes – just happens to exist, or else ethical requiredness is responsible for the matter. There are no further options.[3]

8.6 Some Neoplatonists (Tillich, for instance) are contemptuous about belief in a divine person, but they have little enough reason for this. Fairly popular though Neoplatonism has been among theologians, the thesis that God *is definitely not a person* can scarcely be held to be theologically well proven. Further, as was indicated above (8.1; 8.5), a divine person *might himself owe his existence to his ethical requiredness*, a position defended by the philosopher A. C. Ewing.[4] Neoplatonism might therefore be viewed as carrying the seeds of its own defeat. Once having accepted its point that something's being ethically needful could in at least some case or cases be responsible for such a something's existence, you might next argue that the something in question is a Being who is benevolent, omniscient, omnipotent, and creative of all things beyond himself.

Let us look at this for a moment.

Accepting God-as-a-person need not be the same as thinking that this person exists and has benevolence, omnipotence, omniscience, etc., *for no reason whatever*. God is often held to be 'the source of all explanations', but it strikes me as no compliment to interpret this as meaning that he himself just happens to exist. Absolute inexplicability is no valid ground for worship, although tradition may sometimes have tended to treat it as one. Bear in mind that tradition has also tended to find a ground for worship in sheer power exercised completely arbitrarily – yet Ewing is surely right when he insists in this connection that 'the worship of power as such is evil'.

Besides, there is a strong tradition that God's existence *is necessary*. Now, how are we to interpret this? Would it mean, 'is logically necessary'? Or, perhaps, 'is eternal'? Neither alternative seems acceptable. *The eternal* may not be necessary at all; it is logically possible that a thing should simply happen to exist eternally. On the other hand, it is not logically possible for anything, even a Perfect Being, to have *an existence that is logically necessary*; for a blank, an absence of all existents, is not like a round square. It would seem better for believers in God-conceived-as-a-person to adopt Ewing's suggestion that God would have an existence 'necessary not because there would be any internal contradiction in denying it but because it was supremely good that God should exist'. For as noted in section 8.1, it is at least logically possible that an ethical need or requirement for a thing to exist should bear responsibility for that thing's actual existence: there is no contradiction here. And although its bearing of such responsibility could not be logically necessary, it might be necessary none the less. It might be what philosophers term 'necessary synthetically': necessary absolutely, but not in a way provable by conceptual analysis.

Compare how the inherent badness of misery might be thought to be necessary. Some philosophers have denied that misery has such badness. Conceptual analysis, mere appeals to ordinary language, would seem unable to prove their wrongness. None the less misery could plausibly be thought to have badness of a kind that follows necessarily from its being what it is. It could be thought of as intrinsically bad – i.e. bad if taken all alone, though it might sometimes have causal consequences which made it on the whole worthwhile – in absolutely all possible worlds.[5]

8.7 The reverse of the coin, however, is this. Suppose you are willing to take seriously the idea that an ethical need or requirement *can be creatively powerful* in the case of a divine person's existence. (In other words, this person might owe his existence simply to the ethical need for it. His existence could be eternal despite being explicable in this way. As Aquinas recognized, *creation* need not imply a beginning in time.) You might now come to view *this* position as having in it the seeds of *its* defeat. You might think it attractive to speculate that God, instead of being a person, is the creative ethical need for there to be a universe or universes. Very ordinary Neoplatonist theological thinking, this could allow you to continue to call God 'personal'. For the ethical need or requirement which supposedly requires a universe or universes *with creative success* can be imagined as acting as a benevolent person would, as creating a world for persons to inhabit, and maybe as being specially associated with a particular person, for example Christ.

8.8 Still, what can be said for the paradoxical notion that an ethical need or requirement *might itself be creatively successful*?

Wouldn't it be too purely abstract to act creatively?

Well, if by 'being purely abstract' you just mean 'having no practical power' then you entirely beg the question against Neoplatonism when you classify ethical requirements as always 'purely abstract'. Surely *requirements for the existence of things* are not at all clearly *realities of the wrong sort* for bringing things into existence. (The abstract truth that two and two make four, or the fact that quadratic equations cannot ride horses, would in contrast be realities quite wrong for this task.)

8.9 If it is complained that a requirement which did not issue from some already existing object, such as an inexplicably existing divine person, 'wouldn't be real enough to act creatively', then two things can be said in reply:

(A) *Only* a requirement which *did not issue from some already existing object* could possibly bear responsibility for the general fact of There Existing Something and Not Nothing – i.e. of there being at least one thing which is more than merely possible and which is more than just an abstract truth.

(B) It can look monstrous to suppose that an ethical requirement for the existence of a good world *could ever be unreal.* As if the sudden annihilation of all existing things would necessarily lead to a situation in which *it couldn't really matter* that they had been annihilated! Surely it could instead be really ethically needful that a world should be born again from the void.

Ethical needs, alias requirements, for the existence of various things, for example of good universes (and for the non-existence of other things, for example of a world of unalleviated misery), are not inevitably dependent on the existence of actual people sorrowing (or, in the case of the world of misery, rejoicing) at the absence of those things, or endowed with duties to bring them into existence (or to keep them out of it). Instead they can be real unconditionally. Like the fact that *if* there were two trillion apples and another two trillion then there *would be* four trillion apples, they can be real *no matter what.* (That fact, I take it, is a fact whether or not there are any apples or anybody to count things. Treating it as an example of one such entity, you may conclude that you have long believed in what philosophers sometimes call 'Platonic entities'.)

8.10 If we instead explained our world's existence by reference to the creative activity of an already existing divine person who himself simply happened to exist, then exactly how would this person create things? Would he just *will* the existence of a universe, his act of volition setting up a requirement much more likely to be powerful than any 'mere' ethical requirement? (Couldn't it be preferable to suppose that this act of volition was successful because it was a supremely good one, so that its success was itself ethically required?)

8.11 People new to this area tend to be troubled by a combination of several points:

(a) It is felt that modern thought has somehow established that Ethics is just an arbitrary or subjective matter like the etiquette of handling a soup spoon or whether you like mustard. That it is painfully old-fashioned to believe that there is something *in itself wrong* in, say, burning babies alive for one's amusement.

There is no room here to discuss this.

(b) It is felt that everyday life shows conclusively that ethical needs do not by themselves produce things. Many evil events happen: events whose non-happening was ethically required. Many good events fail to happen. Doesn't that prove Neoplatonism's wrongness?

No; for no Neoplatonist need deny that there are evils or maintain, say, that whenever it would be good for people to have something then that thing appears automatically without anyone's having to manufacture or grow it. Neoplatonism is not the view that *absolutely all ethical requirements* are satisfied.

This leads into the Problem of Evil which will be considered later (8.14 ff.).

(c) It is felt that one would have to identify some *mechanism whereby* ethical needs, requirements, grounds for the existence of this or that, produced their supposed effects. But this misses Neoplatonism's central point. Neoplatonism is the view that some ethical needs *are themselves* creatively effective, unaided by any mechanism. You might just as well ask for a mechanism which made misery intrinsically evil or a mechanism ensuring that two and two made four.

Either some consistent sets of ethical needs are creatively effective, unaided by any act of divine will, or else they aren't. Now, these alternatives *are equally simple*. Why? Well, if ethical needs, alias requirements, *are never* themselves creatively effective, then presumably this isn't just a matter of chance. But it isn't a matter of logic either, like the fact that bachelors are never married: there is no logical contradiction in supposing that some ethical requirement for the existence of such-and-such is actually able to produce its existence. Therefore it can only be a matter of *synthetic necessity* (8.6). Now, the Neoplatonist view is that, yes, there is a synthetic necessity in this area, but it is instead one which makes it true that some ethical requirements *are* creatively effective.

Whether this view is right is something which cannot be settled by conceptual analysis. The matter is not a logical, conceptual matter. But the actual existence of a universe (and of one, what's more, which seems fine tuned for Life) can suggest its rightness.

It is worth adding that there is nothing particularly obvious about the effectiveness of *mechanisms*. Machinery works only because the laws of physics are as they are, and it isn't at all obvious why they are like that.

It could further be added that the absence of all *mechanisms for giving creative effectiveness to ethical requirements* (steam engines, arrangements of superconducting magnets, miniature black holes, configurations of imps waving wands and exerting will-power, or whatever) means that there is no way in which we could determine from our armchairs 'whether the process would be likely to work'. There is no such thing as 'the a priori probability or improbability' of an ethical need's bearing responsibility for the existence of a divine person or of a universe.

(d) It is felt that any fool should be able to see that an ethical requirement *as such* couldn't possibly be creative. That this is just totally straightforward logic, no matter what I or what Mackie may say.

One reply to this objection is that there is certainly *some sense* in which it is correct. Look at the nine words, 'the reality of some particular ethical requirement as such'. You could choose to use those nine words to mean simply this: that it genuinely would be an excellent affair, a fulfilment of a need, if some particular situation were to exist. Now, this really could be so regardless of whether there were any realities of creative activity. So, you might well conclude, ethical requirements as such could obviously never act creatively. But your conclusion would turn on your having chosen to use those nine words in just that way. It is, after all, equally certain that *in some sense* no cow as such is brown, no bachelor as such ever blows his nose, and no judge as such spills ink on his court-room notes. In contrast, cows as such are female; bachelors as such always fail to be bigamists; and judges as such make court-room notes, I suspect, and I know that they sentence criminals. But as we all can see, there is no logical contradiction in a brown cow or a nose-blowing bachelor or an ink-spilling judge. And there is even *some sense* in which a cow *as such* can be brown. It can, for instance, be a brown cow rather than a white cow under brown paint.

This point gets fairly complicated when developed in detail: if interested in pursuing it please turn elsewhere.[6] Not only 'ethical requirement as such' but ''ethical requirement in itself', 'requirement which is merely and purely ethical', and many other such phrases threaten to be ambiguous in ways reflected by 'cow in itself', 'judge acting purely as a judge', and so on.

Remember, ethical requiredness is an abstraction. Now, it is to a large extent arbitrary how you are to cut up The Real when taking your abstractions from it. (Do minds, for instance, have spatial positions? The affair is in dispute even among those who think of our minds as mere aspects of our brains, which obviously do have positions, since they might be considered to be aspects too abstract to be positioned. When a ball rolls across a room, does one of its features, *its redness*, roll across too? Yes, one tends to answer, on the grounds that the redness isn't left behind; but if it does roll, then does *the fact that the ball is red* – or *its being red* – also roll? Here you could well answer No on the grounds that the ball is red no matter what its position. Yet how the ball's redness is any different from its being red you may find hard to say.) Further, whether a requirement of which *being ethical* was at the very least an aspect or feature *would be acting as an ethical requirement* if it acted creatively is not an issue which has very typically occurred to those who developed the ordinary language of Ethics. Why, the ordinary person – not to mention the philosopher of law – might actually have some problems in saying just when a judge *was acting as a judge*.

You can set up more or less what linguistic techniques you please for dealing with this messy area. Don't imagine that you are thereby settling whether Neoplatonism is right.

8.12 Neoplatonism's fundamental idea, that *ethical requirements* can in some cases be *creative ethical requirements*, is a 'metaphysical' one, an adventurous conjecture. It is not being suggested that laws of physics will on a little examination be discovered to be everywhere breaking down in favour of 'laws of teleology' while atoms and light rays will be found to possess some dim conception of goodness. It is not being held that the ethical need that you should continue to live will save you when you fall from a sky-scraper. Yet it is perverse to conclude that Neoplatonism is therefore infected with a speculativeness from which the kind of theory more common in the late twentieth century is immune. As if the actual existence of a universe couldn't possibly count as some kind of *evidence* for the view that some abstract factor – abstract enough, that is, to be a 'Platonic entity', real unconditionally, instead of being just something dramatic inside that universe like a magnetic monopole or a black hole – had acted creatively! As though the world's causal orderliness, which Neoplatonism might hope to explain (since it is the existence *of this causally ordered world* which is supposedly ethically required, and not anything as vague as the-existence-of-something-or-other), could again not count as evidence, so that we ought to prefer a 'non-speculative' view that events fall into Causation's patterns for no reason whatever! As if one ought simply to add to one's stamp album the fact that our universe has physical laws and constants such that minimal changes in them would have made it lifeless! Or as though it were clear that Multiple Worlds and observational selection effect offered a uniquely acceptable, non-speculative way of accounting for such a fact!

8.13 Can it be right, however, for a Neoplatonist to talk of a Design Argument when belief in *a Designer* has been abandoned?

Perhaps it would be better to say 'Teleological Argument', but the point is surely unimportant. Biologists who report that hearts are designed for pumping the blood are not committing themselves to the view that hearts were designed by somebody.

What *is* important, on the other hand, is that Neoplatonism does not find *complexities* specially hard to deal with, in a way forcing us to invoke a Designer. It would (1.32) be absurd to propose that ethical requirements could be creatively effective and then add, 'just so long as they required nothing too complicated'. Hence if it would be a good thing for God-as-an-immensely-intelligent-person to plan and to create a world whose laws very complexly conspired to make Life possible, then exactly such a world could be produced by Neoplatonism's God, a reality which may be 'personal' (8.7) but isn't *a person*. (Think of how immensely complicated mathematical facts can dictate firm limits to what is possible in engineering, for instance, without those facts springing from the mind of an immensely intelligent being or dictating this or that because such a being so willed.) If a world having causal orderliness of some very complicated sort would be better than a blank or than any world lacking such orderliness then that, says Neoplatonism, might be enough to account for the existence of such a world. Neoplatonism is the theory that ethical requirements *can themselves* sometimes be creatively powerful, and the good is the ethically required regardless of whether it is simple or complicated.

Are Evils Conclusive Evidence Against God?

8.14 But why have a causally ordered world at all, with all the ills which this involves – the difficulties of struggling with obstinate materials, the constant threat of broken limbs, famines, earthquakes, the fact that Evolution produces plague germs as well as humans, the narrowing of our experiences by the limitations of our perceptual apparatus, the way in which Time's flow hurries each of us towards annihilation, and so on? Why not have instead a realm of immaterial minds perhaps communicating telepathically – or not communicating at all, for why not have each one filled with a perpetual succession of pleasurable, colourful, interesting experiences, far superior to such tedious matters as our actual loves and friendships?

My main reaction to such questions is that they are so obviously difficult that nobody has a right to be confident about them. I can think of advantages in inhabiting a world ruled by causal laws in which we are free to make our own paths instead of having them made for us through the automatic filling of our minds with an endless succession of visions as in a drug addict's dream. I feel the power of Tillich's remark that creation is (thank heaven) the creation of Life with all its greatness and its danger. I myself would hesitate before exchanging family and friends and shared experiences for the pseudo-life of one of those disembodied brains of science fiction, stimulated with a constant stream of new and interesting patterns by cleverly programmed computers. But to defend against the Problem of Evil we are not required to make out any very powerful case for the goodness of various features of our world: for instance, its causal orderliness. Rather, we need only show (i) that it is far from being clearly stupid to think that these features have considerable goodness, and (ii) that we might therefore reasonably suspect that Reality would be better if it included such things somewhere, despite their being associated with evils.

Let us look at these two points in more detail.

8.15 First, the point that there is no need actually to prove our world's goodness.

My claim is that it isn't up to the theist to show that Pure Reasoners asking themselves what would be a good sort of world for God to create would be well advised to say, for instance, 'Make it a world of causal orderliness, a world ruled by physical laws!' The situation is instead that the idea that ethical requirements could be creatively effective can seem to give a tidy answer to the question of 'why there is something rather than nothing'; that (8.5 and note 3) there just is no other plausible answer to this question, unless you count yourself as answering it when you hold that a universe or a creating deity simply happens to exist; that the answer brings with it other answers to what could well seem to be interesting problems, such as that of why the world is causally ordered and why it seems fine tuned for the production of living beings (for these affairs might be explained either by direct appeal to their ethical requiredness or else by saying that a divine person, himself owing his existence to his ethical requiredness, had judged it good to produce them); and that this explanatory package can look powerful enough to be worth taking seriously even in the face of strong doubts about whether a good world would look much like the world we see. (Think once again of Pauli's decision to believe in neutrinos: 8.2.) Frankly, had I been invited to join Alfonso the Tenth in giving the Creator some advice then I might easily have suggested avoiding causal laws altogether; but this isn't to say that the suggestion would have been justifiably confident.

8.16 Now for the second point: that it might at least be a good thing that Reality should include *somewhere* a world such as ours, despite its evils.

There are two sides to this. (I) There is the recognition that this is a world which does include evils. (II) There is the suggestion that it could none the less be worth having, at least as part of Reality – the implication being that it might perhaps not be true that all of Reality is like this.

It is, I think, not just ridiculous but morally repulsive to suggest that the world contains no evils. The most that could reasonably be held is that evils are the results of conflicts between ethical needs, for instance the needs to which people point when developing the Free Will Defence against the Problem of Evil. The Free Will Defence falls into two parts. First, moral evils (murders etc.) are a result of the misuse of free will. When freely deciding to produce something bad you are evilly ensuring that the ethical need for some good situation to be produced is overruled by the ethical need for the world to be one in which people are free. Second, physical evils (e.g. earthquakes) are consequences of our living in a world ruled by causal laws. Had the world been ruled by magic instead then freedom would be absent or reduced or made into something trivial, perhaps – so runs one version of the Defence – because God's hand would then be too obvious so that we became God's puppets. (This Defence, by the way, is not at all clearly incompatible with believing that our free decisions are themselves determined by causal laws. It is often claimed that freedom is, roughly, being able to make up one's own mind, and that a fully deterministic computer could make up its own mind if its workings were sufficiently intricate.)

Now, what if this meets with the objection that we can imagine causally ordered universes in which it was determined that no evils would ever happen? No getting scratched by thorns, no earthquakes, and even no free decisions taking evil forms (for as noted just now, freedom may be compatible with determinism; hence we might imagine a universe in which it was determined that nobody would ever decide matters badly). (a) It could be answered that this might not in fact be possible in the case of any complex universe. Suppose coin tossing were fully deterministic in the sense that the result of any coin toss could be predicted by a demon who knew enough about the spinning coin, the surface on which it would land, the wind, etc. It wouldn't at once follow that some initial arrangement of a deterministic universe's particles would make it a universe in which none of a billion billion coins ever fell heads when tossed. 'Imagining' such a universe wouldn't settle the question. (b) It could be said as well that even if an absence of all evils were possible in a few universes, it wouldn't follow that these were the only universes worth creating. Known for his slogan that the world 'is the best possible', Leibniz took pains to make clear that by 'world' he *did not* mean just the spatio-temporal region open to our inspection. He meant, he wrote, the totality of existence, the whole sequence of things to infinity.[7]

A world in *that* sense could include any number of small-u universes of the kind considered by modern cosmologists. Leibniz took very seriously the idea that Reality is infinitely rich. The good of variety is central to his thinking.

8.17 What goodness could Variety have, though, when no single thing can carry more than a very limited part of it? Suppose we rather controversially called a man's mind from birth to death 'a single thing' despite how the patterns of his experiences seemed to be carried by hugely many independently existing atoms, atoms replaced at regular intervals (since, like candle flames or eddies in a stream, brain cells constantly renew their constituent particles). Shouldn't we still face the problem that each man's experiences both in space and in time are severely limited?

Why, indeed, would a good world ever include *changes*? Why create situations and then have Time's tooth gnaw away at them?

Well, I find it useful to model Time as *not* gnawing at realities. I take my inspiration from Einstein's statement that it is 'natural to think of a four-dimensional existence, instead of, as hitherto, the evolution of a three-dimensional existence'.[8] That is, I accept what is known as the B-theory of Time, now very popular among philosophers. Past events are no more absent from existence than Africa is absent from existence just because you find yourself in Canada. *Past-ness*, *present-ness*, and *futurity* are as relative as *here-ness* and *over-there-ness*.

Again, I find it useful to picture Reality's elements 'monistically': that is, as less separate in their existence than people tend to think. Inspiration for this could be found in the writings of Spinoza or of F. H. Bradley and other British Hegelians, or in quantum-physical 'Bell experiments' (4.48) which suggest that particles very far apart can still be intimately linked. Maybe the world's parts, and hence the lives of separate individuals, are incapable of existing each in isolation from the others: compare how a length or a colour could not exist all on its own. To suggest this is very different from saying ridiculously that every mind is aware of the experiences of all other minds,

Reality being a large seaside boarding house with no private bedroom in which to take refuge from the society of the place.'

8.18 To see how very hard it could be to make the Problem of Evil a conclusive one, let us look at what might strike someone as an immediately decisive point. Obviously better than our actual experiences, it could seem, would be experiences not of *living*, of selecting paths through dangerous environments governed by causal laws, but of something else: namely, the contents of god-like minds. Instead of having a consciousness which casts a flickering light on only a tiny part of the world's structure, wouldn't it be far better to be a Laplacean demon surveying all space and time? And then, wouldn't it be yet better to be aware of all conceivable world-structures and even of absolutely all facts about possibilities? To perceive all logically possible paintings, poems, symphonies, games of chess, mathematical truths, jokes, and so forth through the omniscience traditionally ascribed to God-as-a-person? But if so, then doesn't Actual Experience refute the theistic vision of Reality?

8.19 Oddly enough, the answer is No. Not even were all this so, would the vision be refuted. An omniscient mind contemplating a possible physical world would know it in all its details, as would a Laplacean demon, yet it would also know exactly how any such world would look to beings inside it: beings experiencing forests, animals, paintings, symphonies, laughter, and *curiosity about many things outside their experience*. But this means that even Eternal Omniscience would have to include *areas of ignorance* in one important sense of those words. For to know just how it feels to be in pain, you have to be or to have been in pain to some extent; and similarly, to know just how it feels to be ignorant of and curious about various things outside your experience you must in some area, part, aspect, or mode of your mind actually be or have been ignorant. It is impossible to have, in one and the same region of one's mental being, both an awareness of having always known everything and an experience of precisely what it feels like to be curious about things.

Hence, as Spinoza saw, no appeal to Experience could easily establish that the actual scheme of things was even different from (let alone inferior to) one in which all experiences were divine ones. For how could a divine mind know just what it would be like to be, say, Spinoza, if there had never been in any part of that mind any feeling of *actually being* Spinoza?

8.20 It could seem, then, that to make the Problem of Evil truly crushing one would have to prove that the experiences of

humans, or, for that matter, dolphins or bats, would be sufficiently worthless for it to be beneath the dignity of any god-like
mind to know just what it would be like – just what it would *feel
like* – to be a human or a dolphin or a bat. But is that even
specially plausible, let alone provable? Despite their unsatisfac-
toriness our experiences are surely not without interest, and in
any case it is untraditional to suppose that the divine mind shields
itself from the 'indignity' of having certain kinds of knowledge. A
Proof that God-as-a-person Cannot Exist because if he did then,
being omniscient, he would have to know just what it felt like to
be *you*, would surely be rather a feeble one.

8.21 The belief that Reality is composed solely of a god-like
mind or minds turns out to be somewhat difficult to distinguish
from the combination of Monism – i.e. the doctrine that single
existents can be complex not just in having complex combinations
of qualities but in actually bearing complex patterns, and that our
universe might itself be a single existent, something whose parts
are too abstract to exist in isolation (8.17) – and the Good-of-
Variety defence against the Problem of Evil.

What I have in mind is this. Suppose we are guided by
traditional views about the properties of God-as-a-person. We
must then accept, first, that a god-like mind or minds would
know everything or at least would know immensely much,
including all the details of all possible law-controlled universes
and of what it would feel like to live in the inhabitable ones; and
second, that any such mind would be not just a collection of
separately existing parts, but a monistic whole. Yet this may be
little different from supposing that creative ethical requirements
have generated one or more centres of experience, any such
centre being a monistic whole, and that the pattern of experience
present in each such whole is immensely rich because experience
is the better for being varied.

8.22 I never saw any argument against Monism that was worth
much philosophically. (Often attacks on it take the form just of
saying that any child can see that Reality is made up of vastly
many distinguishable elements related to one another in complex
ways; but no monist ever denied *that*.) Yet even were Monism
obviously wrong, it could still seem that *varied patterns* could be
very much worth having. And, granted that Variety can contribute to The Worthwhile, it could well be judged a case of silly
fantasizing if the believer in creative ethical requirements were to
decide that what had actually been created was severely limited
in its variety: that, for instance, it was just a single universe
stretching no more than a few billion light years and recollapsing

after only a couple of billion centuries. It would be more plausible to suppose that ethical requirements had created a situation of great (or infinite?) richness, including greatly many different universes obeying different laws. (Plus, conceivably, a great deal more that was not law-controlled universe? Free-floating awareness, perhaps, of how all possible games of chess would end and all possible symphonies sound?)

In the absence of the doctrine that ethical requirements can act creatively, belief in all this richness might itself be very foolish fantasizing. Yet when that doctrine is accepted then any foolishness might instead lie in denying it (cf. 5.37; 8.2). The question of what beliefs about the world are foolish cannot be separated from that of why there exists any world at all.

8.23 Against this background, how unimpressive it can be when someone greets theism with the protest that obviously there could be situations much better than those which Actual Experiences make known to us – perhaps universes obeying other causal laws which led to fewer disasters, or perhaps situations in which there were no laws but only, e.g., free-floating awareness of music! For anyone accepting theism could accept such points also. It is not up to the theist to defend the opinion that Reality is limited to the regions that we can see, or that there are no better regions, or that awareness of all possible music is never had anywhere. Believing either in Neoplatonism's God or in a divine mind whose existence is due to its ethical requiredness, you might find yourself positively forced to believe in an immensely rich Reality which could well contain experiences of lives in immensely many universes – universes governed, maybe, by an immense variety of physical laws. And you might perhaps feel encouraged to believe also in the existence of greatly many experiences *not* governed by such laws.

In respectable philosophical circles it is today becoming possible to make such points: points well understood by such not inconsiderable thinkers as Leibniz and Spinoza but tending until recently to be greeted with blank stares or worse. One of the many reasons for the change is that cosmologists have become increasingly confident that The Real extends very much further than we can see. Another is the now very well-known work of D. Lewis, who argues that absolutely all possibilites exist (4.68). Thus he believes in all the universes which a Neoplatonist could be forced to believe in, and in a great many others too.

See also note 51 to Chapter 4, for attempts by R. H. Kane, R. Nozick, and P. Unger to 'minimize arbitrariness' by supposing that all possibilities exist somewhere.

The Tie Between Basic Laws and Life in a God-Created Universe

8.24 If, despite evils, God manages to be real, either as God-as-a-person or as the God of Neoplatonism, then how would matters stand in the universe which is known to us? What would be the relationship between its basic laws, God, and the existence of living things?

Let us agree that God mustn't be imagined as having selected the world's parts individually to suit particular needs, designing organisms (plague germs included) in all their details or giving the elements their chemical properties in ways unconstrained by any laws (which Mendeleev disproved). The question then becomes: Were the laws selected so that they would generate living things more or less inevitably, or was there a marked element of chance in the affair?

The temptation is to reason as follows. (a) To throw light on how there manages to be a universe fine tuned for Life we could tell a story of multiple universes and of an observational selection effect. A life-containing universe might be expected to come about sooner or later, just by chance variations between the universes. (b) But it could be that vastly many universes would be needed before it could become likely that even one of them would be life-containing. (c) On the other hand, it can safely be assumed that God would ensure that any universes he created were life-containing. (d) Hence believers in God should be specially inclined to see the evolution of living beings in our universe as following more or less inevitably from its basic laws, laws God-selected to ensure this.

However, such reasoning might be faulty. A. R. Peacocke has been arguing recently that God might perhaps have created up to infinitely many universes, confident that at least some (or, indeed, infinitely many) would become life-containing just by chance.

Again, it could be that God, contemplating all the universes which Chance could throw up against the background of some particular set of basic laws, chose for creation just those universes in which Chance led to living things, perhaps because symmetry breakings happened to take place in life-encouraging ways. (I am allowing myself to speak of God as 'contemplating' and 'choosing', although on my preferred, Neoplatonist account of God this could only be very metaphorical talk. Also I am assuming that it makes sense to speak of choosing a universe for creation on the grounds that Chance did this or that in it. This could be so if one had an Einsteinian view about Time – 8.17 – or if one were willing to speak of matters, coin tossings for instance, as involving Chance just because their outcomes were very delicately dependent on initial conditions rather than because they were fundamentally indeterministic.)

8.25 Would it then follow that the God hypothesis should be irrelevant to whether one thinks that Nature's basic laws are life-guaranteeing?

No. For we can say at least this: that in God's absence it would be utterly astonishing if those laws were life-guaranteeing – unless, perhaps, basic laws could themselves vary from one to another of vastly many universes, which is certainly conceivable yet can be thought very implausible (3.11–.12). In God's absence, one would have to tell a story involving variations and an observational selection effect. The variations could most plausibly come about through differences in early symmetry breakings; but no matter how they came about, they would have to be fairly wide variations leading to universes of which many were life-excluding. In God's absence it would be unacceptably strange (1.21–.23; 5.29; 7.8–.9; 7.11) if laws which did not vary within an ensemble of universes dictated force strengths, particle masses, etc. that were life-permitting – i.e. that were precisely such as to suggest, on the one hand, the God explanation, and on the other the explanation in terms of multiple and varied universes and of Observational Selection.

8.26 In contrast, if God were a reality then the basic laws of this and of all other actually existing universes might indeed make it more or less inevitable that living beings would evolve. For one way in which God might fine tune a universe would be (1.22; 2.7; 2.55; 3.11) by choosing laws which dictated a life-encouraging combination of force strengths, particle masses, early expansion speed, and so on, when slightly different laws would have dictated life-excluding combinations.

8.27 Let us sum this up. While we may well not have (A) *that God implies all-dictating basic laws which make Life more or less inevitable*, we could none the less have (B) *that God's ABSENCE almost certainly implies the ABSENCE of any such laws, whereas if God were real then they might be present.*

Contrast this conclusion with the widespread belief that anyone who speaks of God and of our universe's being specially designed for Life must be 'anti-scientific' and *opposed* to all-dictating laws!

It should however be added (cf. 4.77) that any set of all-dictating laws, even if God-selected, would surely *not* be 'so much simpler than its competitors that it just had to be right'. For just as not even God could control the fact that two and two make four, so not even God could bring it about that the simplest all-dictating physical theory was also one which led both to Life and to a very strong appearance of fine tuning. You might almost as well suppose that God could so arrange things that a supremely simple, all-dictating theory covered the rocks with a hundred verses from Genesis.

8.28 Finally, can it be assumed that all God-created universes would be life-containing, no matter how different their basic laws might be?

As indicated in section 4.79, failure to assume it could well be judged too strange *if* by 'a universe' we are to mean a system of causally interacting things entirely disconnected from all other such systems. But as Chapter 4 explained we might instead mean something else. For example, very far separated regions in an infinitely large cosmos or huge domains of differently broken symmetry inside a gigantic inflationary cosmos could count as 'separate universes', and God might be thought to have created even the lifeless regions/domains/universes, so as to give completeness to his creation.

Much might depend on whether you judged that a completeness which no living thing could experience could none the less be good.

Chapter Nine

Conclusions

The chapter reviews various results argued for earlier, developing some a little further. Despite the doubtful nature of many individual items of evidence we see strong signs that our universe is fine tuned to Life's needs. The existence of many and very varied universes supplies a tidy explanation. So, however, does theism when developed sensibly.

At first sight an attractive third alternative is that living organisms take many very different forms even in this universe of ours; the fine tuning is then an illusion due to our seeing everything against the background of the Earthling's biology. But this alternative runs into fairly severe difficulties.

The chapter also draws morals about how scientific and philosophical reasoning ought to work. We need to be guided by analogies and probabilistic arguments, relying on feedback loops to suggest various speculations and to test their success. In their concern for rigour and for knowledge philosophers have too often scorned intelligent guesswork.

The Book's Main Conclusions

9.1 If Chapter 2 was on anything like the right lines then the evidence of fine tuning is impressively strong. True, quite a few of the items listed may easily have been mistakes. Others of them, though, appear fairly well established. Even being wrong by factors of a thousand or a million would scarcely reduce the interest of many items when what is being claimed is a tuning accurate to one part in many billions of billions. Again, the sheer number of the claims is quite a strong insurance that not all of them are faulty. They were culled from the writings of experts. Physicists and cosmologists of today are little inclined to treat our universe's early conditions, and the physically and cosmologically important constants, as brute, inexplicable facts which are to be treated as 'natural' just because they characterize Nature as we find her. And they do not assume automatically that the same facts would be found in all physically possible universes. Instead they puzzle over such things as the early cosmic expansion speed, the cosmic smoothness, the excess of matter over antimatter, and so on.

Admittedly, many physicists and cosmologists are eager to show that this or that is dictated by physical principles so elegant that they just have to be right. There, after all, is the stuff of Nobel prizes. Yet it has come to look quaintly old-fashioned to take it for granted that absolutely all the main cosmic parameters will lend themselves to such treatment. For, first, we have long had indications that physics is probabilistic at a very basic level; second, we now have theories of symmetry breaking which show how force strengths and particle masses might vary probabilistically (2.52–.53; 4.19–.25), the Inflationary Cosmos supplying us with a mechanism which would allow even probabilistic affairs to be settled in the same way for as far out as our telescopes can probe; third, we also have fairly well-developed theories – that of Inflation is only one among many – which indicate that the region visible to us could very well be supplemented by vastly many other huge regions, 'universes' of the small-u kind; and fourth, fine tuning to Life's requirements would be easy to understand in the cases of *observable* universes if there were indeed vastly many universes and if their characteristics were very varied.

Surely no Principle of Pure Reason tells us that what we see *is not* subject to Observational Selection effects set up by Life's prerequisites: by the need, for example, for life-containing universes to be unturbulent or for their early expansion speeds to fall inside a narrow range, or for their force strengths and particle masses to be appropriately distributed. And evidence of fine tuning is plentiful enough to suggest that such observational selection effects are extremely important. (Remember, the words 'fine tuning' are not being used in a way that begs the question of whether there is a divine Fine Tuner. *Evidence of fine tuning* just means (1.4) *evidence that living beings would not have evolved had fundamental conditions been slightly different.*)

At the very least, the apparent fine tuning would seem to reveal that if any theory dictates the values of absolutely all physical constants and other cosmologically important numbers then that theory is not 'so much simpler than its competitors that it just has to be right'. So far as concerns physics, this could be the book's most significant claim. One needs some kind of selection from a wider field: some selection *either* of life-encouraging numbers from among those allowed by a theory which is not all-dictating but leaves these numbers open to variation, most plausibly through random symmetry breaking, *or else* of a life-encouraging all-dictating theory taken from a field of more or less equally simple theories.

9.2 Now, one thing which the above paragraphs illustrate is that scientists try to build up world-pictures which are simple and consistent. Tidy hypotheses present themselves to their minds, together with ideas of what things they might well expect to discover were those hypotheses right. When they do then seem to discover such things, they look on the hypotheses as strengthened.

Still, other hypotheses might explain the same discoveries just as tidily. And in the case of the fine tuning, an account in terms of Multiple Worlds/universes plus Observational Selection may not be the sole one that deserves to be taken seriously. Much of the book has been concerned with two possible competitors. One of them is the God hypothesis: divine selection could replace Observational Selection. The other – it could be thought to have received oddly little attention in these pages when so many people would so much prefer it – is that any fine tuning is just an illusion of us Earthlings. Intelligent living organisms might often be very unlike those on Earth, and much less fussy in their requirements. They might stand in no need of chemistry, for example, or of planetary surfaces to inhabit.

9.3 It was argued (Chapter 8) that the God hypothesis is a strong one. God need not be viewed as a person whose existence and whose powers are utterly reasonless. One possibility is to treat the word 'God' in Neoplatonist fashion. God would then not be a person at all. God would be a creatively effective ethical requirement for the existence of a (good) universe or universes.

Again, even God-as-a-person would not have to exist reasonlessly. His existence, his benevolence, his knowledge, the creative efficacy of his acts of will, might all be accounted for in terms of their ethical requiredness.

There is nothing logically absurd in either of these positions. Just examining the concept of *an ethical requirement for the existence of something* cannot teach us that such a requirement will be creatively effective, yet neither does it reveal its ineffectiveness. *Requirements for the existence of things* could seem to be realities of the right general kind for creative tasks. And if ethical requirements were all of them creatively ineffective then, I reasoned, their *in*effectiveness would involve just as much ontological drama – just as many 'synthetic necessities' (8.6; 8.11[c]) – as would their effectiveness.

True, the Problem of Evil presents a severe challenge to any belief in God. But instead of claiming that evils are unreal the theist can attribute them to conflicts between ethical requirements. (Some of the conflicts would be produced by our misuse of the good of free choice.) Moreover, the teachings of Experience are powerless to refute even Spinoza's theory that all experiences are those of a divine mind (8.18–.20). Knowing everything, such a mind would of course know just how it felt to be *you* and ignorant of many facts, including the fact that your thinkings were only elements in divine thinkings.

I have always felt very uncomfortable when suggesting that the Problem of Evil 'can be solved', i.e. that it fails to be decisive. One's gut feeling is that anyone who suggests this must be defending all manner of horrors. But although (as Hume so convincingly demonstrated) gut feelings have their place in philosophy, they oughtn't to be permitted to triumph immediately over even very strong counter-arguments. Now, the arguments against calling the Problem of Evil decisive do seem very strong.

The God hypothesis, besides being compatible with the hypothesis of multiple universes (for why should God be supposed to have created just a single universe?), can offer to explain affairs which that other hypothesis would appear to leave unexplained. It can offer to explain why natural laws are life-permitting, provided that such things as force strengths and particle masses take appropriate values (Chapter 3). Again, it can offer to explain why there is ever anything worth calling a natural law. *And* why there are things worth the name of *existing objects* (as distinct from mere possibilities and truths about them, e.g. the unconditionally true truth that it would be better that various unalleviatedly evil universes remained in the realm of mere possibility instead of taking on actual existence). Now, its potential ability to explain these affairs might encourage us to accept it despite the qualms that the Problem of Evil arouses.

This is in no way a denial that it ought to arouse them. The Problem of Evil is certainly strong enough to make theism an uncomfortable position.

9.4 The 'Earthling's illusion' hypothesis is in contrast a thoroughly pleasant one. How fascinating it is to speculate about beings not inhabiting planetary surfaces and with bodies not based on chemistry! Further, the notion that talk of fine tuning is all a matter of lack of imagination goes well with my conviction that far too many people have shown crass unimaginativeness when considering what the universe might be like. Yet unfortunately the hypothesis is much less viable than first appearances could suggest (1.27; 2.50–.51; 7.13). For a start, those who oppose it need not be making bold claims about the rarity of living beings in all possible universes. The Fly on the Wall Story (1.24) shows that they need consider only what would have resulted from *slight changes in this universe of ours*. (Slight changes, that is to say, in matters such as force strengths. The argument from fine tuning of course involves the claim – 2.49; 7.12 – that these would lead to great changes in such affairs as whether the universe recollapsed quickly.) Again, there are arguments to show that the only plausible life forms in this universe are those which are chemically based (2.33; 2.50).

Besides, what if we did some day find non-chemical life, for instance inside stars like our sun or in neutron stars? Our universe would still need tuning to considerable accuracy for there to be stars of any type.

9.5 One argument I used in this connection may have been a bit weak. If intelligent life were as easily achieved as some people think, I said (1.27), then why have we no evidence of extraterrestrial intelligent beings? But this could invite the reply that living beings may take many forms not based on chemistry, *none of them* easy to achieve. After all, we do know that organisms based on chemistry are possible; but all the same, we have no evidence of extraterrestrial chemically based life forms. Perhaps Life's beginnings always involve tremendous luck so that it is everywhere very difficult to make the move from an ideally life-encouraging environment – maybe a sun's outer layers or the high interior of a neutron star? – to the actual presence of living things.

Perhaps, too, other life forms would be so different from those on Earth that it would be absurd to expect twentieth-century mankind to have evidence of their existence. Beings based on plasmas could be confined to the depths of the sun and therefore invisible to us. And we might have little hope of detecting neutron star life, life based on the nuclear strong force instead of on the electromagnetism that underlies chemistry, until we had learned how to probe neutron stars with apparatus able to survive there.

The argument by which I set most store is instead the one mentioned a moment ago: that considerable fine tuning – of the cosmic expansion rate, for instance, or of the masses of various superheavy particles (which seem important to the excess of matter over antimatter), or of the degree of turbulence – is needed for there to be such things as stars, whether neutron or otherwise. Life would surely have stood a very poor chance had the universe recollapsed almost at once, or had it quickly become one of light rays only, or of black holes only, or had it expanded very rapidly into cold, enormously dilute gases, etc. (Chapter 2, esp. 2.49–.50).

9.6 Is that right, though? Here you could perhaps point to the speculations of people such as F. Dyson. Dyson suggests that intelligence could survive indefinitely in the enormously dilute universe of a far, far future if it used slow-moving processes cunningly. Even the decay of all ordinary matter would not necessarily spell disaster. Intelligent life might come to be based on positronium states, 'atoms' each consisting of an electron and a positron separated by a distance greater than that between us and the furthest objects seen by our telescopes. Such life would be immensely slow-moving, yet in a sufficiently long-lasting universe this might not matter.

At an opposite extreme, F. J. Tipler has proposed that intelligent life might continue to exist into the final instants of a Big Squeeze if it exploited very-fast-ticking processes. Its thinking would have to proceed even more rapidly than that of any neutron-star person (whose entire life could itself be over in well under a billionth of a second). None the less, such thinking could be very intelligent. Tipler feels that it could be god-like.[1]

My reaction to all this is (cf. 2.50) that it is speculation such as makes both the many-universes hypothesis and the God hypothesis seem extraordinarily tame. And in any case, neither Dyson's slow-ticking life forms nor Tipler's fast-ticking ones are imagined as having evolved in Darwinian fashion. Instead they are the results of planning: planning by our descendants or by other organisms whose origins were Darwinian. Hence without whatever fine tuning is needed for there to be such organisms, there never would be those slow- or fast-ticking entities. We therefore *cannot* argue, for instance, that life of the sort which Tipler prophesies for the final moments of a Big Squeeze could equally well have existed in the earliest instants of a Big Bang so that ours could have been an observed universe even had it recollapsed within a microsecond.

Sometimes, it is true, Dyson-like ideas are developed without any mention of planning by organisms like ourselves. People content themselves with suggesting that while fine tuning could indeed be essential for observers appearing as soon as we have in the history of our universe, it wouldn't be needed by ones evolving later. (For instance, J. D. Barrow has suggested that the cosmic smoothness needed for Life and for Observership, while difficult to achieve at 'early' times such as those we live in, might be an altogether natural condition at late times.) But to this one of several attractive replies would be (cf. 1.27) that it would be very odd if *only life as we know it* required fine tuning.

In short, my conclusion remains that fine tuning can only very implausibly be dismissed as an illusion of Earthlings. We thus seem forced towards the hypothesis of many and varied universes, or the God hypothesis.

9.7 Suppose I am wrong in this, however. Suppose that by far the best way to deal with any seeming evidence of fine tuning would be to flee from the 'over-dramatic', 'absurdly metaphysical', 'wildly speculative' idea of God or of multiple universes, taking refuge in a 'non-speculative' notion that Life can evolve virtually anywhere: for example, at the sun's centre, or in neutron stars, or in frozen hydrogen, or in the near vacuum of interstellar space, or in a universe consisting solely of positronium states. Would this show that all the fuss about fine tuning in present-day books and journals had absolutely no importance? Not at all. Its importance would lie in how it showed that the idea of life in neutron stars, or at the sun's centre, etc. really did need to be taken seriously lest we be driven to the dismal alternative of believing in God or in many universes.

Feedback Loops and Predictions

9.8 Assuming, though, that *God* and *multiple universes* are the only plausible contenders, just what gives them their plausibility?

One of the book's main themes has been that feedback loops of two main types are of great importance here.

First, there are the ones which assure us that various facts really should be treated as problems instead of being shrugged off as 'how things just happen to be'. And second, there are those which affect our views about which alleged facts *are* facts.

Existing in close association, the two kinds of loop lead to theories that are well integrated and sensitive to new evidence. Still, these virtues by no means guarantee that all rational beings will in the end be led to one and the same world-picture.

9.9 Loops of the first type, loops connecting tidy explanations with needs for things to be explained (5.29), are so important that it comes as a shock that they remain unbaptized. Let us call them 'Merchant's Thumb' loops, or loops set up by 'the MT Principle', in honour of Ernest Bramah's story (1.10). All thumbs must be somewhere, yet the positioning of the silk merchant's stands in special need of explanation because a tidy explanation offers itself for its being so positioned. Every fish must have some length, but the catching of a fish of the only length which can be observed is 'special' because it suggests either a benevolent, fish-creating person or the presence of many differently lengthed fish.

It is the MT Principle which suggests the God hypothesis and the hypothesis of multiple universes.

9.10 Loops of the second type are more widely recognized. Putting one's faith in them is often referred to as 'using the hypothetico-deductive method': 'the HD method' for short. Having found out what needs explanation by using loops of the first sort, we then submit various explanatory hypotheses to observational trials by using ones of the second. True enough, we may lack the ability to predict just what observations would result from the correctness of the various hypotheses. (Hypothesizing that someone will murder Mr Smith may not be enough for a prediction that an airgun will be used, rather than an axe.) Aided by common sense, however, we can say that this or that observation was quite to be expected against the background of some hypothesis, whereas some other observation gives the hypothesis grave difficulties.

That allows for the Testing by Experience which is so essential. Yet the testing will not be completely impartial – which is what permits people, all of them genuinely sane, to build up very different pictures of the world. For the feedback loops are not just matters of what general kinds of observation (e.g. Mr Smith-murdered-somehow) could be expected on given hypotheses, and of whether suitable observations are supplied by Actual Experience, observations increasing confidence in those hypo–theses. They are also loops that encourage us to interpret particular experiences in particular ways. Hence what one clever and well-balanced person looks on as an experimental refutation another may treat as experimental error ('Never accept evidence until it is confirmed by theory!') or as a case of actual confirmation.

9.11 How does all this work out in practice?

Consider the hypothesis of many and varied universes and of an observational selection effect. This hypothesis helps to throw light on the truth, if it is a truth, that the observed universe manages to have features that are essential not just to life of the sort we find on Earth but to absolutely all life which we could plausibly expect this universe to contain. It can therefore increase our confidence that the truth *is* a truth. It can encourage us to dismiss claims that life forms made of plasma have been seen through the windows of a spaceship that came from the sun, or that regular radio pulses from neutron stars are generated by advanced civilizations. It can encourage us to predict that studies of galaxy formation will confirm that galaxies would never have formed had the early cosmic expansion speed been slightly different. It can encourage us to resist the idea that some physical theory, so simple that it just has to be right, has dictated all force strengths and particle masses. It can encourage us to expect new instances of fine tuning. And so on. (See Chapter 6, esp. 6.33.)

This kind of thing is of such obvious importance to science that it may today have become merely silly to dismiss all multiple-universe talk as 'mere metaphysics' and thus unworthy of any serious scientist's attention.

Look, for instance, at S. W. Hawking's estimate (2.4) that an expansion speed decrease at early times by one part in a million million would have meant Life's absence. Nowadays, when the God hypothesis is so unpopular, many scientists would initially be very reluctant to accept that Life balanced on such a razor edge. Hawking's estimate would thus suggest to them only that Hawking was wrong. But these scientists could well change their minds when they saw that a varied ensemble of universes and an observational selection effect could do much the same work as God might do. Now, this could be important well outside the galaxy formation studies with which Hawking was concerned. For given many universes, just why should they vary in such things as their expansion speeds? Well, perhaps because force strengths came to be settled probabilistically during symmetry breaking.

The scientists would be being brought to remember two facts which many of them could prefer to forget: that even probabilistic physics can be physics, and that talk of observational selection effects can be good science. The user of 'anthropic' explanations (Chapter 6) is not just making the trivial prediction *that we will never find anything that proves that we cannot exist*, or resorting to *a stop-gap method of reducing our puzzlement* until genuine physics removes that puzzlement entirely by showing how all such things as force strengths are dictated by some Theory of Everything.

9.12 Many of the expectations of an atheist who believes in multiple universes will be shared by the believer in God. Looking down the points listed in section 6.33 should convince you of this. It seems clear, for instance, that theists ought to be open-minded towards the suggestion that the universe is fine tuned to Life's needs. Must they hurry to reject Hawking's idea that the early expansion speed required tuning to one part in a million million? Presumably not. Again, theists may well be inclined to expect more instances of fine tuning to be discovered. Further, God could have strong grounds for creating Variety: hence theists could well believe in many and varied universes. On this and many other points there could be complete harmony.

On other points, however, there would tend to be disagreement. There could be times when one might have to be judged irrational, schizoid, if one's way of doing physics was not in the slightest affected by a deeply held belief in God. The theist has, I argued, rational grounds for being specially open to the suggestion that basic physical principles dictate all force strengths, particle masses, and so on; for God's method of fine tuning could be to choose fundamental laws that were appropriate for producing Life, these laws forming a unified set which dictated all the right force strengths etc., whereas slightly different laws would have dictated wrong ones (1.22; 2.7; 2.55; 3.11). The theist may want to deny that God created a 'messy' world of laws which were in no way unified and physical constants which were completely free to take just whichever values served the divine ends. In God's absence, on the other hand, could a universe manage to be life-producing if it obeyed unified and all-dictating laws? That could well be thought very unlikely unless there existed many universes obeying different sets of unified and all-dictating laws, so that sooner or later one set would be favourable to Life and Observer-ship. Yet unless there were a God intent on producing the good of variety, what possible reason could there be for fundamental laws to vary from universe to universe?

One reason why belief in God is not irrational is that it encourages interpretations of experience which reduce the Problem of Evil. (That again is a matter of a feedback loop. Belief in God encourages those interpretations, and the inter-pretations encourage one to stand by one's belief in God. Compare how belief in God encourages acceptance of apparent fine tuning, the acceptance then reinforcing the belief.) The Problem of Evil can well seem less overwhelming when, for instance, the lives of the dead, lives which are over *now*, are not viewed as having been removed from Reality; and this, I argued, is possible when the viewer prefers an Einsteinian picture of Time to the one the ordinary person tends to favour (8.17). (Naturally, the miseries of the dead would be as little removed as their joys, so that some people might want to see the theist's difficulties as merely having been increased. But to recognize this is just to admit that no single defence against the Problem of Evil can be sufficient.)

Indirect Observations; Design Arguments

9.13 When earlier chapters spoke of *what is observable* what was meant was what could be observed more or less directly. On that interpretation, obviously, cosmic regions existing beyond our present horizon are not observable by us, at least not yet, while universes causally isolated and perpetually devoid of life will never be observed by anyone. However, the sense of the word 'observation' can vary, and a great many things could be thought of as *observable indirectly*. Things can be said to be indirectly observed when they are needed to account in a tidy way for whatever is observed directly. *Strong evidence for something,* evidence encouraging one to claim that this something 'has been observed', is *whatever causes a puzzlement which the existence of that something would reduce or remove* – assuming, that is to say, that there are no other somethings which would be equally effective at reducing or removing it. Little Mary's passage through the room is observed (indirectly) when we observe (directly) the tiny, muddy footprints on the carpet. There is actual evidence for a theory when it explains a situation neatly whereas other theories don't.

9.14 Unfair though it would be to divide the world into open-minded and well-informed scientists on the one hand and narrow, inflexible philosophers on the other, it seems not unjust to comment that philosophers have often been strangely reluctant to accept indirect observations. For example, they have tended to classify first atoms and then their constituents as only 'useful fiction' and the like, on the grounds that we can never actually *come across* atoms, electrons, quarks, instead of placing them at the ends of long theoretical chains. We see, it is said, only what theory alleges to be the causal consequences of atoms, electrons, or quarks. We lack independent evidence that these things themselves exist. Yet why this insistence on 'independent evidence', evidence which is direct rather than of consequences? Most scientists appreciate that evidence needing much theory for its interpretation can be very good evidence indeed. Sudden slight changes in the rate at which radio pulses arrive from stars hundreds of trillions of miles away can give us great confidence that the equators of those stars – stars agreed to be rotating neutron stars but not because anyone has actually landed on them to take samples – have contracted by some ten-thousandths of an inch. We have persuasively evidenced accounts of events occurring very early on in the Big Bang; of elementary particles which live so briefly that only their decay products can be seen (and at that, they are seen only indirectly, from the tracks they leave in bubble chambers); and so on. Scientists can see – indirectly – that the universe does not just come to an end at the distance beyond which no telescopes can probe, the distance that is the maximum which light rays can have traversed since the beginning of the Bang (4.8). Again, scientists know that when particles fall through the horizons of black holes they do not at once drop out of existence or cease acting in accordance with quantum laws, i.e. with complex unpredictability. They know it despite how nobody will ever have direct evidence of it. They are here told *by science itself* that there exist realities whose details science will never discover.

Meanwhile we philosophers have been having a tough struggle in getting beyond Solipsism of the Present Moment, the ridiculous theory that the only reality is the I and the now. On the grounds, apparently, that factors superior to Chance cannot be experienced in the straightforward way in which a pain can, it has been solemnly held that the idea that events up to date *have not been ruled by Pure Chance* must 'of course' – that's a quotation – be a matter not for any 'assertion' but only for a 'blik', a mere attitude.[2] Camps have warred over whether tables of the sort ordinarily believed in can indeed be 'experienced directly' so that they can become respectable. Bafflement has been common over how a man might arrive at a reasonable belief in Other Minds: minds other than his own. Mustn't it be, it has been suggested, that talk of mental workings just is talk of a body's tendency to behave in certain ways, because how else could anyone have 'any possibility of observational corroboration' for such a belief? For 'of course' the fact that other bodies behave much like yours couldn't itself be genuine evidence for the reality of not-directly-observable workings inside them! Why, even were it found that various brain states and various introspectively observed mental workings always went together, how remote that would of course be from finding that mental states were states (organizational states, 'software' states) of brains! And as for the idea that a life-containing universe might owe its existence to an ethical requirement, why of course such a totally unevidenced speculation . . . !

9.15 Recently it has become popular to suggest that the true cannot be any different from what would be warrantedly assertable 'in the long run': in other words, when all available evidence had been collected. Away go all truths of precisely what happened to this or that individual particle early on in the Big Bang, or about the detailed movements of a given electron after its fall through the horizon of a black hole, or the truth of exactly how many ants the largest-ever individual dinosaur squashed, or the truth that there are, or are not, exactly three billion and fifty universes existing in causal isolation from our own and containing no living beings to experience them![3]

How ought one to react to this? By ploughing through the seemingly endless literature on the subject, trying to weigh a thousand technically difficult claims and counter-claims? No. Philosophers who doubt whether we can meaningfully describe a real world whose details will for ever transcend all Actual

Experience do have their highly intelligent, highly complicated reasons. The precise nature of the right theory of meaningfulness is an altogether tricky affair. Yet as I. Hacking points out in the course of a forceful attack on H. Putnam, 'I do not need a theory of reference in order to refer';[4] now, likewise I do not need one in order to have a strong right to believe that my words are at least meaningful despite any inability to check the facts to which they make reference. The statement *that there really are affairs*, perhaps the existence of three billion and fifty other universes, perhaps particular details of such other universes, perhaps goings-on inside black holes, or perhaps the minutiae of events which are long past, *which must remain for ever unknown to all intelligent beings but which might none the less be made the subject of lucky guesses, guesses that delivered the truth*, ought to seem fairly clearly meaningful. Does it sound at all like talk of a round square? Can there look to be a Truth of Logic that intelligent beings must in theory be able to discover everything, or at any rate everything about which correct guesses could be made? Does it seem as if the snapping of some last causal link with ourselves would send an entire other universe into the realm of unmeaning (4.7; 5.12)? Not so. Not, anyway, to those who remain undazzled by their discovery of how complex the meaning of 'meaning' can be. There is no obligation to solve all the undoubtedly very hard problems of philosophy of language, showing precisely how one's words come to be meaningful, before allowing oneself to say such things as that there might conceivably be exactly seven trillion and thirteen universes causally separate from ours: that this might be *true*. The meaningfulness of that – or of remarks such as that it might perhaps be that some dog in the streets of Rome scratched himself just fifty-one times on the day of Caesar's assassination – is much more to be trusted than any abstruse, highly controversial philosophical arguments. Very valuable while such arguments might be for drawing attention to problems in the philosophy of meaning, they are very poor excuses for dismissing statements as 'meaningless' as soon as they grow speculative enough to be permanently beyond verification. (And like guesses about the minutiae of events long past, statements about the fine details of other universes do very obviously have such speculativeness.)

Besides, how unverifiable speculations can get to be meaningful can I think be glimpsed. A map is in countless respects different from the countryside it represents, and a picture of a mountain or a rabbit is in innumerable ways unlike any actual mountain or rabbit. Maps and pictures are two-dimensional, for example, whereas countrysides and rabbits are not. But toddlers

– aided by mothers who manage to reduce ambiguities by exploiting a common sense, a preference for the simplest inter-pretation,[5] which leads a child to assume, say, that a rabbit is what is in question and not just a rabbit-skin – do learn rather quickly what it is, roughly, that makes a picture of a rabbit 'of' a rabbit and which picture is instead of a rabbit-skin or a cow. After a little teaching a drawing of a black volcano can fairly clearly 'be of', i.e. be such as might well correspond to, a black volcano rather than an iceberg. And there is little reason to think that very much the same relationship of correspondence (what-ever the exact meaning of 'correspondence' may be) couldn't possibly hold between a picture of a mountain and some actual mountain in another (small-u) universe existing in addition to our universe. There is even little mystery in what could be meant by mountains that existed in universes entirely devoid of conscious beings.

9.16 Associated with many philosophical demands for 'actual evidence' is grave head-shaking over 'mere Arguments from Analogy'. Even a defender of God and of Design will be struck, for instance, by how he can hit on 'nothing better than' the kind of analogical reasoning one might use in connection with Other Minds; now, of course nothing as weak as *that* could be useful for knocking sceptics down! So he will feel forced to adopt a tactic popular among modern defenders of religion, of saying that a way of looking on things, while of no earthly use for persuading any who are reluctant to share it, can still be 'not irrational', intellectually viable. New events experienced in accordance with this 'way of looking on things' can even strengthen it much as my initially disapproving attitude towards massacres may excite me to ever greater indignation as I watch them. Well, this book has certainly used analogies: firing squads and fishing and shooting at flies and being hit by arrows, buying a silk robe with a hole which the merchant's thumb is covering, seeing a sonnet which a monkey has typed, finding words in granite, and so forth. But that does not mean that it has been intended as just another addition to the literature of viable beliefs and attitudes.

'Argument from Analogy' tends to be used like 'Classical Physics'. If we still approve of a nineteenth-century way of doing physics then we call it 'modern physics' instead, and when we think an analogy strong then we talk of 'valid inductive generaliz-ation' or 'adopting a simple and consistent world-picture' rather than of 'reasoning analogically'. When analogical arguments are developed sensibly, the only thing wrong about them is their name. A great many of them are just means of reminding us about principles of everyday reasoning which we have managed to forget (7.9), but even those which are more nearly of the form, 'Thing number 1 has properties *A, B, C, D, E*; thing number 2 has properties *A, B, C, D*; and therefore thing number 2 quite probably has property *E* also', are not without their uses in a world in which no two apples, babies, or cats are ever precisely alike. Recognizing their uses is not equivalent to underwriting the move from 'My love is like a red, red rose' to 'My love will probably soon wither and die, as the rose will', neither need it lead straight to the conclusion that the world was designed by a blundering committee of demigods complete with the ulcers that torment human designers. Arguments from analogy only become disgracefully weak when they are handled in disgraceful ways. And there are sensible ways of handling the Design Argument while still leaving it as something perhaps worth classifying as an argument from analogy – although (7.8) that may well not be the most helpful way of classifying it.

9.17 It is high time we philosophers took the Design Argument seriously. Whether the evidence of fine tuning points to multiple universes or to God, it does do some exciting pointing; and it does it through being just the sort of evidence which too many of us have tended to dismiss as uninteresting. Too many philosophers construct such arguments as that if the universe were hostile to Life then we shouldn't be here to see it, and that therefore there is nothing in fine tuning for anyone to get excited about; or that obviously there could be only the one universe and that therefore, because probability and improbability can be present only where repetitions are possible, its basic laws and conditions cannot be in any way 'improbable'. Again, too many have confused being rigorous with rejecting everything not directly observable.

My argument has been that the fine tuning is evidence, genuine evidence, of the following fact: *that God is real, and/or there are many and varied universes.* And it could be tempting to call the fact an observed one. Observed indirectly, but observed none the less.

Counting the Possibilities; Inverting Probabilities

9.18 It might be judged, though, that two things should be troubling me.

First, there is the problem of counting possibilities. We must do this if we are to find that life-permitting conditions are hard to achieve, i.e. are rare among the possibilities and so would not be expected in a universe taken at random. But how is it to be done?

Second, even if life-permitting conditions were rare, how could we conclude anything without committing the blunder of 'inverting a probability'?

9.19 Bertrand's paradox illustrates the problem of counting possibilities. A chord is to be selected at random inside a large circle on the roadway; with what probability will it be longer than the side of an equilateral triangle inscribed in that circle? Answers vary with the means adopted for selecting chords randomly. When we wait for a raindrop to mark the chord's midpoint then the probability of its being longer is one in four. When we roll broom handles from afar until one of them marks the chord, it rises to one in two. Now, if circles had only finitely many chords then some one means of random selection might be *right* – because, say, exactly one in four of the twenty billion chords were longer. But if the number of chords is infinite then the infinitely many longer chords cannot be compared in number with the infinitely many shorter ones. It might seem that talk of *estimating a probability rightly* would therefore be nonsense here, as would any idea that God interfered with our chord selections so as to give results which 'defied Chance' through their failure to reflect 'the true probability'. And wouldn't the same difficulty be raised by the question of whether a universe taken at random would be a life-permitting universe?

9.20 Well, I suggested a way of escape from any such difficulty (4.11; 4.69). Possibilities not straightforwardly countable can still be compared with respect to their *ranges*. It may make no literal sense to say there is a larger number of points in a longer line, but the range of the points is certainly larger. If your life depended on rolling a broom handle so that it stopped on a very long line or else on a very short one, it could be suicidal to roll the thing towards the very short one. Again, an inexpert dart thrower gets little hope from the reflection that the infinite number of points inside the bull's-eye is no smaller than the infinite number outside. And if discovering MADE BY GOD written all over the world a reasonable man would be unmoved by the thought that messages of much this kind might have appeared in infinitely many infinitesimally different positions. The Cicero who, flinging a great many letters into the air, then actually finds they have fallen so as to form the *Annals* of Ennius, cannot reasonably exclaim, 'There's nothing remarkable here since there were countless slightly different ways in which this could have happened.'

Notice that the idea of randomness, even if it is relative to particular procedures for selecting randomly, can be adequately specific once we have specified some such procedure, e.g. rolling broom handles. Furthermore, certain outcomes can be expected of a given procedure before any actual experiments. Few writers on Bertrand's paradox can actually have dismantled brooms or prayed for rain. Once having built up a general idea of what laws operate in our world we can say, before actually tossing the tetrahedral dice of ancient Egypt, what the chances are that their red-marked points will fall uppermost. Again, we can rightly refuse to join A. J. Ayer in making the following weird claim: that in card-guessing experiments 'doing better than Chance' would not itself be startling evidence of anything because only Actual Experience of card-guessing could show how often card-guessers would be likely to guess correctly if unaided by paranormal visions of hidden cards.[6]

9.21 But, you may object, if what results are to be expected depends on what laws and conditions are in effect, e.g. the laws governing letters flung into the air on a windy day, then how could Nature's most basic laws and conditions themselves be something astonishing, a God-produced defiance of Chance, or a sign of a vast ensemble of universes?

The objection is much less powerful than one might think, for reasons like these:

(a) *Of course* physical laws might have given strong grounds for astonishment. Their operation might have inscribed the Koran's prohibition of wine on every grapeskin. Nothing else would then have been *physically possible*, given the actual laws of physics, but we should have had our grounds for suspecting that Allah had chosen those laws.

(b) You don't need to know *all about* natural laws before judging what could be expected if matters were left to chance. Before ever seeing darts thrown you can know that bull's-eyes are hard to hit. The knowledge doesn't depend on mastery of atomic physics. You can calculate the probabilities, roughly at any rate, when you appreciate that flying darts will not turn into miniature winged pigs intelligently speeding towards the target.

(c) Well reasoned judgments of what is likely need not be dogmatic assertions about probabilities 'out there' in the world, but neither need they be mere reports on anything as personal as the strengths of our beliefs. They can be genuinely well reasoned and undogmatic. In making them we are often in effect judging that *if* certain situations were governed only by the factors so far believed to be relevant then such-and-such outcomes *really would be* probable 'out there'. For instance, if the die is in fact falling in obedience only to laws of dynamics and not to those governing a die with an internal iron lump which is being attracted by a powerful hidden magnet, then . . . .

When their well-reasoned predictions turn out to be regularly mistaken, good reasoners change their theories. Startled by the unexpected smoke they begin to think there is a fire and expect more smoke. Given a little knowledge of how things work we can make probability estimates which *through turning out to be wrong* give us more knowledge of how things work. The gambler starts to look for the hidden magnet. Initially expecting to find that Life *did not* 'balance on a razor edge', the cosmologist later comes to believe in multiple universes and an observational selection effect, or in God.

(d) The laws which give Space and Time their structure can themselves divide possible events into ranges whose sizes can be roughly compared so that investigators can decide what cries out for explanation. Thus, the markings * ** *** **** ***** ****** have a spacing which clearly needs to be explained.

The 'investigators' include babies. They need have no ideas about what the laws are which give Space and Time their structure.

(e) Asking whether it would be likely in the absence of Design that natural laws would have led to living beings in a one and only universe, we need not consider all logically possible universes. As has already been said many times, we need look only at 'the local area' of universes slightly different from ours (Fly on the Wall Story: 1.24). Now, the universes of this local area are *by definition* all sufficiently similar to allow ranges of possibilities to be measured and probabilities estimated, albeit only roughly. (Differences like that between a one-in-four and a one-in-two chance are unimportant to this book's arguments.) The situation is of course much less easy to handle than that of throwing darts, where it can readily be seen that very slight changes would lead to very different outcomes. Yet this is no excuse for yawning at, say, an apparent discovery that Life depended on fine tuning of the early cosmic density to one part in ten followed by fifty-four zeros (2.5) or that changing the balance between gravity and electromagnetism by one part in ten followed by thirty-nine zeros would have made stars burn too fast or too slowly (2.19). Yes, many such findings may be mistaken; but it can seem altogether unlikely that all of them are when they form a list as long as the one which Chapter 2 gave.

(f) We cannot be quite sure of what would happen to all other natural constants and to Life's prospects if one of the actually observed constants were altered slightly. It is as if we had found a tube balanced on a razor edge with the help of sliding weights and suspected that these were interconnected by rubber bands inside the tube. Mightn't moving one weight make the others move in such a way that the tube continued in balance?

Perhaps it might; yet this can look none too likely. Again, the fact that the balance might perhaps be restored if two weights were moved simultaneously in appropriate ways (cf. 2.51) need not make the tube's balancing act look any the less impressive.

How about the suggestion that moving several weights could lead to the razor edge's being replaced by something much broader? (In other words, that life forms of unimagined sorts would evolve without any need for fine tuning in universes whose mixtures of force strengths etc. differed markedly from the mixture in our universe, but which might none the less be counted as 'universes in the local area' since they did contain forces recognizable as gravitation and electromagnetism, particles recognizable as electrons and quarks, and so forth.) Well, not even the arguments of section 2.51 can quite rule out that possibility – but it can still be very impressive that the tube *as actually observed* is positioned *in a way so strongly suggesting* that any moving of its weights would upset things. Look again at the ingenious philosopher's hypothesis in the Story of the Message in Granite (1.21). That hypothesis was comparable to saying that the weights on our tube were fixed so rigidly that they could never be moved, and that the point at which the tube touched the razor edge was similarly unalterable, and that therefore nothing but balancing 'was really possible'. The answer to this must surely be that it would be utterly amazing if *the single real possibility* were one suggesting a very delicate balancing act. Now, similarly with the notion that *the single possibility actually before our eyes* just happens to be one giving the illusion of such an act. In all such cases our presumption must be (1.11; 5.29; 7.11) that neither Blind Necessity nor Chance has created a situation wrongly suggesting a tidy explanation.

9.22 The claim that Blind Necessity is involved – that universes whose laws or constants are slightly different 'aren't real physical possibilities on a par with a dart's falling outside the bull's-eye' – is in any case eroded by the various physical theories, particularly theories of random symmetry breaking, which show how a very varied ensemble of universes might be generated. But the really strong point against such a claim is the one made in the previous paragraph. You could not use a claim of that sort to undermine all possible evidence of fine tuning, any more than you could use it to suggest that the prohibition of wine on the grapeskins (9.21[a]) was nothing to be excited at.

9.23 Next, the objection about 'inverting a probability'.

Suppose you know of an urn only that it contains two balls, each either red or blue. You then draw a red ball from it. Can you argue that if the urn had held two red then you would have drawn a red with 100 per cent probability; that you did draw a red; and that therefore, with 100 per cent probability, two red is what it held? Clearly not. Nor can you argue that because a sonic boom will shatter a window 70 per cent of the time, 70 per cent of shattered windows must be shattered by such booms. Each case would illustrate the blunder of inverting a probability.

Now, it could be asked, mustn't such a blunder, or something approaching it, be committed by the Design Argument and by the rather similar argument for multiple universes? For what if we granted that there would be a high probability or a certainty that a God-created universe would be life-containing? How could we move from that to any conclusion about whether our life-containing universe was God-created? If we were to do more than just 'invert a probability', wouldn't we need to use some estimate of God's *intrinsic likelihood*? And from just where would we get that? Didn't I myself suggest (8.11[c]) that there was no a priori likelihood or unlikelihood to be found in this area?

9.24 My reply is that section 1.23 tried to forestall this objection. Suppose that, as was imagined there, you repeat the draw from the urn a hundred times. After each draw you replace the ball and give the urn a good shake. Every single time a red ball is drawn. With each new draw after, let's say, the fifteenth, it would get more and more insane to believe that one of the balls in the urn was blue. This would be so despite your perhaps having had absolutely no information about, e.g., whether the man who filled the urn had any special liking for one colour. To avoid insanity, there is no need to treat *absence of knowledge* of the man's likes and dislikes as *knowledge of the absence* of certain likes and dislikes. All that is needed is the open mind which treats lack of information as a good excuse for not adhering, utterly arbitrarily and in defiance of the evidence, to a belief that he may well have been extremely likely to put in a blue ball. Technical talk about misuse of the probability calculus – of the crime of believing in 'prior probabilities' for which there is no evidence, of the wrongness of using any Principle of Indifference for setting up such probabilities, of the Fallacy of Inverting a Probability, and so on – must not be allowed to blind us to so obvious a point. Otherwise experience will never teach us anything. You are not 'forced to resort to putting totally unknown probabilities into Bayes's formula' when experience has given you evidence of precisely the kind which makes probabilities knowable. After a hundred reds you could be as certain about the urn's contents as if you had looked inside it. *Possibly* you would be wrong. Possibly the urn was filled by tossing balls at it from a hundred yards away, with enormously many blue balls being tossed and hardly any red. But possibly, too, a demon deceives humans whenever they look inside urns. There can be no learning from experience if you are impressed by such possibilities.

9.25 One moral becomes plain at something like the twelfth draw. When there is no special reason not to adopt some hypothesis, and when no other viable hypothesis is in sight, then that hypothesis ought to be adopted at least provisionally if the alternative is amazement. It would certainly be amazing if red just happened to be drawn twelve times in the first twelve draws.

Now, much evidence suggests that Life's prerequisites could only amazingly have been fulfilled anywhere unless this is a truth: *that God is real and/or there exist vastly many, very varied universes*. Independently of all such evidence it is certainly hard to give a figure for the probability of that truth. Yet when we see the evidence, the conclusion to be reached can be plain enough.

Notes

In the cases of works listed in the References at the end of the book, references will be only by name, date, and perhaps a letter.

1 World Ensemble, or Design

The chapter draws on Leslie, 1988d. As in the cases of later chapters which also draw on various of my papers, I thank all those whose criticisms led to changes.

1 See Adams's, *The Education of Henry Adams* (New York, 1931), esp. p. 429. 'If he were obliged to insist on a Universe, he seemed driven to the Church' – so he opted for a 'multiverse' of largely or entirely separate worlds with very different characteristics.

2 I consider the Argument for Multiple Worlds in many places. See esp. Leslie 1982, 1983a and b, 1985, 1986a and b, 1987, 1988a, b, c, d, and e, and 1989a and b. In early treatments of the Argument, 1978a and 1979 (ch. 7), I underestimated its power.

3 Neoplatonism is defended in my *Value and Existence* (Leslie, 1979) and in several articles, esp. Leslie, 1970, 1978b, and 1980. Also see Leslie, 1972, for the ethical theory underlying it, and 1986c for a reply to J. L. Mackie's chapter discussing *Value and Existence* in his *The Miracle of Theism* (Oxford, 1982).

4 Guth and Steinhardt, 1984.

5 Linde, 1983, p. 245. Compare Weinberg, 1983, p. 140: 'Did the universe freeze into domains? Do we live in one such domain, in which the symmetry between the weak and electromagnetic interactions has been broken in a particular way?'

6 For all this and also the Little Puddle tale, see G. Feinberg and R. Shapiro, *Life Beyond Earth* (New York, 1980).

7 Here and in section 1.28 I particularly have in mind Sylvan, 1986, pp. 160–8. (While J. Earman's paper in *American Philosophical Quarterly*, October 1987, pp. 307–17, could seem to revolve around similar reasoning, I believe that the key to this paper is instead Earman's doubts about whether such things as carbon really are essential.) Sylvan also challenges the point made in section 1.12: that those fish need to be *actual* fish.

8 Cf. p. 664 of S. Coleman, *Nuclear Physics* B310, 12 December 1988, pp. 643–68: 'When we describe a phenomenon as unnatural we may

mean either that it requires fine tuning of short-distance physics or that it requires fine tuning of initial conditions. The original cosmological-constant problem was unnatural in the first sense; the slightest alteration in the parameters of microphysics would produce an enormous cosmological constant.'

2 The Evidence of Fine Tuning

The chapter is largely a reworking of material in Leslie 1988c.

1 Newton, *Opticks*, Query 28.
2 Ibid., Query 31.
3 Newton, first letter to Bentley.
4 Leibniz, letter to the Princess of Wales, November 1715.
5 A Neoplatonist Creative Principle (see Chapter 1, section 1.3) is defended in many of my writings, esp. Leslie, 1970, 1978b, 1979, 1980, and 1986c.
6 Newton, second letter to Bentley.
7 Newton, fourth letter to Bentley.
8 Davies, 1980, pp. 160–1, 168–9.
9 Penrose, in Isham *et al.*, 1981, pp. 248–9.
10 Dicke, *Gravitation and the Universe* (Philadelphia, 1970), p. 62.
11 Dicke and P. J. E. Peebles, in Hawking and Israel, 1979, p. 514.
12 Hawking, in Longair, 1974, p. 285.
13 B. J. Carr, *Irish Astronomical Journal*, vol. 15, no. 3, 1982, p. 244; cf. Davies, 1983, p. 20; or Barrow and Tipler, 1986, p. 411.
14 A. H. Guth, *Physical Review D*, vol. 23, no. 2, 1981, p. 348.
15 Barrow and Tipler, 1986, p. 433; cf. Guth, op. cit. (note 14 above), p. 352.
16 See Gibbons *et al.*, 1983, pp. 271, 393; or A. D. Mazenko, G. M. Unruh, and R. M. Wald, *Physical Review D*, vol. 31, no. 2, 1985, pp. 273–82.
17 Davies, 1983, pp. 28–30.
18 See Barrow and Tipler, 1986, p. 413; or Gibbons *et al.*, 1983, pp. 6, 26, 475–6.
19 S. W. Hawking, in McCrea and Rees, 1983, p. 304.
20 Davies, 1983, p. 28.
21 Barrow and Tipler, 1986, p. 434. For a general review of Inflation's problems, see T. Rothman and G. F. R. Ellis, *Astronomy*, February 1987, pp. 6–22. Ellis has further argued (*Classical and Quantum Gravity*, vol. 5, 1988, p. 891) that Inflation by no means guarantees spatial flatness.
22 Wheeler, *American Scientist*, vol. 62, no. 6, 1974, p. 689.
23 Dyson, 1971; Idlis, *Izvestiya Astrofizicheskogo Instituta Akademii Nauk Kazakhskoii SSR*, vol. 7, 1958, pp. 39–54 esp. p. 47.
24 Davies, 1984, pp. 183–205.
25 Newton, *Opticks*, Query 31.
26 R. Penrose, in Isham *et al.*, 1981, pp. 244–72; P. C. W. Davies, *God and the New Physics* (London, 1983), pp. 50–4, 177–81.

27 Newton, *Opticks*, Query 11.
28 Ibid., Query 30.
29 Dyson, 1971, p. 56.
30 Ibid.
31 Davies, 1980, pp. 176–7.
32 Demaret and Barbier, 1981, p. 500.
33 M. J. Rees, in McCrea and Rees, 1983, p. 317.
34 J. D. Barrow and J. Silk, *Scientific American*, April 1980, pp. 127–8.
35 Davies, 1983, p. 8; and I. L. Rozental, *Elementary Particles and the Structure of the Universe* (Moscow, 1984, in Russian), p. 85.
36 Dyson, 1971, p. 56.
37 F. Hoyle, *Astrophysical Journal,* supplementary, vol. 1, 1954, p. 121; E. E. Salpeter, *Physical Review*, vol. 107, 1957, p. 516.
38 I. L. Rozental, *Structure of the Universe and Fundamental Constants* (Moscow, 1981), p. 8.
39 Carr and Rees, 1979, p. 611.
40 B. Carter, in J. H. Sanders and A. H. Wapstra (eds), *Atomic Masses and Fundamental Constants: 5* (New York, 1976), p. 652.
41 Atkins, 1981, p. 13.
42 Davies, 1983, p. 7.
43 M. J. Rees, *Quarterly Journal of the Royal Astronomical Society*, vol. 22, 1981, p. 122, with the figure of about 1 per cent coming from a conversation of that year; cf. Hoyle, op. cit., and Salpeter, op. cit. (note 37 above).
44 Barrow and Tipler, 1986, pp. 252–3.
45 Ibid., p. 327.
46 Rozental, *On Numerical Values of Fundamental Constants* (Moscow, 1980), p. 9: on atomic weights above four Rozental cites E. E. Salpeter, *Astrophysical Journal*, vol. 140, 1964, p. 796.
47 Press and Lightman, in McCrea and Rees, 1983, pp. 323–36.
48 V. Trimble, *American Scientist*, vol. 65, 1977, p. 85; Rozental, 1980, esp. p. 303.
49 Carter, in Longair, 1974, pp. 296–8.
50 G. Gale, *Scientific American*, December 1981, pp. 154–71, esp. p. 155.
51 R. T. Rood and J. S. Trefil, *Are We Alone?* (New York, 1982), p. 21.
52 Davies, 1984, p. 242.
53 Rozental, 1980, pp. 303, 298.
54 Teller, *Physical Review*, vol. 73, p. 801.
55 Dicke, *Reviews of Modern Physics*, vol. 29, no. 3, 1957, pp. 375–6: Dicke has written to me that his remarks about the dielectric constant are to be read in this way, given what is said elsewhere in the paper.
56 McCrea and Rees, 1983, p. 312.
57 R. Breuer, *Das Anthropische Prinzip* (Munich, 1983), p. 228.
58 Ibid.
59 Carr and Rees, 1979, p. 611.

60 Barrow and Tipler, 1986, p. 339.
61 Silk, *Nature*, vol. 265, 1977, p. 710.
62 I. S. Shklovskii and C. Sagan, *Intelligent Life in the Universe* (New York, 1966), p. 124.
63 Hawking, *Physics Bulletin: Cambridge*, vol. 32, 1980, p. 15.
64 Barrow and Tipler, 1986, pp. 371, 399–400; Davies, 1983, pp. 9–10, and *The Forces of Nature* (Cambridge, 1979), pp. 100–2, 172; Rozental, op. cit. (note 35 above), pp. 78–83.
65 Rozental, 1980, p. 298.
66 Rozental, op. cit. (note 35 above), pp. 78–83.
67 Newton, *Opticks*, Query 31.
68 Davies, 1984, pp. 137–8.
69 Newton, *Opticks*, Query 31.
70 Ibid.
71 Barrow and Tipler, 1986, pp. 403–7; G. G. Ross, in Isham *et al.*, 1981, pp. 304–22.
72 Demaret and Barbier, 1981, p. 489.
73 H. Pagels, *Perfect Symmetry* (New York, 1985), pp. 275–9.
74 Demaret and Barbier, *Revue des Questions Scientifiques*, vol. 152, no. 2, 1981, p. 199; Weinberg, 1983, p. 87.
75 Carr and Rees, 1979, p. 610; Demaret and Barbier, 1981, pp. 478–80, 500; D. V. Nanopoulos, *Physics Letters*, vol. 91B, no. 1, 1980, pp. 67–71; Davies, 1983, pp. 24–7; Barrow and Tipler, 1986, p. 418.
76 Goldhaber, in Pagels, op. cit. (note 73 above), pp. 275–9.
77 Weinberg, 1983, p. 157.
78 Barrow and Tipler, 1986, pp. 358–9.
79 Newton, *Opticks*, Query 31.
80 Misner *et al.*, 1973, p. 1215; and G. Toraldo di Francia (ed.), *Problems in the Foundations of Physics* (Amsterdam, 1979), p. 441.
81 CERN bulletin 65-26, 2 July 1965, pp. 2–3, 12.
82 Ward, in J. Oro, S. L. Miller, C. Ponnamperuma, and R. S. Young (eds), *Cosmochemical Evolution and the Origins of Life* (Dordrecht, 1974), pp. 7, 24.
83 Kahn, in W. C. Saslaw and K. C. Jacobs (eds), *The Emerging Universe* (Charlottesville, 1972), p. 79.
84 Barrow and Tipler, 1986, p. 297.
85 Regge, *Atti del Convegno Mendeleeviano* (Turin, 1971), p. 398.
86 Wald, in Oro *et al.*, op. cit. (note 82 above), pp. 23–4.
87 Davies, 1984, p. 131.
88 Rozental, *On Numerical Values*, op. cit. (note 46 above), p. 14.
89 Rozental, 1980, p. 298.
90 Barrow and Tipler, 1986, p. 298.
91 Atkins, 1981, pp. 86–7; C. Rebbi, *Scientific American*, vol. 240, no. 2, 1979, pp. 76–91; Z. Parsa, *American Journal of Physics*, vol. 47, 1979, pp. 56–62.
92 Ehrenfest, *Proceedings of the Amsterdam Academy*, vol. 20, 1917, p. 200; for discussion of many other authors, see Barrow and Tipler, 1986, pp. 258–76. Hawking, *A Brief History of Time* (Toronto and New York, 1988), pp. 163–5.

93 Wheeler, in Misner *et al.*, 1973, p. 1205.
94 Barrow and Tipler, 1986, pp. 248–9, p. 283 n. 95.
95 Davies and Unwin, *Proceedings of the Royal Society of London*, vol. 1377, 1981, pp. 147–9.
96 Linde, 1984, p. 974.
97 M. Turner and F. Wilczek, *Nature*, vol. 298, 1982, p. 633; Wilczek, in Gibbons *et al.*, 1983, p. 27.
98 Newton, General Scholium.
99 Newton, *Opticks,* Query 31.
100 Davies, *The Forces of Nature*, op. cit. (note 64 above), pp. 229–30; Rozental, 1980, p. 301.
101 Drawn in part from such classics as V. F. Weisskopf, *Knowledge and Wonder* (New York, 1962), and H. F. Blum, *Time's Arrow and Evolution* (Princeton, 1968).
102 Davies, *The Forces of Nature*, op. cit. (note 64 above), p. 160.
103 Dyson, 1971.
104 Squires, *European Journal of Physics*, vol. 2, 1981, pp. 55–7.
105 Newton, first letter to Bentley.
106 Wheeler, in Misner *et al.*, p. 1206.
107 Eigen and Winkler, *Laws of the Game*, trans. R. and R. Kimber (New York, 1981).
108 Davies, 1983, p. 15.
109 Atkins, 1981, pp. 10–12.
110 Islam, *The Ultimate Fate of the Universe* (Cambridge, 1983), pp. 130–1.
111 Wald, in Oro *et al.*, op. cit. (note 82 above).
112 Rozental, 1980, p. 296.
113 D. Goldsmith and T. Owen, *The Search for Life in the Universe* (Menlo Park, 1980), pp. 220–1; G. Feinberg and R. Shapiro, *Life Beyond Earth* (New York, 1980), is a rich source of speculations like this.
114 Ibid., pp. 221–2.
115 Rozental, Novikov, and Polnarev, *Izvestiya Akademii Nauk Estonskoii SSR Seriia Fiziko-Matematicheskii*, vol. 31, no. 3, 1982, pp. 284–9.
116 See note 48 above (Trimble, Rozental).
117 Several authors discuss all this in *Los Alamos Science*, no. 11, 1984; and in McCrea and Rees, 1983: see esp. C. H. Llewellyn Smith on pp. 253–9. Also G. 't Hooft, *Scientific American*, June 1980, pp. 104–38; S. Weinberg, *Physica Scripta*, vol. 21, no. 5, 1980, pp. 773–81; W. Willis, *New Scientist*, 6 October 1983, pp. 9–12; C. Quigg, *Scientific American*, April 1985, pp. 84–95; M. J. G. Velt-man, *Scientific American*, November 1986, pp. 76–84.
118 Weinberg, 1983, p. 140.
119 Newton, *Opticks*, Query 31.
120 Newton, third letter to Bentley.
121 Atkins, 1981.

3 Further Evidence

The chapter draws on Leslie, 1978a, 1979, 1985, and 1988c, in particular.

1 Leslie, 1979, ch. 6. (See also Leslie, 1973.)
2 Wigner, *Communications in Pure and Applied Mathematics*, vol. 13, no. 1, 1960, p. 227.
3 Leslie, 1979, sects. 7.12, 7.13.
4 Particularly rich sources include: Rozental, 1980; E. J. Squires, *European Journal of Physics*, vol. 2, 1981, pp. 55–7; Atkins, 1981; Barrow and Tipler, 1986.
5 Rozental, 1980, p. 302.
6 At any rate, many see the matter in that way; some details are given in Leslie, 1976.
7 Penrose, in Hawking and Israel, 1979, p. 594.

4 Multiple Worlds

The chapter draws on Leslie, 1982 and 1989b.

1 Weinberg, 1983, p. 105.
2 Ellis and Brundrit, 'Life in the infinite universe', *Quarterly Journal of the Royal Astronomical Society*, vol. 20, 1979, pp. 37–41.
3 Hart's argument appears in *Quarterly Journal of the Royal Astronomical Society*, vol. 16, 1975, pp. 128–35; and in M. Hart and B. Zuckerman (eds), *Extraterrestrials: Where Are They?* (New York, 1982), pp. 154–64 (reprinted in Leslie, 1989a).
4 Ellis in, for instance, *General Relativity and Gravitation*, vol. 11, no. 4, 1979, pp. 281–9.
5 See Linde, 1985. $10^{1,000,000}$, one followed by a million zeros, could seem large enough, yet figures far larger suggest themselves. A. H. Guth has said ten billion zeros: see his contribution to Gibbons *et al.*, 1983, p. 185.
6 Davies, 1984, ch. 12, esp. pp. 194–5; Guth, in Gibbons *et al.*, 1983, p. 186; Guth and Steinhardt, 1984, esp. p. 128; Barrow and Tipler, 1986, p. 618.
7 Narlikar, *Journal of Astrophysics and Astronomy*, vol. 5, 1984, p. 67. Cf. Linde, 1984, esp. pp. 973, 981 and his 'Eternally Existing, Self-Reproducing Chaotic Inflationary Universe', *Physics Letters B*, 14 August 1986, pp. 395–400; Guth and Steinhardt, 1984, p. 128; Gunzig, Geheniau, and Prigogine, *Nature*, 17 December 1987, pp. 621–4.
8 Linde, 1984, p. 948. An earlier paper of his suggested $10^{3,240}$ cm.
9 Even the comparatively cautious Guth and Steinhardt, 1984, whose domains stretch only about 10^{26} cm when Inflation ends, place us in a domain which would by now measure 10^{35} light years, some 10^{25} times further than we can see.
10 First reported on in CERN Preprints of 1984.
11 Kibble, in M. J. Duff and C. J. Isham (eds), *Quantum Structure of Space and Time* (Cambridge, 1982), p. 395.
12 The best introduction to this area is Linde, 1985. See Linde's contribution to Gibbons *et al.*, 1983, pp. 244–5, for a picture of 'mini-universes with all possible symmetry-breaking patterns', making

Inflation's universe 'the only lunch at which all possible dishes are available'. Linde, 1984, gives further details.

13 On domains with different dimensionalities, metric signatures, gauge groups (such as SU[4] × U[1]), and vacuum energy densities, see Linde, 1984, pp. 967–9, 974, 981, and Linde, *Physics Letters B*, 14 August 1986: 'an enormously large number of possible types of compactification which exist e.g. in the theories of superstrings should be considered not as a difficulty but as a virtue of these theories, since it increases the probability of the existence of mini-universes in which life of our type may appear'. Also, for example, V. A. Kuzmin, M. E. Shaposhnikov, I. I. Tkachev, in M. A. Markov and P. C. West (eds), *Quantum Gravity* (New York, 1984), pp. 231–48.

14 For more details, see the works listed in note 117 of Chapter 2.

15 Linde, 1985, p. 16.

16 Davies and Unwin, *Proceedings of the Royal Society of London*, A 377, 1981, pp. 147–9.

17 Tryon, 'Is the universe a vacuum fluctuation?', *Nature*, 14 December 1973, pp. 396–7.

18 Some main papers are: R. Brout, F. Englert, E. Gunzig, *Annals of Physics*, vol. 115, 1978, pp. 78–106, and *General Relativity and Gravitation*, vol. 10, 1979, pp. 1–6; D. Atkatz and H. Pagels, *Physical Review D*, vol. 25, 1982, pp. 2065–73; J. R. Gott III, *Nature*, 28 January 1982, pp. 304–7; Ya. B. Zel'dovich, *Pontificia Academia delle Science Rome Scripta Varia*, vol. 48, 1982, pp. 575–9; A. D. Linde, *Lettere al Nuovo Cimento*, vol. 39, 1984, pp. 401–5, and also his other above-cited writings; L. P. Grishchuk and Ya. B. Zel'dovich, in Duff and Isham, op. cit. (note 11 above), pp. 409–22; A. Vilenkin, *Physics Letters*, vol. 117B, 1982, pp. 25–8, and *Physical Review D*, vol. 30, 1984, pp. 509–11; V. A. Rubakov, *Physics Letters*, vol. 148B, 1984, pp. 280–6. Tryon returns to the theme in *New Scientist*, 8 March 1984, pp. 14–16.

19 Hartle and Hawking, 'Wave function of the universe', *Physical Review D*, vol. 28, 1983, pp. 2960–75.

20 Doubts about this area are expressed by T. W. B. Kibble, in McCrea and Rees, 1983, p. 300 and by Zel'dovich, op. cit. (note 18 above), p. 578. At a September 1987 workshop at Castel Gandolfo, C. J. Isham stressed that the theories of quantum gravity which Hartle and Hawking exploit are plagued by such ill-defined expressions that no creation account like theirs is likely to be even mathematically consistent in its present form.

21 See Barrow and Tipler, 1986, pp. 494–5. Though they are here discussing Everett's approach to quantum mechanics, the point applies to virtually any theory which accepts a Bang or Bangs.

22 J. Silk, *The Big Bang* (San Francisco, 1980), p. 311.

23 See Dicke and Peebles, in Hawking and Israel, 1979, pp. 504–17.

24 See, e.g., Wheeler, in Misner *et al.*, 1973, ch. 44.

25 See esp. the last two pages of S. W. Hawking, *Scientific American*, January 1977, pp. 34–40. Other reasons for thinking that the law of

entropy increase would fail include Linde's suggestion (Linde, 1984, pp. 378–9) that all particles must vanish in the final stages of a Squeeze.

26 Hawking, op. cit. (note 25 above), p. 40.

27 Barrow and Tipler, 1986, pp. 248–9.

28 A. Shimony, *Scientific American*, January 1988, pp. 46–53.

29 Prigogine, *From Being to Becoming* (San Francisco, 1980). Contrast the more enthusiastic discussion of Prigogine's points in A. Rae, *Quantum Physics: Illusion or Reality?* (Cambridge, 1986), ch. 9.

30 R. Penrose, in Isham *et al.*, 1981, p. 267.

31 See, e.g., the conflicting interpretations in *Noûs*, November 1984.

32 Everett, *Reviews of Modern Physics*, July 1957, pp. 454–62.

33 B. S. DeWitt and N. Graham (eds), *The Many-Worlds Interpretation of Quantum Mechanics* (Princeton, 1973), p. 190.

34 As is recognized by B. Skyrms, *Philosophical Studies*, November 1976, pp. 323–32.

35 Davies, 1980, pp. 29, 67–9, 84–5, 111, 122, and 149, exploits the notion of 'jostling', and is echoed in J. D. Barrow's review in *The Times Higher Educational Supplement*, 22 August 1980. Mukhanov's words appear in his paper in M. A. Markov, V. A. Berezin, and V. P. Frolov (eds), *Proceedings of the Third Seminar on Quantum Gravity* (Moscow, 1985); and Deutsch's in *Proceedings of the Royal Society of London*, A 400, 1985, p. 111.

36 Deutsch, *International Journal of Theoretical Physics*, January 1985, pp. 1–41. See also his paper cited in note 35 above, and his 'Three connections between Everett's interpretation and experiment', in C. J. Isham and R. Penrose (eds), *Quantum Concepts in Space and Time* (Oxford, 1986), pp. 215–25.

37 See Hoyle's *Astronomy and Cosmology* (San Francisco, 1975), ch. 18.

38 Sato *et al.*, *Physics Letters*, vol. 108B, 14 January 1982, pp. 103–7.

39 Linde, in Gibbons *et al.*, 1983, p. 240.

40 See Markov's paper in Markov, Berezin, and Frolov, op. cit. (note 35 above).

41 Mukhanov, op. cit. (note 35 above).

42 Gale, in his useful paper in Leslie, 1989a.

43 See the last two pages of the paper cited in note 19 above. Wheeler is similarly aware that his oscillations may better be treated as 'side by side' rather than 'successive': see his contribution in J. Mehra (ed.), *The Physicist's Conception of Nature* (Dordrecht, 1973), pp. 204–47, esp. 231.

44 Wilson, *Dialogue*, June 1973, pp. 199–216; Einstein, often quoted as saying that his main motivation was to find 'whether the dear Lord had any choice when he created the universe'; Dirac, *Proceedings of the Royal Society of Edinburgh*, vol. 59, 1938–9, part 2, pp. 122–9; Eddington, *The Philosophy of Physical Science* (London, 1939), and *Fundamental Theory* (London, 1946); Wheeler, *The Monist*, vol. 47, 1962, pp. 40–76, esp. 65, 69, and in Misner *et al.*, 1973, pp. 1208–12; Chew, *Science*, vol. 11, 1968, pp. 762–5; Trimble, *American Scientist*,

vol. 65, 1977, esp. pp. 85–6; Penrose, *New Scientist*, 13 May 1979, pp. 734–7, esp. the closing words; Barrow and Tipler, 1986, pp. 105, 257–8, and Tipler's contribution to the September 1987 Castel Gandolfo workshop; DeWitt, *Physical Review*, vol. 160, 1967, p. 1113; Hartle and Hawking, op. cit. (note 19 above); and Hawking, in C. DeWitt (ed.), *Les Houches Lectures 1983* (New York, 1984).

45 For attacks on it, see L. J. Henderson, *The Order of Nature* (Cambridge, Mass., 1917); E. McMullin, *American Philosophical Quarterly*, July 1981, esp. pp. 178–81; D. Goldstick, in G. J. D. Moyal and S. Tweyman (eds), *Early Modern Philosophy* (New York, 1986), pp. 177–92.

46 The point is elegantly developed by C. W. Misner, in W. Yourgrau and A. D. Breck (eds), *Cosmology, History and Theology* (New York, 1977), pp. 96–7.

47 Jaki, *Irish Astronomical Journal*, March 1982, p. 257.

48 Barrow and Tipler, 1986, challenge this: p. 108, for instance. So do C. M. Patton and J. A. Wheeler, in C. J. Isham, R. Penrose, and D. W. Sciama (eds), *Quantum Gravity* (Oxford, 1975), pp. 538–605. Opposing them are generations of philosophers; I tackle the point in Leslie, 1978b, pp. 182–3.

49 See P. Hut and M. J. Rees, 'How stable is our vacuum?', *Nature*, 7 April 1983, pp. 508–9.

50 See Lewis, *Philosophical Papers* (Oxford, 1983), esp. pp. 21–5, and *On the Plurality of Worlds* (Oxford, 1986).

51 See R. H. Kane, *American Philosophical Quarterly*, January 1976, pp. 23–31; R. Nozick, *Philosophical Explanations* (Cambridge, Mass., 1981), pp. 123–30; P. Unger, *Mid-West Studies in Philosophy*, vol. 9, 1984, pp. 29–52.

52 Lewis knows of this difficulty but denies its seriousness: *On the Plurality of Worlds*, op. cit. (note 50 above), pp. 116–23, urges that all users of Induction are in essentially the same boat.

53 Leslie, 1988e, is a debate with Goldstick. See A. C. Michalos, *The Popper–Carnap Controversy* (The Hague, 1971), on systems of R. Carnap and others allowing non-zero probabilities for universal hypotheses in infinite universes.

54 Jevons, *The Principles of Science*, 2nd edn (London, 1877), pp. 257–61.

55 Boltzmann, *Nature*, 28 February 1895, pp. 413–15, esp. the closing paragraphs; and a paper in *Annalen der Physik*, vol. 60, 1897, trans. p. 238 of S. G. Brush, *Kinetic Theory: Vol. 2* (Oxford, 1966).

56 Leslie, 1976, p. 118.

57 Penrose, in Hawking and Israel, 1979, p. 634.

58 Davies, 1980, pp. 162–70; and Davies, 1983, p. 37, for the tie between local and global.

59 See note 3 above.

60 Steigman, in Longair, 1974, pp. 347–56, esp. 355.

61 Weinberg, quoted by M. J. Rees, *New Scientist*, 16 August 1987, p. 47. Elsewhere Weinberg has greeted anthropic reasoning more favourably, in particular in connection with why 'theoretical expecta-

tions for the cosmological constant exceed observational limits by some 120 orders of magnitude': see his 'The cosmological constant problem', *Reviews of Modern Physics*, January 1989, pp. 1–23; or his 'Anthropic bound on the cosmological constant', *Physical Review Letters*, vol. 59, no. 22, 1987, pp. 2607–10.

5 The Need to Explain Life

The chapter draws above all on Leslie, 1983a.

1 An argument grim enough to be banished to a footnote has been toyed with by cosmologists. The human race might be expected to survive for many million years not just on Earth but in numerous large colonies throughout the galaxy. Looking at the entire history of the race – future history included – we should then find ourselves to be very unusually early humans: we could well be in the first 0.00001 per cent to live their lives. Yet suppose that the race is instead about to die out through nuclear war or runaway greenhouse effect or . . . (choose your disaster). We are then altogether ordinary humans. Recent population growth has been such that, of all human lives lived so far, getting on for a half are being lived today. Conclusion: to promote the reasonable aim of making it unsurprising that we exist so soon after the dawn of human history, let's assume that the human race will indeed quickly die out. It is to be hoped that this argument has a flaw! Yet arguments designed to show *that the apparently surprising is not surprising in the last analysis* are good common sense. (The rumbling sounds from behind the door you were about to open become unsurprising in view of a rumour that a lion has escaped from the zoo; therefore hesitate before rejecting the rumour!) Further, it could be weak to protest that a race surviving for billions of years would have some earliest members who would be misled by an argument on the above lines. It could be weak because probabilistic arguments can be powerful despite being sure to mislead those rare people who are in statistically very unusual situations.
    Note that the above 'Doomsday Argument' (which may first have been suggested by Brandon Carter) is of course not conclusive: it is just for a *shift* in any estimate of the probability that our race will soon die out, a shift which could be counteracted if we took enough extra care to avoid risks to its survival. But the shift really is needed – and so, therefore, is the extra care! *Living early* would be like having one's ticket drawn early in a raffle: for instance on the first draw. Now, when I won $300-worth of books, first prize in a raffle held recently, my hunch that few would bother to enter the raffle was thereby strengthened, justifiably. While every raffle has to be won *by somebody*, the winner always has *more reason than before* to think that there were few names in the hat. These points are developed at some length in Leslie, 1989d, and in 'Is the end of the world nigh?', to appear in *The Philosophical Quarterly*.

2 Mellor develops the point in 'God and probability', in K. E. Yandell (ed.), *God, Man and Religion* (New York, 1973), pp. 472–81.

3 Similar open-mindedness has led to a search for messages from extraterrestrials in the nucleotide sequences of very simple organisms. Being very stable, these sequences might reproduce themselves unchanged until Earth's scientists had developed the skills for decoding them. See H. Yokoo and T. Oshima's technique-pioneering paper, 'Is bacteriophage ØX174 DNA a message from an extraterrestrial intelligence?', *Icarus*, vol. 38, 1979, pp. 148–53.

4 R. Swinburne, *The Existence of God* (Oxford, 1979).

5 Chapter 8 will give just a hint of them. *Value and Existence* (Leslie, 1979) discussed them more thoroughly but still not nearly thoroughly enough.

6 Anthropic Explanations

The chapter draws on Leslie, 1982, 1983b, 1986a and b, 1987, and 1988a.

1 Carter, 'Large number coincidences and the anthropic principle in cosmology', in Longair, 1974, p. 291; reprinted in Leslie, 1989a.

2 Ibid., pp. 293, 294.

3 Dicke, *Nature*, 4 November 1961, p. 440: also reprinted in Leslie, 1989a.

4 Carter, op. cit. (note 1 above), pp. 295–6, 298.

5 Ellis, *General Relativity and Gravitation*, vol. 11, no. 4, 1979, pp. 281–9.

6 Marochnik, *Astrophysics and Space Science*, vol. 89, 1983, p. 61.

7 Hart, in M. H. Hart and B. Zuckerman (eds), *Extraterrestrials: Where Are They?* (New York, 1982), pp. 154–64, reprinted in Leslie, 1989a.

8 Polkinghorne, *One World: The Interaction of Science and Theology* (London, 1986), p. 105.

9 Hawking, in Longair, 1974, pp. 283–6.

10 See H. R. Pagels, 'A cozy cosmology', *The Sciences*, April 1985, pp. 35–8, reprinted in Leslie, 1989a.

11 Hacking, *Mind*, July 1987, pp. 331–40, replied to by Leslie, 1988a. Reasoning similar to Hacking's is central to J. Katz's paper in *Dialogue*, vol. 27, no. 1, Spring 1988, pp. 111–20: see esp. p. 118 on 'making more probable'.

12 See Hacking, 'Coincidences: mundane and cosmological', in J. M. Robson (ed.), *Origin and Evolution of the Universe: Evidence for Design?* (Montreal, 1987), pp. 119–38; and Leslie, 1986b, which replies to this.

13 Barrow, *Quarterly Journal of the Royal Astronomical Society*, vol. 24, 1983, pp. 146–53.

14 Leslie, 1979, ch. 10, suggests that Neoplatonists might accept a sense in which the universe in fact contains nothing beyond minds and their experiences; see also Leslie, 1986c.

15 A fine account of Carter's Anthropic Principle, and especially of his use of such words as 'must', is given by M. Munitz, *Cosmic Understanding* (Princeton, 1986), pp. 236–57, esp. p. 255.

16 Pagels, op. cit. (note 10 above).

7 The Design Argument

Much of the chapter draws on Leslie, 1985.

1 Advocated by A. C. Ewing, *Value and Reality* (London, 1973), ch. 7; and by R. Swinburne, in Leslie, 1989a. See in addition Leslie, 1978a: the Design hypothesis could also be viewed as 'gaining its authority, much as scientific ones often do, through giving a constant explanation of widely varied facts'.

2 Some have reasoned that God's own life would contain so much goodness that giving lives to others would be superfluous. Like Abelard, I find this hard to reconcile with the picture of a morally admirable God, but here is not the place to argue this. (I argue it in *Philosophy*, July 1983, pp. 329–38, and develop the basic ethical point further in *Philosophia*, vol. 19, no. 1, 1989.)

3 As does, for instance, K. V. Nelson, *Religious Studies*, vol. 14, 1978, pp. 423–44.

4 Mellor's argument on these lines was mentioned in Chapter 5 (section 5.13 and note 2). A theist who thinks such an argument forceful is J. Hick: see his *Philosophy of Religion*, 2nd ed (Englewood Cliffs, 1973), pp. 27–8.

8 God

The chapter is based largely on Leslie, 1970, 1978b, 1979, 1980, and 1986c.

1 Mackie's *The Miracle of Theism* (Oxford, 1982), ch. 13. I am grateful to D.Parfit for suggesting to him the need for this chapter. Neoplatonism's 'greatest strength', he says, lies in its seemingly very paradoxical central claim that 'the mere ethical *need* for something could *on its own* call that item into existence' (p. 232), in particular when the something was an entire universe; the need for the creation of a good world could then be satisfied without the operation of any already existing person or mind 'that was aware of this need and acted to fulfil it'. Considering the Leibnizian question of why there exists any universe at all, Mackie comments that while he himself thinks that such a question does not need an answer, to explain a universe in terms of its ethical requiredness could give what might easily be the best answer (p. 235). For (pp. 233, 237) it could indeed be 'a gross error' to argue 'that merely because ethical requirement and creative requirement are conceptually or logically distinct there cannot be a real, and perhaps necessary, connection between them'; it is right to resist 'the prejudice that it can be known *a priori* to be impossible'. 'In calling something good we do commonly imply that it is intrinsically and objectively required or marked out for existence, irrespective of whether any person, human or divine, requires or demands or

prescribes or admires it' (p. 238); and although this of course cannot guarantee the creative success of ethical requirements, it can suggest it. Mackie's own judgment is that the concept of being intrinsically required or marked out for existence 'is a very strange concept' and so should be rejected; but this is, he admits, a case of his going against the common view and even against Ordinary Language. He is fully aware of how odd he sounds to most non-philosophers when he declares that no act is ever *in itself* better than any other.

A discussion somewhat similar to Mackie's is that of J. J. C. Smart, *Our Place in the Universe* (Oxford, 1989), ch. 7. (The same chapter discusses fine tuning and multiple universes.) Like Mackie, Smart is intrigued by my Neoplatonist bid to explain the world's existence just by reference to its ethical requiredness, without appeal to how that requiredness is recognized by any divine being (who, says Smart, could create the natural world only if 'of at least equal complexity' so that no explanatory advantage is gained by introducing him). But, again like Mackie, Smart rejects the idea that anything is ever intrinsically ethically required: 'Putting it a little crudely, I regard talk of values as an expression of our attitudes, our likes and dislikes.' And he has strong doubts not only about eternal ethical needs, but about all other such unconditionally real 'Platonic entities'.

An important variant on Neoplatonism is provided by N. Rescher, *The Riddle of Existence* (Lanham and London, 1984): I give an account of this in *Philosophy of Science*, September 1985, pp. 485–6. Rescher suggests that Value or fittingness can itself be powerful without aid from 'a creator-god', but sees it not as directly creative but rather as setting up elegant abstract principles, of which the fundamental equations of physics might be examples. These principles make it either certain or altogether probable that a world should come to exist, emptiness being 'unstable' at best: compare Tryon's quantum vacuum fluctuation story about our world's origin. The background to all this is the quasi-Kantian 'Conceptual Idealism' developed in many of Rescher's writings.

2 *Value and Existence* (Leslie, 1979). After an introductory chapter summarizing the main themes, chs 2–4 develop Neoplatonism. Chs 5, 9, and 11 discuss the Problem of Evil and a world-model which could be useful in defending against it. On Neoplatonism, see also Leslie, 1970, 1978b, 1980, and 1986c.

3 Some alleged further options are described and rejected in Leslie, 1978b.

4 See Ewing, *Value and Reality* (London, 1973), ch. 7.

5 Nowadays people often say that 'logically necessary' simply means 'true in all possible worlds'. This tends to destroy the very important distinction between *the conceptually necessary* and *what is necessary synthetically*.

6 Perhaps to Leslie, 1980.

7 Leibniz, *Theodicy* (1710), sects 8 and 202. Often criticized by people who have never troubled themselves to open it, this book also

contains a long defence of Leibniz's view that freedom is compatible with determinism and that the need for one good may very unfortunately overrule the need for another, for instance if we use our freedom badly; hence belief in God and in the world's goodness does not involve what his *Discourse on Metaphysics* (first published in 1846) describes as 'waiting ridiculously with folded arms to see what God will do'. Leibniz's 'best possible' world is by no means a perfect world, a world without evils. (I discuss this in *Studia Leibnitiana*, vol. III, part 3, 1971, pp. 199–205.)

8 Einstein, *Relativity: The Special and the General Theory*, appendix 5 to the 15th ed (New York, 1920).

9 Time is discussed in Leslie, 1976, and in Leslie, 1979, ch. 9; ch. 11 of the same book considers various kinds of Monism.

9 Conclusions

The chapter draws in part on Leslie, 1983a.

1 For Tipler's ideas, see Barrow and Tipler, 1986, esp. pp. 658–77. These pages further contain some discussion of Dyson's musings about positronium. See also ibid., p. 651, for the gigantic size and slow-ticking nature of positronium states: the orbital velocities of electron and positron about one another are in the neighbourhood of a ten-thousandth of a centimetre per century. A popular account of all this, and of similar ideas in others, is T. A. Heppenheimer, *Omni*, August 1986, pp. 37–40. For a little more, see Dyson, *Reviews of Modern Physics*, vol. 51, 1979, pp. 447–60.

2 See R. M. Hare's contribution to the discussion in *University*, 'Theology and falsification', reprinted in A. Flew and A. MacIntyre (eds), *New Essays in Philosophical Theology* (London, 1955), pp. 101–2.

3 Mustn't I be misinterpreting what people of H. Putnam's eminence have been saying? Alas not. Consult J. J. C. Smart's fine writings on this subject: e.g. his short piece in *Analysis*, vol. 42, 1982, pp. 1–3, which points to possible cosmological truths of kinds which could never be experienced, or his paper in *Philosophy*, vol. 61, no. 237, 1986, pp. 295–312. Or W. P. Alston, 'Yes, Virginia, there is a real world', *Proceedings and Addresses of the American Philosophical Association*, vol. 52, no. 6, 1979.

The arguments of section 9.15 are expanded in Leslie, 1989c.

4 Hacking, *Representing and Intervening* (Cambridge, 1983), p. 106.

5 'A preference'? 'A fortunate stupidity' could be more accurate. Philosophers have long known that an infinite variety of very complex laws could in theory account for any given finite sequence of events, much as an infinite variety of equations could describe curves passing through any finite series of points (Leibniz, *Discourse on Metaphysics*, first published in 1846, sect. 6). But aided by how humans are too brainless to find laws an archangel might see at a glance, scientists do manage to make progress. Similarly, children

manage to learn the language of pictures or of words despite the infinitely many consistent interpretations which could conceivably be given to pictorial or linguistic patterns.

6 See Ayer's article 'Chance', *Scientific American*, October 1965, pp. 44–54.

References

Atkins, P. W. (1981) *The Creation*, Oxford: W. H. Freeman.

Barrow, J. D. and Tipler, F. J. (1986) *The Anthropic Cosmological Principle*, Oxford: Clarendon Press.

Carr, B. J. and Rees, M. J. (1979). 'The anthropic principle and the structure of the physical world', *Nature*, 12 April, pp. 605–12.

Davies, P. C. W. (1980) *Other Worlds*, London: Dent.

—— (1983) 'The anthropic principle', *Particle and Nuclear Physics*, vol. 10, ed. D. Wilkinson, pp. 1–38 (A further development of the arguments of his *The Accidental Universe*, Cambridge: Cambridge University Press, 1982.)

—— (1984) *Superforce*, New York: Simon and Schuster.

Demaret, J. and Barbier, C. (1981) 'Le principe anthropique en cosmologie', *Revue des Questions Scientifiques*, October, pp. 461–509. (Continues a two-part paper begun on pp. 181–222.)

Dyson, F. (1971) 'Energy in the universe', *Scientific American*, September, pp. 51–9.

Gibbons, G. W., Hawking, S. W., and Siklos, S. T. C. (eds) (1983) *The Very Early Universe*, Cambridge: Cambridge University Press.

Guth, A. H. and Steinhardt, P. J. (1984) 'The inflationary universe', *Scientific American*, May, pp. 116–28.

Hawking, S. W. and Israel, W. (eds) (1979) *General Relativity*, Cambridge: Cambridge University Press.

Isham, C. J., Penrose, R., and Sciama, D. W. (eds) (1981) *Quantum Gravity 2*, Oxford: Oxford University Press.

Leslie, J. (1970) 'The theory that the world exists because it should', *American Philosophical Quarterly*, October, pp. 215–24.

—— (1972) 'Ethically required existence', *American Philosophical Quarterly*, July, pp. 109–21.

—— (1973) 'Does causal regularity defy chance?', *Idealistic Studies*, September, pp. 277–84.

—— (1976) 'The value of time', *American Philosophical Quarterly*, April, pp. 109–21.

—— (1978a) 'God and scientific verifiability', *Philosophy*, January, pp. 71–9.

—— (1978b) 'Efforts to explain all existence', *Mind*, April, pp. 181–94.

—— (1979) *Value and Existence*, Oxford: Blackwell.

References

—— (1980) 'The world's necessary existence', *International Journal for Philosophy of Religion*, vol. 11, no. 4, pp. 207–23.

—— (1982) 'Anthropic principle, world ensemble, design', *American Philosophical Quarterly*, April, pp. 141–51 (with some misprints corrected in the October number).

—— (1983a) 'Cosmology, probability and the need to explain life', in N. Rescher (ed.), *Scientific Explanation and Understanding*, Pittsburgh: Center for Philosophy of Science, and Lanham and London: University Press of America, pp. 53–82.

—— (1983b) 'Observership in cosmology: the anthropic principle', *Mind*, October, pp. 573–9.

—— (1985) 'Modern cosmology and the creation of life', in E. McMullin (ed.), *Evolution and Creation*, Notre Dame: University of Notre Dame Press, pp. 91–120.

—— (1986a) 'The scientific weight of anthropic and teleological principles', in N. Rescher (ed.), *Current Issues in Teleology*, Lanham and London: University Press of America, pp. 111–19.

—— (1986b) 'Anthropic explanations in cosmology', in *PSA 1986: Volume One* (Proceedings of the Philosophy of Science Association), Ann Arbor: Edwards Bros, pp. 87–95.

—— (1986c) 'Mackie on Neoplatonism's "replacement for God"', *Religious Studies*, September/December, pp. 325–42.

—— (1987) 'Probabilistic phase transitions and the anthropic principle', in J. Demaret (ed.), *Origin and Early History of the Universe*, Liège: Institut d'Astrophysique, University of Liège, and Presses of the University of Liège, pp. 439–44.

—— (1988a) 'No inverse gambler's fallacy in cosmology', *Mind*, April, pp. 269–72. (A reply to I. Hacking.)

—— (1988b). 'The Leibnizian richness of our universe', in N. Rescher (ed.), *Leibnizian Inquiries*, Lanham: University Press of America, pp. 139–48.

—— (1988c) 'The prerequisites of life in our universe', in G. V. Coyne, M. Heller, and J. Zycinski (eds), *Newton and the New Direction in Science*, Vatican City: Specola Vaticana, pp. 229–58. (To be reprinted in *Truth*, 1989, in an issue on the cosmological argument edited by W. L. Craig.)

—— (1988d) 'How to draw conclusions from a fine-tuned universe', in R. J. Russell, W. R. Stoeger, and G. V. Coyne (eds), *Physics, Philosophy and Theology*, Vatican City: Vatican Observatory, pp. 297–311. (Coming from a September 1987 papal workshop at Castel Gandolfo; distributed by University of Notre Dame Press.)

—— (1988e) 'Dialectics and metaphysics', *Explorations in Knowledge*, vol. 6, no. 1, pp. 1–12. (A debate with D. Goldstick.)

—— (1989a) *Physical Cosmology and Philosophy* (edited, with introduction and annotated bibliography), New York: Macmillan.

—— (1989b) 'Multiple universes', to appear in R. F. Kitchener (ed.), *The Origin of the Universe*. (Coming from a September 1988 conference of Colorado State University.)

—— (1989c) 'Demons, vats and the cosmos', to appear in *Philosophical Papers*.

—— (1989d) 'Risking the world's end', *Bulletin of the Canadian Nuclear Society*, vol. 10, no. 3, May/June.

Linde, A. D. (1983) 'The new inflationary universe scenario', in G. W. Gibbons, S. W. Hawking, and S. T. C. Siklos (eds), *The Very Early Universe*, Cambridge: Cambridge University Press, pp. 205–49.

—— (1984) 'The inflationary universe', *Reports on Progress in Physics*, vol. 47, no. 8, pp. 925–86.

—— (1985) 'The universe: inflation out of chaos', *New Scientist*, 7 March, pp. 14–18.

Longair, M. S. (ed.) (1974) *Confrontation of Cosmological Theories with Observational Data*, Dordrecht: Reidel.

McCrea, W. H. and Rees, M. J. (eds) (1983) *The Constants of Physics*, volume A310, pp. 209–363, of *Philosophical Transactions of the Royal Society, London*.

Misner, C. W., Thorne, K. S., and Wheeler, J. A. (1973) *Gravitation*, San Francisco: W. H. Freeman.

Rozental, I. L. (1980) 'Physical laws and the numerical values of fundamental constants', *Soviet Physics: Uspekhi*, vol. 23, pp. 293–305.

Sylvan, R. (1986) 'Toward an improved cosmo-logical synthesis', *Grazer Philosophische Studien*, vols 25 and 26, pp. 135–79.

Weinberg, S. (1983) *The First Three Minutes* (2nd edn with afterword), London: Fontana.

Index of Concepts

Index of Names